Multicultural Education

Routledge Education Books

Advisory editor: John Eggleston
Professor of Education
University of Warwick

Multicultural Education
Principles and Practice

James Lynch

Dean of the Faculty of Education,
Sunderland Polytechnic

Routledge & Kegan Paul
London, Boston and Henley

First published in 1986
by Routledge & Kegan Paul plc

14 Leicester Square, London WC2H 7PH, England

9 Park Street, Boston, Mass. 02108, USA and

Broadway House, Newtown Road,
Henley on Thames, Oxon RG9 1EN, England

Set in 10/11 Times Linotron 202
by Inforum Ltd, Portsmouth
and printed in Great Britain
by Billing & Sons Ltd
Worcester

Library of Congress Cataloging in Publication Data

Lynch, James.

   Multicultural education.
(Routledge education books)
Bibliography: p.
Includes indexes.
1. Intercultural education.   2. Intercultural
education—Great Britain.   I. Title.   II. Series.
LC1099.L964   1986   370.19'6   85–18325

British Library CIP data also available

ISBN 0–7102–0768–9 (pbk)
       0–7102–0411–6

Contents

Contents

Tables and figures

Acknowledgments

Several publishers and individuals have agreed to the reproduction of copyright and other material in this book, for which I should like to express my sincere thanks. Carlton Duncan, Headmaster of Wyke Manor Comprehensive School, Bradford gave permission for the reproduction of materials concerning his school's policy statement on multicultural and antiracist education and the description of the implementation of staff development to address that policy. The Editors of *Education Review* have kindly permitted the reproduction of limited sections from my article 'Human Rights, Racism and the Multicultural Curriculum' which appeared in the June 1985 edition. Professor Lou Cohen, Lawrence Manion and Croom Helm Ltd, Publishers, agreed to the publication in Chapter 5 of my adapted version of their classification of objectives for multicultural education, which appeared in *Multicultural Classrooms*, published in 1983. The National Council for the Social Studies gave permission for the inclusion of an adapted version of the guidelines for multiethnic education, which first appeared in James A. Banks, Carlos E. Cortés, Geneva Gay, Ricardo L. Garcia and Anna S. Ochoa, *Curriculum Guidelines for Multiethnic Education*, Washington DC: National Council for the Social Studies, 1976, and B.T. Batsford Ltd kindly gave permission for me to re-use the diagram for constructing a multicultural curriculum, first used in *The Multicultural Curriculum*, published by them in 1983.

Preface

It is a pleasure for me to acknowledge the intellectual debt which I owe, in the writing of this book, to many cherished colleagues in different parts of the world. Their work has assisted in challenging the parochialism and myopia which has surrounded so much of the development of multicultural education in the United Kingdom. In that process, however, of challenging the ethnocentric nature of much that has passed for multicultural education in the United Kingdom, I have needed to be eclectic, and it is inevitable that the choice involved has been, to some extent, personal. It has certainly not been possible, in spite of extensive bibliographies, to include reference to all colleagues who have 'laboured' in this field. Subsequent work may be expected to express more explicitly my continuing debt to others and, hopefully, my own better and more complete appreciation of the extent of all my intellectual debts and the growth of the field.

There are many views of multicultural education, and I am conscious that some, perhaps many, leading groups and persons in my own country feel, in very many cases, little or no commitment to the implementation of any concept of multicultural education, but would prefer to aim for assimilation of other cultural traditions. On the other hand, I am equally conscious that many of my colleagues and friends consider multicultural education a new placebo for the continued injustice and inequality in education and society; too slow to promise real change; too inadequate to right the wrongs.

For my part, I am convinced that a middle way is both possible and desirable, which recognises the pernicious effects on all of prejudice and discrimination, of inequality and injustice, but which seeks to change this deplorable situation by rational social action, persuasion and discourse rather than through nihilistic exhortation to utopian revolution. In my view, the former is the only really viable and constructive course, if democracy, freedom and justice for all are to be safeguarded. Equally, of course, I realise that, in spite of my immense debt to others, what follows in the pages of this book is one person's construction of reality, as it is, and as it might be, or in some cases, should be. In a democracy, there will always be a pluralism of views about how we can best proceed and even indeed in what direction and why. I welcome the discourse which this implies as an indispensable characteristic of multicultural education.

The central aim of this book is to present the argument that multicultural education for all is essential in a pluralist democracy, as a preparation for that discourse which is an indispensable support for continued freedom and justice in a culturally diverse society, and as guarantor of the human rights of all. Teachers are at the very fulcrum of this struggle, through discourse, to preserve and renew creatively, for all our children, those values of freedom, justice and democracy, without which that very diversity, which is our cultural treasury and the source of positive human progress and change, would be submerged by those who would stifle and silence the human spirit rather than liberate it. With all its inadequacies, therefore, I dedicate this book to my colleague educators.

James Lynch
Ilkley
January 1985

Part One

Goals and concepts: definitions and debates

Chapter 1

Cultural pluralism and the educational response

Introduction

In this chapter I want to look at some of the basic terminology which often proves so difficult and confusing for teachers who are attempting to plan and develop multicultural education in their schools. I also want to paint in the background scenario of what I call democratic cultural pluralism, why British society and many other Western societies have begun to be perceived as 'culturally pluralist' and what educational responses have been made by the major democracies to this more recent perception. By the major pluralist democracies I mean those societies of Western Europe, of North America and of Australasia which, over the past two decades, have increasingly had to face the problems, issues and challenges surrounding the arrival of new cultural groups in their society and which have adopted strategies such as multicultural and intercultural education to respond to this.

I do not wish to imply that this focus on more recently arrived ethnic minorities is the outer limit of the cultural pluralism with which multicultural education is concerned. Far from it, for it is apparent that there are old-established and indigent ethnic, racial, religious and other cultural minorities, blacks and Mexicans in the United States, Aborigines in Australia, Welsh and Gaels in the United Kingdom, Gypsies and travelling people in various countries and many other cultural minorities within Western democratic societies which contribute to the cultural mosaic of those societies, and many racial minorities have a long history of presence in some of these countries.[1]

Multicultural education is concerned with all these minorities and their educational needs, as also with the needs of majority students of both sexes and all linguistic, credal and racial groups to learn how to live in creative harmony within a multicultural society. But,

3

whilst the cultural mosaic has been formed of a linguistic, ethnic and religious diversity over centuries, it has to be recognised that the spur to newer perceptions of Western democratic societies as being multicultural has occurred in the decades since the end of the Second World War.

An initial classification

Watson has classified countries adopting multicultural education policies into three groups: those with a deep-rooted racial and cultural mix, such as the Soviet Union; those with a cultural mix largely as a result of colonialism, for instance, France and Holland; and those which have become multicultural mainly as a result of voluntary immigration, for example, West Germany.[2] According to this classification, Britain falls within the second category. Newer perceptions of such societies as being multicultural have been caused to a major extent by the impact of new and, at that time, foreign cultures on nation states which had previously considered themselves monist, and by what has been termed in the United States the ethnic revival movement, which focussed national attention on the injustices inherent within its diversity and the way in which that diversity was responded to.

Multicultural education is one major way in which those societies have attempted to reconcile the dual goals of democratic society within a pluralist context and to overcome thereby what Bullivant has called the pluralist dilemma.[3] These twin goals are *social cohesion*, that is, provision for the maintenance of reasonable social and political stability, on the one hand and, on the other, *cultural diversity*, that is, not just toleration but active encouragement of and support for diversity of legitimate cultures. As I shall be arguing later in this chapter, policies tending to either polarity are usually legitimated by reference to one of the common values of these societies such as equality and freedom.

Varying patterns of migration

With regard to post-war migration into Western European societies and notwithstanding the already existing cultural mosaic referred to above, Castles has identified the following patterns:

1   Return migration of settlers from former colonies such as the British from India, the French *pieds noirs* from Algeria and the Dutch from Indonesia.

2   Immigration of ethnically distinct citizens of colonies and
    former colonies.
3   Labour migration mainly of manual workers from such areas as
    the Mediterranean.
4   Migration of skilled employees between highly developed
    countries.
5   Entry of foreign refugees seeking political asylum.[4]

Most European countries have now severely constrained new
immigration except of a consequential, adoptive or refugee kind,
and immigration to all countries has been made more difficult since
the beginning of the 1970s. The above five forms which post-war
migration into Western societies has taken should be seen at the
side of continued mass migration to countries of the New World
such as the United States, Canada and Australia, continued informal immigration into the United States from Spanish-speaking
countries in the New World, and increasing refugee settlement
particularly of those seeking political asylum from the so-called
Third World.

The pattern and content of these forms of migration differ from
country to country as does also the political structure, administrative organisation, cultural context and historical aetiology which
form the reception country location for the settlement of immigration groups. These differing factors in turn have, over time and
place, caused different perceptions of the arrival of cultural pluralism
in the countries concerned and have distinctively influenced the
kind of educational and broader social strategies which have been
adopted.

Options faced by ethnic minorities

In general, however, ethnic minorities have been seen as facing four
options in their response to the surrounding society: assimilation or
the complete abandonment of their cultural differences; pluralism
involving the acceptance and toleration of their differences by
dominant and majority populations; secession or complete independence or apartheid; and militancy in an attempt to take over
power from the majority group.[5] Gordon refined the concept of
assimilation by identifying seven dimensions or levels:

– cultural, i.e. adoption of the cultural patterns of the majority;
– structural, i.e. entrance into the social, organisational and
  institutional groups of the majority;
– marital, i.e. intermarriage;

- identificational, i.e. adoption of a sense of peoplehood based on the majority community;
- attitude receptional, i.e. the absence of prejudice;
- behaviour receptional, i.e. the absence of discrimination;
- civic assimilation, i.e. the absence of power and value conflict.[6]

The problem with these models is their focus on the minority group. Moreover, recent years have seen the almost wholesale rejection of assimilation as a viable strategy for interethnic relations at any level, and the growth of policies consciously labelled pluralism, multi-ethnicity, and multiculturalism. Gordon, for instance, writing almost a decade later, envisaged two kinds of pluralism: liberal, where toleration of all cultural differences is practised but where there is no 'official' recognition of cultural criteria of any kind as a basis for the allocation of resources; and corporate pluralism, where ethnic groups have explicit recognition as legal entities in society and act as a basis for the allocation of economic rewards.[7] More recently, Bullivant has reinforced the second of these as he has argued that an ethnic group may have to establish some separate structures and institutions in order to survive.[8] He also emphasises that dominant groups in society will tend to resist such tendencies in pursuit of the maintenance of their own cultural hegemony. Such an analysis may seem to be confirmed by the strategies adopted towards linguistic pluralism in such countries as Belgium, Canada and Switzerland and towards such minorities as the Danes in Germany and the Germans in Denmark and Belgium. These situations, however, have been perceived as being fundamentally different – in terms not least of geographical concentration – from those of the more newly arrived ethnic minority groups.

The responses of majority communities

Thus, as a generalisation, and with certain notable exceptions which I shall refer to later in this chapter, the responses of majorities to the perceived presence of ethnic minorities in their midst have been essentially defensive, restrictive and exclusive; they have sought to defend their hegemony, restrict or marginalise the influence of minority culture where they have recognised it at all, and 'exclude' in the sense that there has been little or no attempt to engage ethnic minorities in potent and equal discourse as a means of interaction and the resolution of conflicting interests. More recent economic crises have only served to accentuate the vicious circle leading from xenophobia to legal scapegoating and marginalisation and ultimate alienation and breakdown of social cohesion. It is the paradox of culturally pluralist societies which wish to pursue democracy that they must foster cultural diversity to maintain and legitimate social cohesion.

Based on a six-country analysis, I have identified elsewhere the major characteristics of the above responses as:

- legal scapegoating;
- imposition of gross social and economic equality;
- subjection to harassment, discrimination, and, on occasions, violence;
- ethnic encapsulation of the dominant group;
- cultural recalcitrance and lack of potent dialogue;
- economic predestination in the educational sphere;
- bracketing out minority cultures, e.g., by neglect of home language;
- educational marginalisation of ethnic minority children;
- teacher stereotyping and ability underestimation and minimisation;
- structural overrepresentation in special education;
- sedimentation of minority children into lower streams;
- structural underrepresentation in prestigious forms of education;
- undercredentialisation of minority children;
- grade retardation;
- additive and impotent curriculum change;
- culture bias in the control mechanisms of education.[9]

Three basic ideological orientations

But there are a few indications of changes and, broadly speaking, it is possible to identify three major ideological orientations underlying current perceptions of cultural pluralism and the educational strategies for which they provide the theoretical moorings. Democratic societies have need of ideologies in order to justify and sustain support for and motivation towards the policies which the state wishes to implement. Such ideologies also act as the motivation for individuals and groups for their actions *vis-à-vis* those policies and they are, therefore, of fundamental and practical importance to teachers in their ordinary, everyday, professional lives. All teachers will be aware of the sentiment that schools should provide equality of educational opportunity for all children. Equally apparent, however, is the fact that not only are all schools not equal in their facilities, staffing etc., but that some schools have the specific function of providing privileged, i.e. unequal, educational opportunities. Notwithstanding that reality, however, the ideological commitment remains a powerful motivator of individual action and state policy and a legitimator of national and institutional policies and efforts. But the social system continues to reproduce itself through the educational system and to frustrate efforts at so-called democratisation and equalisation of opportunities.

Broadly speaking, three ideologies have been used in this way to respond to post-war migration and to legitimate policies. These have been those associated with *economic efficiency*, the development of *greater equality of educational opportunity* on the basis of existing structures, philosophies and values, and those which have been concerned with the development of *interdependence and partnership* by means of negotiation and social discourse.[10]

Each of these ideologies which represents a different and alternative conglomeration of values, ideals and attitudes to cultural pluralism may be seen in terms of its influence at four different levels of human existence: firstly, the level of values and philosophies; secondly, the structures of knowledge which are built on and derived from those values and philosophies; thirdly, the human social structures which are tailored to fit those structures of knowledge; and, lastly, the control mechanisms which lock the values, structures of knowledge and social organisation into a coherent system.[11] If we take each of the three ideological orientations in turn, it is possible to identify the policies which they represent in responses to cultural pluralism. Table 1.1 attempts to illustrate, by means of a typology and specific examples, the relationship between the ideological orientations and the levels of human cultural and social organisation indicated above.

It is not intended to suggest that the typology of relationships represented by the examples given in Table 1.1 is static or discrete or indeed that they represent a chronological sequence. It is quite possible to see co-existing within the same society values of both an economic and interdependent orientation. For example, there can be little doubt that the early preoccupation in almost all European countries with host country language provision by means of reception centres or concentration on special language provision in schools derived more from reasons of economic efficiency than from any concern with equality or interdependence.

Likewise, as demonstrated more recently, in isolated examples such as Sweden,[12] the new-found commitment to partnership is quite clearly something beyond a mere acceptance of the need for involvement of all sectors of society or to take account of diversity which would be advanced as part of a democratic value orientation. It is, in other words, a commitment to education *for* linguistic and cultural diversity and to a higher level of social discourse as a means for the regulation of human behaviour than that which is available through existing economic and social class hierarchised norms or

TABLE 1.1: *A typology of policy options for responses to cultural pluralism*

Ideology	Economic	Democratic	Interdependent

Values	elitist
	technocratic
	instrumental
	purposive-rational
	hierarchical
	production-
	  oriented
		egalitarian
		subjective
		sponsorship
		traditional
		individual-
		  oriented
			community
			dialectic
			intersubjective
			partnership
			emancipatory-
			  oriented

Knowledge	dominant culture
	economic-literacy
	traditional
	  subjects
	compartment-
	  alised
	unilingual
		learner-centred
		multidisciplinary
		additive change
		mother-tongue
		'false' demo-
		  cratisation
			new paradigms
			interdisciplinary
			community-
			  centred
			global
			bilingual
			human rights

Structures	economic
	  solidarity
	social class
	stratification
	traditional roles
	given
	hierarchical
		social cohesion
		systemic
		  homogeneity
		equality
		traditional –
		  evolutionary
		roles earned
			cultural diversity
			organic separation
			equity
			evolutionary –
			  revolutionary
			roles changed

Social
  Controls
	economic
	  exigency
	materialistic
	coercive
	administrative
	multinationalism
		formal
		  participatory
		individual/self
		  control
		representative
		  democracy
		national
			community norms
			negotiatory
			decentralised
			social discourse
			international

even the traditional democratic structures and processes,[13] proposed as a *placebo* alternative.

This is not to suggest that any of these ideologies holds exclusive sway at a particular moment in time, still less that there is a chronological sequence whereby one of them is now a historical relic and there is an alternative and exclusive focus on one of the others. Rather, all three can be observed in currently existing policies in major Western societies and also, and perhaps more importantly, in the broader educational curricula and more narrowly pedagogical strategies which are currently adopted as part of the formal school system and the training of personnel for that system. In most cases, however, the dominant ideological orientation is one based on an economic investment view of education closely allied to reproduction of the social class hierarchy deriving from that system. At any moment in time, these ideologies may be used in order to justify competing and even contradictory goals for the education system. There may, for example, be a continued emphasis on host-country language teaching at the same time as an overall commitment is made to revising curricula to teach for prejudice reduction and eradication. (This has not by and large happened yet except in isolated cases.)

Some initial implications for schools

The implications for teachers are that all teachers must scrutinise their own curricula and activities including the organisational patterns and structures within which they work, to lay bare and expose the real underlying value positions inherent within their current activities and professional aims. This must involve teachers studying their own practice individually, in pairs and in groups, and extending the criteria which they use in order to judge that professional practice. It is important, for example, for teachers to understand that the pupils whom they teach in school will also have been influenced by the kinds of ideological influence typified, either directly or via their parents. These ideologies will have formed an important motivator for the multiple acculturation within which all members of a society achieve their personal, cultural and social biography. What is meant by this is that the process of obtaining those skills, expertise and that knowledge which results in a child becoming an adult should not be envisaged as a unilinear process, nor even the result of influences which all have the same directionality. Rather, it is inevitable, within a multicultural society, that children, from whichever cultural group, will have been influenced by a series of groups, individuals and broader social and cultural pressures which we describe as a process of *multiple acculturation*.

The major goals

It is within this pluralist context of prevailing and countervailing influences that schools fulfil their functions of educating children towards two major goals, those of the maintenance of *social cohesion* and those associated with encouragement of *cultural diversity*. It will be apparent that without education towards social cohesion society would disintegrate. Yet, without an opportunity for cultural diversity within a pluralist society there would inevitably be discontent, alienation and possibly revolution. The dilemma, therefore, which education in a multicultural society faces, is how to reconcile the often competing aims within these overall goals, and to express them in the very core of its cultural transmission: its schools.

Stephan has suggested that it might be useful to look at a number of different dimensions in multicultural societies in order to classify them. These he refers to as the political dimension, the social dimension, the economic dimension, the cultural dimension and the socio-psychological dimension.[14] Altering these slightly yields a series of six dimensions against which we can identify differences in goals between those addressed to the achievement of aims of social cohesion and those which address the goal of cultural diversity. In their extreme form these two sets of goals are mutually incompatible. For example, it could well be that the implication of cultural diversity in its environmental dimension is, at the extreme, social apartheid and ghettoisation. On the other hand, at its extreme, social cohesion across the environmental dimension would lead to a situation intolerable within a democratic society, where everyone has to assimilate into fully mixed social, cultural and economic communities, which would only be achieved by a level of directiveness and negation of freedom of choice, incompatible with democratic practice.

The practical task faced by teachers in a democratic multicultural society, and indeed by the whole of the education system, is to reconcile the tension between goals of social cohesion and those of cultural diversity and to weld these within an overall commitment to greater equality of educational opportunity, expressing this commitment through the structure of knowledge and organisation within the education system or narrower institutional base.

This is a very complex problem and we shall be dealing with it in greater detail in Part Two of this book. For the moment, it is important to clarify the meaning of certain basically emotive terms which are associated with these two goals. We often hear, for example, the slogans integration or, on the other hand, no integration; assimilation or no assimilation! It is important for teachers to realise that these are vastly oversimplified rhetoric, for, as we have argued above, all societies must have certain levels of integration and assimilation in order to continue to exist as cohesive societies. On the other hand, if that level of assimilation and integration within all dimensions of human life is too great, then this will inevitably represent cultural and social oppression to an extent which is unacceptable in democratic society and the upshot will be an unavoidable motivation and legitimation crisis.[15] According to Habermas, governments may only have two options in response: repression and coercion to enforce policies, or the opening up of policies to further democratic discourse. It is for this reason that this book advocates the latter strategy, discourse, as one of its central approaches to the resolution of educational dilemmas inherent within democratic cultural pluralism. Education has to seek a balance to sustain commitment through discourse across the ideologies and the balance will be different according to the different dimensions of the typology which are given in Table 1.2.

TABLE 1.2: *The conflicting goals of multiculturalism seen across six major dimensions*

Dimensions of Multiculturalism (Directionality)	Social Cohesion (Centripetal)	Cultural Diversity (Centrifugal)
Cultural	Similarity	Difference
Socio-Psychological	Unity	Differentiation
Social	National Partnership and Commonality	Community Separateness and Directiveness
Economic	Association	Segmentation
Political	Representation through Existing Forms	Separate Representation
Environmental	Integration	Dispersal

It is perfectly possible for there to be a minimum of social integration and assimilation where, for example, marriage between various cultural groups is rare for religious or other reasons, whilst, at the same time, economic or political co-operation and interaction between those groups continue to exist. This may range from tacit acceptance of the commonalities according to which their lives will be governed, such as the acceptance of the rule of law, the right to private property etc., to the broader commitment to the political system of the nation state within which they live. It is possible for there to be dispersal in the environmental dimension with different cultural and/or socio-economic groups living in different areas, without destroying the ultimate cohesion of the nation state and without destroying the effectiveness of the units of local, regional and national government within which those various cultural groups live. Mallea expresses it like this:

all societies require elements of centripetality if they are to function effectively, but multiethnic societies have to learn to live with greater measures of centrifugality than their more homogenous counterparts.[16]

The ethnic encapsulation of majorities

It is thus possible for groups within a multicultural society to be in favour of relative political stability; a dynamic stability and not merely the maintenance of the *status quo*, but at the same time to foster and support cultural divergence and diversity. A major problem which faces most Western societies at the moment is that a large number of the population, perhaps even the vast majority, are living within what James Banks has called 'ethnic psychological captivity' or 'ethnic encapsulation'. These are the first two stages in a six-part typology which Banks has developed to illustrate the stages of ethnicity within multiethnic societies. The remaining four stages are ethnic identity clarification, biethnicity, multiethnicity and reflective nationalism, and globalism and global competency.[17]

Banks considers his 'ideal' typology to represent a series of hypotheses, seen particularly from the point of view of members of ethnic minority communities. For our purposes, it is useful to hypothesise that the vast majority of members of British society – indeed of members of most Western societies – from both minority and majority communities are probably living at Stages One or Two within that typology. It is useful to refer back here to the cultural and social reproduction thesis introduced earlier and to use the relationship between cultural and social pluralism proposed by Schermerhorn.[18] He hypothesises that the two are virtually symbiotic, and thus ethnic or cultural encapsulation inevitably leads to social encapsulation or apartheid of one kind or another. Moreover, if the 'rules for life', which Schermerhorn uses as a shorthand for culture, are lacking in sufficient overlap between cultural groups, as would be the case in cultural encapsulation, then the crystallised relationships, which Schermerhorn proposes as relating people to the major institutional activities of society, will be conducted on the basis of different rules and understandings. Inevitably conflict in society is thereby accentuated and existing legitimation crises are inflamed and sharpened for as long as discourse is not facilitated to attenuate them. This process then results in further alienation which, in turn, means a deterioration of prospects for inter-communication and the discourse which is necessary to break the cycle.

The task of multicultural education

The task of multicultural education in a democratic society is therefore, to assist the individual by means of emancipatory curricular and educational pedagogies which appeal to and extend rational judgement, to reach out to and achieve a higher stage of ethnic and cultural existence than is the case initially, so that there exists sufficient cultural and social overlap for society to function, and for discourse across areas of crisis and conflict to take place. As is explained in Chapter 5, this is one major reason why multicultural education must aim continually for higher levels of intellectual functioning and for affective and social competence increments. For ethnic captivity is a state which is debilitating both to members of minority communities, because of the negative self-images which they will have absorbed, and to members of majority communities, because they do not recognise as negative the self-images which they have absorbed and the relationships which these imply with other cultural communities within a pluralist society as being destructive of the social cohesion which is necessary for cultural diversity to thrive.

Thus, for example, English middle-class attitudes tend to be inimical to the legitimate existence of cultural values and life styles alternative to those which are embraced by the English middle classes. These values, and persons socialised into them, dominate the major institutional activities of society and, therefore, tend to exclude minority participation and success in educational, occupational and economic spheres.

It is important to emphasise that such persons may or may not be culpably conscious of their values and actions. It is quite possible for them to be unprejudiced and yet by their silence or acquiescence to discriminate against members of ethnic minority communities. As Merton argued long ago, discrimination is not always or necessarily related to individual, prejudiced (i.e. exclusive) attitudes.[19] And reinforcing the point, Hall draws our attention to the fact that racism does not necessarily derive from conscious intentions, but may arise from well-intentioned but false stereotyping and patronising attitudes. It may become 'explicit' only in acts of indifference or omission which further reinforce the cultural hegemony of exclusive, prejudiced and monist values.[20]

It is for this reason that multicultural education is necessary for all children in all schools,[21] state and private, denominational and non-denominational, co-educational and single sex, primary and secondary, comprehensive and differentiated, compulsory and non-compulsory. Put simply, the task of teachers in multicultural education is to enable all pupils to achieve a higher stage of cultural competence and sensitivity than that at which they entered the school so that both cultural and social interaction can take place and recognition of the positive value of cultural diversity may grow.

Summary

To summarise and conclude this chapter, it may be useful to define the central focus of this book. Multicultural education, as defined in this book, is that education which is appropriate to democratic cultural pluralism. By democratic cultural pluralism I mean the commitment to the existence of different legitimate cultural groups as legally sanctioned entities which maintain some separate structures and some structures held in common with all other groups in society. Such groups are recognised as legitimate categories for the allocation of economic rewards and political power. The principles of such a society are those associated with pursuit of rationality, respect for persons, commitment to discourse for the resolution of conflict, encouragement for human emancipation and freedom, including the freedom to choose to be – or not to be – a member of a particular cultural group, acceptance of equality before the law and mutuality of instrumental regulation, acceptance of negotiated common values and structures as also of the existence of some separate structures and commitment to political unity at the level of the nation state, combined with engagement for the above values globally. All this adds up to a big job for education with some fundamental changes to traditional goals, forms of knowledge, structures and policies.

To set this in a slightly simplified way, education which seeks to articulate to cultural pluralism and to support and not destroy that pluralism needs to weave together the interrelated principles of commitment to freedom, discourse and rationality. With the decline of absolute standards covering the way in which individuals and groups relate in a culturally pluralist society, and the inadequacy of legal measures alone and a movement to instrumental regulation for all aspects of life in detail in a democracy, the need arises for new norms and mores to be generated. This can only be achieved by discourse, which includes all cultural groups, conducted on a rational basis without compulsion or coercion, i.e. in a context of maximum freedom. Freedom in turn needs rational discourse to set its bounds or the consequence is licence and, for there to be rationality, free discourse has to be available or the rationality becomes 'slanted' as the rationality of only one group. These three elements are, as illustrated in Figure 1.1 not only symbiotic but thus jointly indispensable to a society committed to democratic cultural

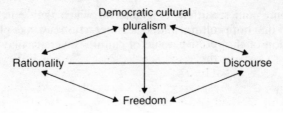

FIGURE 1.1: *Principles of decision for democratic cultural pluralism*

pluralism. It is from this nexus of relationships that education in such a society has to draw and on which it has to build in determining its aim, forms of knowledge, structures and procedures. In many of the multicultural societies referred to in this chapter, there are indications of a stirring for something more significant than formal democratisation in response to the rationality crisis occasioned by the more widespread recognition of cultural diversity.[22] As the momentum to achieve democratic cultural pluralism mounts, the struggle for more wide-ranging and pluralist means to reconstruct continually a national covenant challenges the continuing cultural dominance of traditional elite groups and the stratifying and segregating functions of education conducted in the service of their cultural and economic advantage. Teachers are at the very heart of the cultural process and the implications for their professional development are as far-reaching as they are inescapable.

To the extent that the wider social and community context within which they work is unpredictable and continually changing, new intellectual and social skills are required to enable teachers to come to terms with the explosive dynamic of that uncertainty. Insofar as they are required to respond to that dynamic in their professional context, they will need to learn to relate meaningfully in community with pupils and parents as well as the wider social environment, not merely technically tolerating but positively valuing cultural diversity. And, for as long as they must learn to work with the provisionality, relativity and negotiability of human values and institutional forms, and the fact that the teacher no longer has exclusive possession of knowledge, they will need to develop professional expertise and processes which can make conflict creative rather than seek to stifle it.

Viewed internationally, a number of significant contemporary formulations have been made to subject the goals of education and curricular and institutional forms to radical reappraisal and to work out the conventions and cultural values which may be maximally appropriate to democratic cultural pluralism. Chapter 2 picks up this relay and considers current approaches to multicultural edu-

cation, seen in international perspective and some of the categorisations of such approaches. From a consideration of these wider
speculations and approaches, the way in which similar goals have
been addressed in the United Kingdom is then mapped out in
Chapter 3. From that base, the book proceeds to identify the way in
which schools may respond in their assumptions and values, in their
curriculum and their organisation, in their examinations and their
relationships with the community, to the task of constructing a
multicultural education for democratic cultural pluralism, to
replace current cultural and social tendencies to political secession,
ethnic segmentation, cultural alienation and social intolerance.

Chapter 2

Approaches to multicultural education: international perspectives

Introduction

In Chapter 1 of this book I outlined the responses of industrialised societies to the crisis of rationality, which the perception of their own cultural pluralism evokes in their social and political structures. I defined the role of multicultural education as being indispensable to the education of individuals in preparation for the discourse which, in turn, is essential to overcome that rationality crisis. But whilst the basic cultural phenomena are the same in all societies, the educational and broader social responses, and the perception of those phenomena, have varied in different Western societies, and this has meant that there has been a pluralism of approaches to the task of constructing multicultural education. Different experts working within the field have emphasised different goals for multicultural education and this has resulted in a *pluralism of paradigms* in Western societies, in constructing an education system appropriate to those perceptions of cultural pluralism. Some educationists have embraced differing kinds of multicultural or multiethnic education, while others have favoured intercultural and still others anti-racist education as the organising label for their proposed reponse.

In this chapter, I want to draw out the thread of that diversity of responses to cultural pluralism into greater detail. I want to elaborate what I said in Chapter 1 by describing, analysing and comparing the responses of the major Western nations and of some of the major advocates of multicultural education working within those nations, before describing some of the major attempts to categorise the manifold views of what multicultural education is.

18

The international context of human rights

First, however, I want to set these developments within individual nations and regions, such as Europe, in a wider international context. Indeed, in order to gain perspective, it is essential that democratic societies recognise, outside of themselves and their own legislation and regulation, overarching values and principles which are at the core of a commitment to democratic cultural pluralism and their educational support for that pluralism: multicultural education. One of the major weaknesses in the field has been the intellectual and moral parochialism within which it has been launched and pursued, and the consequent impoverished and blinkered responses of the various nation states, usually in isolation from one another.

While the influence of international instruments for the achievement of human rights should not be underestimated, neither should the ingenuity of signatory nations in attempting to circumvent some of their provisions when it suits them. By 1983 there were well over fifty of these declarations, covenants and agreements, not all of which by any means had been signed, nor indeed ratified after signature, by all nations.[1] The main international instruments, however, may be summarised as centring around the United Nations Declaration of Human Rights, dating from 1948, the European Convention on Human Rights (1950), the Convention on Consent to Marriage, Minimum age for Marriage and Registration of Marriages (1962), the International Convention on the Elimination of all Forms of Racial Discrimination (1965), together with the United Nations General Assembly Declaration of 1965, the International Covenant on Civil and Political Rights (1966), the Unesco Declaration on Race and Racial Prejudice, dating from 1978 and the Convention on the Elimination of all Forms of Discrimination Against Women (1979).

To begin with a basic example, the Universal Declaration states in Article 2:

> Everyone is entitled to all the rights and freedoms set forth in this Declaration, without distinction of any kind, such as race, colour, sex, language, religion, political or other origin, national or social origin, property, birth or other status.[2]

Of course, the cynical may well say that we are still a long way from achieving that goal. But the force of an international agreement is that it provides a basic ethic of humanity which must underpin any commitment to multicultural education. In a sense, such agreements are the modern instrumental equivalent of previous religious covenants, not replacing them but identifying,

19

universally, common human rights that in some cases derive from their highest ideals. They provide us with tentative answers to questions such as 'What is acceptable and legitimate in a multi-cultural society and what is not?' and 'Who is to decide whether this value, action or behaviour is acceptable and legitimate for a nation committed to multicultural education?'.

Similarly, the Convention on Consent to Marriage, Minimum Age for Marriage and Registration of Marriage states: 'No marriage shall be legally entered into without the full and free consent of both parties, such consent to be expressed by them in person after due publicity . . . ' And the subsequent General Assembly Resolution adds (Principle II): 'Member States shall take legislative action to specify a minimum age for marriage, which in any case shall not be less than fifteen years of age . . .'[3] It must be added that this declaration had received the support of only thirty-four signatory nations, including the United Kingdom, by 1984.

The United Nations Declaration on the Elimination of All Forms of Racial Discrimination (1963), signed and/or ratified by 123 nations by April 1984, declares: 'Discrimination between human beings on the ground of race, colour or ethnic origins is an offence to human dignity and shall be condemned . . . ' (Article I), and further, 'Particular efforts shall be made to prevent discrimination based on race, colour or ethnic origin, especially in the fields of civil rights, access to citizenship, education, religion, employment, occupation and housing' (Article 3.)[4]

Racial prejudice and/or discrimination are thus not only morally wrong according to a religious belief, or national legislation, or local authority policy, or school rules, but because they offend against humanity as codified in an international moral instrument.

Endorsing and updating this latter convention, the Unesco Declaration on Race and Racial Prejudice, adopted and proclaimed by the General Conference of Unesco at its twentieth session of 27 November 1978, states:

> Any distinction, exclusion, restriction or preference based on race, colour, ethnic or national origin or religious intolerance motivated by racist considerations, which destroys or compromises the sovereign equality of States and the right of peoples to self determination, or which limits in an arbitrary or discriminatory manner the right of every human being and group to full development is incompatible with the requirements of an international order which is just and guarantees respect for human rights.[5]

On the twenty-fifth anniversary of the adoption of the Universal Declaration of Human Rights, the United Nations convened, in

New York, a special General Assembly on 10 December 1973, which officially launched the decade for action to combat racism and racial discrimination. Such international agreements, covenants, conventions and declarations are an indispensable but not sufficient identification of the ethical base and criteria for personal and professional judgement in multicultural education.

Some nations have also legislated a Bill of Rights for their citizens and in a few cases, e.g. Europe, this has been done on a regional basis. But seeking redress and endorsement of civil rights and liberties where there is no such national codification is lengthy, daunting and expensive. In addition, therefore, to any international and regional instruments, all democratic countries should have a Bill of Rights for their citizens, so that the rights and freedoms of their citizens cannot be easily infringed or denied, nor lightly altered. Many countries, the United Kingdom included, do not yet have a Charter of Rights and Freedoms.

It is in this wider international and regional context that teachers wishing to implement policies of multicultural education have to see their task. They need some considerable knowledge of human rights instruments, particularly those concerned with race and racism and women's and children's rights. Human rights transcend frontiers and entitle individuals to claim authority for their liberties beyond the state. Equally, they impose duties beyond frontiers, not to exploit the civil rights of others. For the political and economic interdependence of peoples in a 'shrinking' world ensures that global and international issues are context-setting for multicultural education.

It is illogical and unethical, as well as an infringement of the human rights of others, to claim for ourselves, or support by our actions or lethargy, economic exploitation, racism, discrimination against other countries, whilst declaring ourselves committed to those principles in implementing multicultural education in our own societies. Multicultural education is thus inevitably set within a wider global context, which provides moral definition for its implementation.

Developments in the United States

Turning now to other nations let us take a brief look at developments in the United States where approaches to multicultural education have to be seen in the context of the birth and growth of slavery in society, and the ethnic revival and civil rights movements which arose in the United States in the 1950s and 1960s. The institutionalisation of slavery brought about a legitimation of racism which continued long after legislation had been introduced to abolish slavery. Thus, whilst the institutionalisation of slavery was eliminated, the institutionalisation of racism in American society continued. This discrimination was not restricted to blacks but included immigrant groups such as Chicanos and indigent communities including the native peoples.

As in a number of nations, race riots led, in the early 1940s, to the development of the Intergroup Education Movement in the late 1940s and early 1950s, a major aim of which was to reduce racial and ethnic prejudice and misunderstanding. This movement tended to be a defensive reflex reaction by dominant groups. As Banks has pointed out in a recent paper,[6] the Intergroup Education Movement was essentially assimilationist in intent, not aimed at the maintenance of cultural difference. Its major advocates were from the dominant white community. The result was that intergroup education came to be seen as a palliative for the *status quo*, rather than as a means of achieving social and racial justice for minority groups.

Gradually, stimulated by legislation dismantling segregation and the provision of allegedly 'separate but equal' educational facilities, a Civil Rights Movement emerged to give expression to the black revolt which erupted in the 1960s. In the response to the riots of the mid and late 1960s, a whole series of federal and state initiatives was taken to give effect to civil rights and to lessen racial tension. In 1964 the Civil Rights Act was passed, which forbade discrimination on the basis of race, colour, religion or national origins in American public accommodation and education, in federally assisted programmes and in most areas of private employment. One of the big lessons of the Act was that something more positive than legislation was needed to give effect to substantive social equality. Legislation was necessary but not sufficient. The assumption that the Act would make race increasingly irrelevant was turned, through implementation strategies such as quotas and affirmative action, into a reality where race became more important and prominent. The Civil Rights Movement also spawned what later became known as the multiethnic dimension of educational provision.

The predominant thrust was compensatory, as is evidenced by the Title I amendments to the Elementary and Secondary Education Act (ESEA) of 1965, providing assistance for the education of low income families' children, and the Bilingual Education Act of 1968, which provided special funds for the school instruction of those with other than English mother-tongue. The Title IX Amendment, the Ethnic Heritage Studies Act of 1972, was slightly different insofar as the aim was to foster the development and dissemination of materials on the history and culture of ethnic groups and to encourage appropriate teacher training.

One distinctive feature of the historical process of the development of education in the United States, largely absent in other countries, is the participation of federal and district courts and their decisions in shaping educational policy. Two decisions, in the 1970s, for example, Lau versus Nichols of 1974 and Martin Luther King Junior Elementary School Children versus Ann Arbor School District in 1979, focussed on the language issue and provoked heated debate.

Later the focus broadened to include the civil rights of women, handicapped individuals and senior citizens, and at each stage vigorous debate was evoked. As a consequence, substantial improvements were achieved, including the revision of textbook materials, the introduction of criteria for training teachers, the appointment of staff in teacher training with a predominant interest in multiethnic education, including at professorial rank, and the appointment of a small number of black academics from other ethnic minority communities to professional appointments in higher education, including teacher education. Many school boards and professional organisations also developed policy statements and initiatives in this field and a whole programme of ethnic heritage studies material was developed with aid from a federal department, the Ethnic Heritage Studies Department of the Department of Health, Education and Welfare.

A second, consequent and distinctive characteristic of the American development in this field has been the wide array of imperatives which have faced educational providers. These imperatives include legislation, policy demands and statements of ethnic and cultural groups and professional organisations, regulations at federal, state and local level, judicial decisions and the requirements of professional and accreditation organisations, such as the National Council for the Accreditation of Teacher Education (NCATE). As the number of interest groups increased, however, the focus of the movement became more blurred and energies were more dissipated, so that there were those who argued, by the early 1980s, that the movement had lost its direction and momentum.

With the advent of the Reagan administration, the Ethnic Heritage Studies Department of the Department of Health, Education and Welfare was abolished and multiethnic education became a decreasing concern. Multiethnic education was no longer high on the agenda of educational policy-making and national reports indicated a deterioration in the position of blacks in society in general.

Turning now to the major advocates of multiethnic education in the United States, possibly the most eminent and consistent exponent of this field has been Professor James A. Banks of the

University of Washington, Seattle. The most important aim of multiethnic education for him is to reform all major variables in the school environment so that students from all ethnic and racial groups will experience educational equality.[7] Banks argues for a *holistic, multifactor paradigm* as a basis for policies of multicultural education, to facilitate the conceptualisation of the *total school environment* as a system, consisting of a number of identifiable factors, each of which would need to be changed to reflect ethnic, cultural, social class and sex equality. These factors include the ethos of the school, including its norms and values, its curriculum and teaching materials, its assessment and testing procedures, its language policy, its teaching and motivational styles and its approach to racism and racism elimination.

His holistic approach to multicultural education, considering schools as dynamic, social systems, draws attention to the interdependence of a multitude of factors in the school environment, each of which needs to be addressed according to multicultural criteria. This approach provides a baseline for both acculturation and accommodation, enabling children from ethnic minority communities to maintain their separate identities, but also to achieve socialisation sufficient for peaceful, effective and satisfying interaction with students from other ethnic minority communities. The process is one of mutual acculturation rather than exclusive accommodation by the minority to majority culture. Thus, students will achieve the competences to become successful citizens of their own cultural communities, their nations and the global world community.[8] His analysis and proposals contain three major dimensions, indispensable for any commitment to multicultural education in a pluralist democracy: maintenance of a dynamic diversity; acceptance of the need for social cohesion; and a commitment to greater equality, albeit one subject to redefinition.

Gollnick and Chinn consider that multicultural education should be conceptualised to include a very wide range of interests, including ethnic, credal, social class, age group, sex and language as well as racial and handicapped considerations.[9] Gay, on the other hand, sees such a broadening as potentially distorting and even destructive of the major purposes of multicultural education.[10] It is also argued that the diffuse focus detracts attention away from major issues of prejudice, discrimination and equality *vis-à-vis* ethnic groups in general and blacks in particular in American society. Baker sees the aim of multicultural education as a process of growing self – and other-culture awareness and the development of skills in individuals to participate in as many cultural groups as they choose. She envisages multiethnic education, concerned with such groups as blacks, Hispanic and native Americans as being at the centre of multicultural education, concerned with broader cultural groupings such as religious groups, women, the handicapped, etc., located within international education.[11]

Grant, a past director of the Teacher Corps Associates, sees multicultural education as implying three major expectations for teachers: self-understanding; understanding and acceptance of the concept of pluralism; and affirmation of the principles of pluralism in the total school environment: staffing patterns, curricula, language policy and instructional materials.[12] He believes that appropriate teacher education is a key element in the introduction of multicultural education and that only strategies of *normative re-education* change can achieve the necessary and fundamental value, habit and meaning reorientation.[13]

One of the major strengths of the American literature in this field is the wide diversity of views which have focussed on issues of ethnicity. The so-called neo-conservatives, for example, who have included such well-known figures as Jean Kirkpatrick, Senator Daniel Moynihan and the distinguished sociologist and prolific writer, Nathan Glazer, have consistently expressed doubt about major issues of public policy in American society, not least those of race, ethnicity and culture.[14] At the centre of such doubts have been items from the liberal agenda of the 1960s and 1970s such as affirmative action, group, as opposed to individual rights, bi-lingualism, the need to continue to create from an indigent society a common American identity, etc. Bowles and Gintis adopted a neo-Marxist critique of schools in the United States,[15] the implications of which are that the school cannot be effective against the pressures to inequality in the broader capitalist society: a view of the limitations of schooling put more influentially perhaps by Jencks.[16]

All of this has made for a very rich and open debate and the demolition of taboos. More progress has, for example, also been made than in almost any other Western country in identifying the causes of racism and advancing strategies for its elimination[17] and in beginning to comprehend the importance of teaching and learning styles, locus of control and language in educational performance[18] and the role of media in multicultural education.[19] The discourse has drawn back the curtain of secrecy and ignorance from issues which are still in intellectual purdah in some other countries.

Developments in Canada

In Canada, there are long-established black communities which, together with the surrounding dominant cultures, provided an early haven for escapees from slavery in the United States. Ontario alone

25

provided sanctuary for 40,000 runaway slaves. The British Empire's first anti-slavery law was passed in Ontario in 1793, preceding by forty-one years the Imperial Emancipation Act and by seventy-one years, Abraham Lincoln's declaration.[20] The Ontario Racial Discrimination Act was passed in 1944, preceding the United Nations Declaration on Human Rights by four years; a Canadian Bill of Rights was passed in 1960; and that same province, Ontario, established a Human Rights Commission and Code in 1962. On the other hand, slavery was practised in Canada and blacks have had to fight job discrimination, segregated schools and housing and refusal of service in hotels and restaurants. Not until the major immigration influxes of the early post-war period stimulated discussion of issues of citizenship and pluralism was the task tackled of developing a more encompassing policy to include all Canada's cultural communities.

With the appointment of the Royal Commission on Bilingualism and Biculturalism by the late Lester B. Pearson, on 19 July 1962, the pursuit of a broad and comprehensive policy was commenced. In spite of the endorsement of Common Law Rights in the 1960 legislation and federal and counterpart legislation at provincial level, the 1950s and early 1960s had been a period marked by violence and unrest, and this had led to the establishment of the Royal Commission, with the task of reconciling the maintenance of the two basic cultures in Canadian Society, British and French, with a commitment to the numerous other cultural groups. Book Four of the Royal Commission's Report was submitted to the Governor General on 23 October 1969, and on 8 October 1971 the Prime Minister, Pierre Trudeau, tabled his government's official response in the House of Commons, which was accepted unanimously. Thus began a period of political aspiration to a policy of *multiculturalism within a bilingual framework*, which is unique in Western nations.

In 1972 a Minister of State responsible for Multiculturalism was nominated and one year later the Canadian Consultative Council on Multiculturalism was constituted, in May 1973, as an advisory body to the Minister of State for Multiculturalism.[21] From 1972, a Multiculturalism Directorate was established within the Department of the Secretary of State, reporting to the Minister of State for Multiculturalism with regard to its main objective, namely to encourage and assist, within the framework of Canada's official language policy and in the spirit of existing human rights codes, the full realisation of the multicultural nature of Canadian society, through programmes that promote the preservation and sharing of cultural heritages and which facilitate mutual appreciation and understanding among all Canadians.

From 1982, a Race Relations Unit was established with the task of supporting efforts to improve understanding among Canadians of various racial backgrounds and, from 1983, a special parliamentary committee on the participation of visible minorities in Canadian education was constituted, with the task of reporting to Parliament in 1984. That committee presented its first report entitled *Equality Now!* in March 1984.[22] It contained eighty major recommendations on social integration, employment, public policy, justice, the media and education. It was almost immediately greeted by the Minister of State for Multiculturalism, David M. Collenette, with a positive and supportive response,[23] and, within 120 days, a major response of the government to the report was published, including details concerning action on each of the eighty recommendations.[24]

Meanwhile, as part of the patriation of the Canadian Constitution, a list of rights and freedoms, the Canadian Charter of Rights and Freedoms, was included as part of Canada's new Constitution.[25] The Government also set out a national strategy for race relations, allocating $81.5 million immediately in 1981 to that task, and encouraging school boards to act.[26] Many school boards established policies and structures for the implementation of good race relations, dealing with racial and ethnic incidents in schools.[27] Teachers' assocations have drawn up policy guidelines[28] and, at the federal level (as well as provincial), Human Rights Commissions exist throughout Canada, with explicit Human Rights Codes such as that proclaimed as Law on 15 June 1982 for the province of Ontario.[29]

In November 1981, a National Conference on Multicultural Education, organised in Winnipeg by ad hoc committees from each of the provinces and territories of Canada, with the support of the Multicultural Directorate, founded a new organisation, the Canadian Council on Multicultural and Intercultural Education (CCMIE), with representatives from various provincial and territorial committees. As well as fostering a commitment to multiculturalism and equal recognition and consideration in educational institutions of all cultures, one of the tasks of the Council is to combat racism and discrimination. The organisation represents a coalition of political, academic, lay, administrative and other representatives from different cultural and racial groups.

Canadian academics have begun to acquire an international reputation for their work in the field of multicultural education. In particular, a group of younger academics at the prestigious Ontario Institute for Studies in Education (OISE) have made important empirical and conceptual advances possible. The work of Dr Jim Cummins has focussed on the effects of bilingualism on children's cognitive development, language planning and public policy on bilingualism and bilingual education, the effects of pedagogical strategies on the development of language and literacy and issues of bilingualism and special education.[30] Professor Michel Laferrière broadened the focus of bilingualism by including consideration of issues of racism,[31] while Professor Fernand Ouellet of Sherbrooke University, Quebec, sought to investigate the area of values and religion. Others, such as Dr John Kehoe and Dr John Mallea, also of OISE, have aimed to document and develop the field conceptually and analytically, drawing on sociology and comparative ethnic studies.[32] Dean Wood has sought to produce materials for ethnic studies,[33] whilst many others, such as Professor Kogila Moodley of the University of British Columbia and Professor Joti Bhatnagar of Concordia University, have attempted to introduce greater critical reflexivity into policy development.[34]

In the permeation of commitment to multiculturalism and anti-racism, Canada has gone further than any other Western nation in achieving a national consensus. In particular, the multifaceted nature of the approach has ensured that, in addition to legislative measures to achieve equality of educational opportunity and to outlaw racialism, financial and political support has been forth-coming for major initiatives at all levels, even taking into account the criticisms which Canadians themselves make of the Canadian policy of multiculturalism.[35]

Developments in Australia

After a long historical development in which indigent minorities were subject to racial persecution and extermination and a *de facto* white Australia policy was pursued, with ideologies of assimilation and integration towards new immigrants dominant, Australia gradually became committed in the 1970s to a policy of multi-cultural education. The reasons for this change were both demo-graphic and political.

Whilst, for example, in the early post-war period successive waves of immigrants had been predominantly composed of British stock with a small admixture of other Europeans and a total ex-clusion of Asians, the white Australia policy of the inter-war period was effectively continued. With the surge of British and Northern European migrants drying up, an increasing number of migrants from Southern European countries arrived, and from the mid-1960s immigrants from the Middle East were actually sought. Australia's population increasingly took on a more pluralist com-position, not only ethnically and linguistically, but also racially.[36] It was not, however, until the autumn of 1975 that, with the support of all political parties, the Racial Discrimination Act was passed.

In 1970 a five-year Child Migrant Education Programme was commenced with a budget of over a million Australian dollars per annum. Special migrant education programmes were also introduced and bilingual education programmes, including also Aboriginal children in the Northern Territory, date from the early 1970s. The year 1976 saw the establishment of a national Aboriginal Education Committee and in 1975 the Schools Commission produced a report suggesting extensive changes in educational provision, including the development of multicultural education.

A seminal document in this development was the brief but influential response of the Australian Ethnic Affairs Council, which had been established in January 1977, to the Green Paper on immigration policies and Australia's population. It was entitled *Australia as a Multicultural Society*.[37] Whilst a major focus of the document was on the area of language, it also included proposals for the development of ethnic studies programmes for all children, teacher education and material production.

A review group was established in September 1977 to look at post-arrival programmes and services to migrants and to report back to the Commonwealth government. This body produced its report in April 1978, proposing a major Commonwealth initiative to ensure that greater priority was given to multicultural education for all children and recommending substantial financial support. It also made structural proposals for the co-ordination of Commonwealth policies and programmes with regard to schools and school systems in the field of multicultural education, and the inclusion in courses at all tertiary institutions of appropriate multicultural dimensions. It recommended the establishment of an institute of multicultural affairs to be directed by a small group of experts in the field. The guiding principles in these recommendations were those of equality of opportunity, the right to the maintenance of personal culture without prejudice or disadvantage, the need for special services and programmes to ensure equality of access and provision for migrants and client involvement in the design and operation of services and programmes with the encouragement of self-help as much as possible.[38]

Almost simultaneously with the publication, a high level group was established to clarify the concept of multicultural education. The group made an important contribution to the debate in defining the commonalities of Australian society, whilst at the same time firmly embracing the concept of structural pluralism.[39] Other measures contributed to a torrent of initiatives and publications, advocating the development of Australia as a multicultural society and the introduction of multicultural education.

The Curriculum Development Centre, set up in the mid-1970s in

Canberra as an independent statutory body, instituted in 1977 a small grant scheme for school and community groups involved in education for a multicultural society, and the Educational Research and Development Committee also contributed by supporting research into multicultural education. Both of these institutions were, however, abolished in 1981, as part of the government's spending cuts. The Australian Ethnic Affairs Council, established in January 1977 to advise the Minister for Immigration and Ethnic Affairs, operated three committees, including one on multicultural education, another on community consultation and ethnic media and a third on settlement programmes. In 1977 it published its influential paper *Australia as a Multicultural Society*,[40] which centred around three key issues, *social cohesion*, *equality* and *cultural identity*.

Meanwhile, the Galbally Report recommendation on the establishment of an Australian Institute of Multicultural Affairs was implemented with the setting up, in 1979, of such an institute with Mr Frank Galbally as chairman of the Council. The review which it immediately conducted of multicultural initiatives has been criticised for ideological bias and highly selective research. Such criticism preceded the resignation of the Director and proposals for changes in the charter, the name and mode of operation of the Institute.[41]

Notwithstanding such initiatives, there is increasing concern about racism and prejudice within Australian society.[42] There has, however, been progress in the development of a more viable approach to multicultural education as a result of the initiatives taken by the Ethnic Affairs Task Force of the Australian Council on Population and Ethnic Affairs established in April 1981. This involved a series of public fora and consultations, resulting in two major publications which appeared in late 1982.[43]

Possibly the most prolific and influential writer in the field of multicultural education in Australia is Dr Brian Bullivant, a long-term critic of simplistic approaches to multiculturalism, who has proposed an analysis which includes both the establishment of a *polyethnic survival curriculum* and the recognition that racial, cultural, ethnic, class and gender differences are being adopted as boundary markers in processes of exclusion and inclusion which are overlapping and multifaceted means of attempting to maximise social rewards and economic resources.[44] Above all, he has been responsible for a much more self-critical, reflexive and rigorous approach to the identification of educational initiatives, appropriate to a dynamic and changing view of ethnic and class groups as non-homogeneous entities and the development in education of a much more power-sensitive approach. Sociologists such as the late Dr Jean Martin, Professor Jerzy Zubrzycki and psychologists such as Professor Ronald Taft were early contributors to the field and influential in the development of subsequent policy. More recently, educationists such as Dr Jerzy Smolicz have made extensive contributions through their research, writing and curriculum development work.[45]

The dominant characteristics of the development of multicultural education in Australia centre on its acceptance and support from the mid-1970s by all political parties. The policies of governments at both federal and regional levels, the structural accommodations and changes which have been made in order to implement the policy, the presence of a small number of academics who have contributed to the theoretical development and, more recently, the inclusion of issues of racial prejudice as being among the more dominant within the progress towards a multicultural society also locate it culturally.

Marked characteristics include a more open debate and wide national consultations and discussions concerning the content and directionality of policies of multicultural education. Equally, issues of racism and anti-racist education have been increasingly highlighted in the late 1970s and early 1980s. Each state now has an official advisory committee on multicultural education and there is co-ordination at federal level by the National Advisory and Co-ordinating Committee on Multicultural Education. There is also growing awareness of the complexity of the issues inherent in education for cultural pluralism, and the need to avoid naive, folkloric, simplistic and romantic approaches to multi-cultural education. Bullivant reports, however, that the teaching of multicultural education in most schools is confined to minor additive courses rather than a major reconstruction of the whole curriculum and that virtually nothing is being done to make multicultural education more politically sensitive and the curriculum more appropriate to the needs of ethnic minority children's life chances.[46]

European developments

Whilst there are a number of distinctive differences in the development of educational responses to the perception of cultural pluralism in Europe from those which we have noted in the case of North America and Australia, there are also certain commonalities, such as the mounting concern with issues of race relations in the late 1970s and early 1980s. Additionally, although the extent of interaction between theoreticians and academics in the three aforementioned countries should not be underestimated, there has probably been greater emphasis on international (particularly

European) initiatives than is the case in the other three countries. Thus, notwithstanding significant bilateral and national initiatives, it is international initiatives such as those launched from the early 1970s by the Council of Europe and from the mid-1970s by the European Economic Community which have dominated policy-making.[47] The preference in a European context has, in any case, been for the concept of *intercultural education*.[48] Intercultural education tends to focus on home and host country language provision, preparation of teachers for this task, the special problems of migrant workers' children and folkloric and highly marginal changes to the curriculum in response to problems 'caused' by immigrants.

The Directive on mother-tongue instruction has been neglected, if not actively disregarded, by many of the countries of the European Community.[49] A report prepared for the European Community, concerned with three of the countries of the EEC, graphically documented a vicious cycle of economic deprivation, social and legal scapegoating and educational marginalisation as the lot of children of migrant workers, and the generalisation could be applied to most countries in Western Europe.[50]

The European Convention, signed on 4 November 1950, which came into force on 3 September 1953, and the second protocol conferring on the European Court of Human Rights competence to give advisory opinions have been increasingly utilised by United Kingdom citizens in the absence of a national Bill of Rights of their own.[51] Although the United Kingdom did not grant its citizens right of individual petition for the first ten years of the Convention, it has been 'found guilty' in twice as many cases as any other single country and more 'provisional files' are opened against it each year than against any of the other member states. Moreover, the Council of Europe's work in the field of human rights education in schools, which dates from a resolution by the Committee of Ministers in 1978 and which the Committee has addressed in a specific objective of its second media term plan and in its declaration of 14 May 1981, is important in setting an ethical context in schools for the implementation of measures of multicultural education.[52]

Significant theoretical advances have recently begun through the work of such academics as Professor Louis Porcher [53] and M. Maurice Mauviel[54] in France, but the language barrier has proved an effective inhibitor to the transmission of such theoretical advances across national boundaries. Individual scholars and groups have begun to make a contribution, such as Professor Camilleri, working on intercultural phenomena, at the psychological laboratory at the University Paris V – René Descartes; Dr Pierre Dasen of the University of Geneva, attempting to bridge anglophone and francophone research in the area; and the Alfa group in the Federal Republic of Germany has sought to develop internationally valid evaluation of the field.[55]

But the European country which has probably moved furthest in its commitment to genuine partnership and dialogue as a basis for multicultural education is Sweden. In 1974, with the publication of the *Invandrarutredingen*, the country forsook its previous assimilationist policy and the following year adopted a new policy, embracing the principles of equality, freedom and partnership. This was followed by the home language reform of 1977, placing a responsibility on local authorities to provide mother-tongue teaching and, with the subsequent establishment of national commissions to look into issues such as ethnic prejudice and discrimination, the way was paved for the publication of the Report, *Different Origins: Partnership in Sweden*, in 1983, which included a commitment to intercultural training for all school staffs.[56]

With few exceptions, the development of educational policies for cultural pluralism still rests at a very immature stage, where the focus is predominantly on foreigners, immigrants and language issues, although substantial progress has been made in recognising and implementing international statutes concerned with human rights and the elimination of racism,[57] and beginning to teach human rights in the curriculum of some schools.

Categorisations of multicultural education

From the brief overview above it is clear that there is a wide diversity of positions across nations, among authorities and in the ranks of academics and other advocates of multicultural education. But whilst there are major differences, there are also major similarities and even commonalities. Spurred by such considerations, a number of writers have sought to achieve a coherent overview of the field by developing categorisations of different approaches.

In the United States, Gibson, drawing predominantly on American material, has distinguished five major approaches:

1 Education of the culturally different or benevolent multiculturalism;
2 Education about cultural differences or cultural understanding;
3 Education for cultural pluralism;
4 Bicultural education;
5 Multicultural education as the normal school experience.[58]

Taking her point of departure primarily in the anthropological literature on cultural pluralism, ethnicity and acculturation, the author analyses the five approaches and their assumptions and delineates the underlying values, change strategies, intended outcomes and target populations. The first four approaches derive from the educational literature on bicultural and multicultural education, whereas the fifth derives from key concepts of education and culture and draws particularly on sociological definitions and anthropological concepts. Education is no longer equated with schooling, nor is culture restricted to ethnic group, and she argues that efforts to support ethnically separate schools are antithetical to the purposes of multicultural education.

A second categorisation is that developed by Williams, describing alternative perspectives on the multicultural curriculum. She identifies three types of justification for such a curriculum developing a typology in order to clarify the debate concerning differing ideologies and practices.[59] The three approaches which she identifies are the *technicist* approach, the *moral* approach and the *socio-political* approach. She considers each of these approaches in terms of five major dimensions: their educational ideologies; their definition of the educational problem to be remedied; the types of programme they recommend; the curriculum emphases; and their central value assumption.

The technicist approach rests upon the assumption that the main problems and solutions relate to the development of educational skills and are best resolved by experts within the teaching profession. It is of the 'compensatory education' tradition, sharing many of its basic values and approaches. She identifies the moral perspective as aimed at improving the ability of individuals to understand themselves and so to foster intergroup co-operation. It is aimed at all pupils within schools and cherishes a concern to diminish prejudice and discrimination. The third perspective, the socio-political, Williams identifies as being the most common in sociological comment and research, deriving particularly from a sociology of knowledge perspective. She emphasises that none of the perspectives is straightforward, unambiguous or without problems and critics.

Lynch has developed two typologies. The first, identifying different *strategies of innovation* aimed at introducing multicultural education into teacher education curricula, derives from an empirical study of multicultural teacher education in Australia. The second looks at the *global ideologies* underlying different approaches to multicultural education. In the first, six major innovatory curricular tactics are identified, described and analysed. These are *parallel* approaches such as Black studies, Asian studies, Caribbean studies; *additive* approaches which involve small units or modules or components being added to existing curricula, in already existing subjects or areas such as art, history, religion, etc.; *permeation* approaches involve the internal rearticulation or redesign of the structure of knowledge of existing courses; *materials production* approaches represent predominantly knowledge-based approaches to more effective educational strategies, as, for example, in the 'race pack' of the Humanities Curriculum Project; *consultancy* approaches are institutional tactics, where a dialogical partnership is adopted, involving local advisers, syndicates, teacher education tutors, etc.; and an *action research* approach takes account of power and policy issues in the implementation of deliberate strategies to change and monitor the curriculum.[60]

In a more recent categorisation, deriving from extensive consideration of initiatives in Europe, Lynch proposes three basic underlying ideologies, motivating attempts to implement multicultural education. These, he identified as *purposive-economic*, *egalitarian* and *interdependent*. He examines each of these ideological orientations underlying multicultural education in terms of six major areas: their implicit value orientation; their major aims; their approach to issues of language; their curricula; their view of the structure of education; and their approach to the control of education.[61] He concludes his analysis by arguing that the major ideology, which has underlain the predominance of efforts to develop multicultural education, has been one based on economic motivation as a means to hold the school and the education which it provides, on course to the needs of industry and, through that process, to serve the demands of dominant groups in society.

Nixon, looking at the way in which policies may be interpreted into practice, identifies two broad organisational structures within which the curriculum may be developed, in order to meet the needs of a multicultural society. These he identifies as *accretion* and *permeation*. Under accretion he sees three possibilities which he labels multicultural education as an *optional extra*, as a *common core* and as *piecemeal development*. Under permeation, an alternative strategy to the accretion approach, all approaches involve a rethinking and restructuring of every aspect of the curriculum. Adopting a partially developmental perspective on the permeation process, he envisages three phases: *small scale innovation*; *co-ordination and development* and *consultation and evaluation*.[62]

In a very early conceptualisation, Gay also seeks to adopt a developmental perspective on the evolution of multicultural education, whilst at the same time advocating rapid movement into the stage where multicultural education is seen as *process*. She identifies three major prestages to this development: *Stage One*, where varying concepts of multicultural education co-exist simultaneously in different parts of the country because of its differential stages of development; *Stage Two*, where in a similar way to the intermediate stage of development for living organisms the concept of multi-cultural education becomes broadened in complexity and the concept becomes more definitive; and, *Stage Three*, where the recognition is born that the educative process, concerned with cultural differences, has to include more than just the acquisition of cognitive information. It requires equal attention to instructional strategies and learning activities, the environments in which they live and learn, the structural organisation of the schools and the institutional values, its commitments and academics policy priorities.[63] Her overview was written in 1977, focussed on developments which had taken place in the previous two decades in the United States.

In one of the most major recent attempts to categorise and analyse comparatively responses to cultural diversity in various societies, Stephan has set up a sophisticated typology, which includes, in the one dimension, five major aspects of multiculturalism: the *political, social, economic, cultural* and the *socio-pyschological* dimensions;[64] and on the other axis, the three major types of socio-historical situations out of which multiethnic societies have emerged, derived from Watson's previous classification, concerned particularly with educational policies.[65]

In a comprehensive and developmental analysis, Banks attempts to correlate four phases in the development of ethnic revitalisation movements with the responses which schools have made to those phases, emphasising that these response paradigms might develop within a nation at different times and indeed even co-exist at the same time. He sees only one being dominant, however, at any particular point in time. He identified ten major response paradigms which he labels *ethnic additive, self-concept development, cultural deprivation, language, racism, radical, genetic, cultural pluralist, cultural difference* and *assimilationist*. Each of these, then, is located in terms of their major assumptions, their major goals and school programmes and practices.[66]

Whilst there is insufficient space here to describe, in detail, the approaches adopted by Banks, they represent perhaps the most extensive categorisation of approaches to multicultural education developed so far. It is important to emphasise that Banks regards the situation as continuing to be very fluid and emergent, where one dominant paradigm replaces another and a 'Kuhn' scientific revolution takes place.[67] More frequently, however, he sees a new paradigm emerging from the challenge which is levied against an older one, but which it does not replace. In this context of a scientific attempt to marshal our current information and approaches to multicultural education, it seems important to repeat Banks's

TABLE 2.1: *A collection of categorisations of multicultural education*

Author	Gibson	Williams	Nixon	Lynch 1	Lynch 2	Gay	(Watson) Stephan	Banks
Categor-isation	*Education*	*Approaches*	*Broad Organisation Curriculum Approaches*	*Curricular Tactics*	*Ideologies*	*Stages*	*Dimensions*	*Paradigm Change*
	1 Culturally Different	Technicist	Accretion	Parallel	Purposive-	1 Simulta-neous variety	Political	Ethnic
	2 About Cultural Difference	Moral	Optional Extra	Additive	Economic	2 Refined, broadened and Definitive	Social	Additive
	3 Cultural Pluralism	Socio-political	Common Core	Permeation	Egalitarian	3 Gestalt Holistic	Economic	Self Concept
	4 Bicultural Education		Piecemeal Development	Materials Production	Inter-dependent	4 Process Approach	Cultural	Cultural Deprivation
	5 Multicultural Education for All		*Permeation* (Phases)	Consultancy			Socio-psychological of *Multicultural Societies* (Watson)	Language Assimilation-ist
			1 Small-scale Innovation	Action Research			Amalgamation	Genetic
			2 Co-ordination and Development				Assimilation	Cultural Pluralist
			3 Consultation and evaluation				Quasi-immigration	Cultural Difference
								Racist
								Radical

judgement that, whilst the radical critics of multicultural education tend to be cogent and explicit in their criticism of schools, they are vague and ambiguous in proposing strategies for school reform. They thus provide practising teachers with few insights, techniques and methods that can be used, either within the classroom or the school, in order to bring about appropriate and legitimate reform.

I have collected the above categorisations into an overview and presented them in Table 2.1. Although it is beyond the scope of this chapter to give a detailed analysis, and the categorisations have only been identified by key words, there are clearly major similarities in all approaches, but also major differences of emphasis and approach related often to the *Weltanschauung* of the individual.

Summary: some implications for educators

Measuring initiatives and arguments within the United Kingdom against those described briefly above must inevitably evoke a certain feeling of *déjà vu* in an outside observer. The fixation with untenable monocausal explanations of underachievement is one example. There is, thus, much that can be learned from the work of policy-makers, academics and teachers, viewed internationally, which would enrich the way in which pedagogies of multicultural education might be attempted. So what can practising teachers learn from what has happened abroad? And, are there lessons, resources, information and research on which they could draw?[68]

A number of tentative principles arise from this very brief international survey, which might act as principles of procedure for the next part of this book, where we consider, in greater detail, the development and implementation of strategies of multicultural education. They might be briefly and provisionally summarised as follows:

1 Issues of global, development and international education are an indispensable context for the launching of multicultural education;
2 Each country needs a Bill of Rights and liberties itself, in addition to international or regional instruments in this field;
3 Whilst it will not lead automatically to increased commitment, a knowledge of the international and national context of human rights and anti-racist instruments is essential knowledge for teachers;
4 Legislation and policy statements are necessary but insufficient instruments to achieve greater quality and social justice; active implementation strategies are needed, particularly in education;

5   Open and rigorous debate is an essential prerequisite to the development of realistic, practical initiatives in the field and this applies at all levels: national and international codifications of human rights and liberties should provide guidelines for that discourse and for the safeguarding of a variety of legitimate views;

6   Evidence from a number of societies indicates that strategies for multicultural education cannot be effectively based on simplistic, monocausal explanations of the achievement of ethnic minority children;

7   Language issues are important and there is a need to achieve a better balance between home and national language policies in education;

8   A genuinely multicredal society is incompatible with an established religion;

9   Multicultural education must be pursued on a 'whole-institution' and 'whole-system' basis;

10   Staff development should address both cognitive and affective gains through normative-re-educative strategies;

11   Normative re-educative approaches to racism and prejudice reduction in schools for teachers and pupils are inevitably long term and necessitate continuing reinforcement throughout the school life of the child and the professional life of teachers; they demand a knowledge of the sources of prejudice reduction and of appropriate pedagogical strategies for prejudice-reduction and elimination;

12   Multicultural education cannot be a separate subject; it concerns all subject areas throughout the curriculum;

13   An understanding of differing learning styles, of issues of field dependence and independence, of locus of control research and of the assumptions behind teaching styles is essential to achieve better teaching/learning strategies and greater educational equality;

14   Multicultural education implies the development of new and alternative means of assessment;[69]

15   All of the above imply major and fundamental reforms in teacher education.

In the next chapter, I examine and analyse policy and practice in multicultural education in the United Kingdom, as it has grown since the end of the Second World War, against the background of international initiatives and developments described in this chapter. The principles identified above also provide us with guidelines for Part Two of this book, where I attempt to describe and analyse appropriate responses to cultural pluralism in the form that we call multicultural education.

Chapter 3

The development of multicultural education in the United Kingdom

Introduction

In Chapters 1 and 2 I have attempted to sketch the international background of educational responses to newly perceived cultural diversity. I have sought to identify and categorise the policy statements and theoretical and conceptual writings which have accrued, their advocates, critics and underlying ideological orientations. Against this background, this chapter attempts to look more closely at policy and practice in the United Kingdom since the end of the Second World War, as a basis for more detailed professional and practical issues in Part Two.

There seem to me to be five clearly identifiable chronological and conceptual phases in the development of multicultural education in the United Kingdom in the post-war period, ranging from a period of almost total *laissez-faire*, commencing at the end of the Second World War, to the present time and its broader and diversifying concerns with the emergence of a multicultural curriculum and pedagogy, including antiracist teaching strategies and prejudice reduction approaches. Whilst there is overlap between these phases and some characteristics of one period co-exist with others, it is nonetheless possible to identify overall characteristics of the following five phases.

1 *The 'laissez-faire' phase*

This period lasted approximately from the end of the Second World War until the beginning of the 1960s. It was a time of neglect and non-perception of the new social and cultural phenomena, either deriving from passive or active ignorance of the problems, or dominated by a nineteenth-century policy of *cultural hegemony*.

2 *The immigrant and ESL phase*

From the early 1960s, because of social pressures and unrest, a phase of apparently mounting, but largely passive, educational *assimilationist* concern commenced, where the first social initiatives were taken to put 'immigrant children' and issues associated with them on the educational agenda. Strategies in the school system included a heavy emphasis on English as a second language, dispersal policies and, in some cases, bussing, syphon-use of special education, marginalisation of ethnic minority children, etc. This period lasted until approximately the mid-1970s and it overlapped with:

3 *The deficit phase*

This transitional phase saw mounting awareness of the legal, social and school problems of ethnic minorities and the first *integrationist* developments of a folkloric multicultural education, striving towards an acknowledgment of the presence of alternative, legitimate and valid cultures. The emphasis was on life styles rather than life chances, on self-esteem and identity rather than curricular or structural disadvantaging.

4 *The multicultural phase*

From the late 1970s multicultural education entered a substantially different phase, where holistic issues of curriculum design, including assessment, pedagogical strategies and systemic reform were seen as central to the development of a harmonious but culturally heterogeneous society. This *cultural pluralist* phase, addressing all children, led to and continues in parallel with the contemporary phase.

5 *The anti-racist phase*

Issues of racism, prejudice acquisition and reduction were gradually recognised as central concerns for the school and the curriculum. This period has been characterised by mounting politicisation and criticism of multicultural education both from the right and the left; on the one hand, because it appeared to some members of ethnic minority communities as a solely no-change, social control strategy and, on the other hand, because it appeared to many establishment figures as an undermining of traditional British values and standards; a threat to the traditional epistemological mould.

I should now like to consider each of these phases in greater detail, giving illustrations and exemplifications of the characteristics and approaches typical of each phase.

Phase 1: the 'laissez-faire' phase

In the early post-war period, British society perceived no apparent schooling difficulties in the fact that thousands of migrants had come to Great Britain in response to the demands of productive industry and the labour needs of the service sector of the economy. At first, as is well known, predominantly adults and mostly men came, and the few children who arrived could be easily 'absorbed' into the normal school system and anglicised or, alternatively, filtered off into the special school system. The period was, by and large, one of ignorance and neglect, combined with a deliberate but secret commitment to racial discrimination on the part of some English dominant groups and governments, and the expectation of assimilation.[1]

The United Kingdom was felt to have a long and honourable tradition in the reception of migrants who, for various reasons, had come to its shores. In almost all cases, these migrants had settled down fairly easily and become culturally absorbed within one or two generations, even if, in some cases, they still maintained their own clubs, churches, Sunday Schools, etc., and observed their own festivals. They posed no apparent threat to the political or social orders. No special measures were instituted for them in the school system.

This experience of 'trouble-free' assimilation lasted into the first full decade after the end of the War. New migrants, it was hoped, would accommodate to the existing society and school system as earlier ones had. Determined by an ideology of assimilation and a conviction of cultural superiority, with an admixture of subliminal prejudice, an unplanned social policy of separation emerged in such areas as housing. As the bulk of the newcomers settled into the poorest quarters of the inner city areas of a small number of large cities, like other immigrants had done before them, a situation of social ghettoisation and separation came to pass.

At the same time, the other side of the 'Janus' policy, unsparing cultural assimilation was being pressed through *de facto* in an educational system which endorsed *corporate pluralism*[2] for other cultural groups, specifically built into such national legislation as the 1944 Education Act. Thus, whilst Jeffcoate is correct that central government did not explicitly espouse a policy of assimilation, neither did it endorse a pluralist policy.[3] The expectation of assimilation was built into the fact that the system remained unchanged and did not therefore articulate to the increasing pluralism of society. 'Doing good by doing little' is how it was characterised by one foreign observer.[4]

Gradually, however, as economic pressures mounted and needs diversified, male migrants began to bring wives and children, their relatives and families. With the major disturbances which took place in Nottingham and London in 1958, deep-rooted problems of skin colour, race, religion and life style began to become more evident. The presence of other cultures could no longer be ignored. But what should the state do and how should it react?

The whole history of the recognition of the implications of newer perceptions of British society as being multicultural was overshadowed by the process of legislation concerning British nationality.[5] From the middle ages until the middle of the twentieth century, all those who were subjects of the British crown enjoyed British citizenship, regardless of where they were born. New legislation and regulations were introduced at the beginning of this century in order to stem the flood of East European Jews, and a little 'fine tuning' was applied as the century progressed. Yet the situation of the 'Colonial peoples', remained unaltered. They were all British subjects with the right, even if they did not have the means or the opportunity, to enter the United Kingdom. Only gradually, as international travel became easier, did a series of so-called British Nationality and Status of Aliens Acts such as those of 1904, 1918, 1922, 1933 and 1943 begin to react in an *ad hoc* and piecemeal way.

In 1948, with the passage of the British Nationality Act, it became possible to have dual citizenship, and members of the Commonwealth, and naturally also of the Colonies, could continue to come to Britain. In the context of this 'generous' legislation, the first mass migrations of West Indians, Indians and Pakistanis began to come to the United Kingdom to settle. By the end of the 1950s, however, it became politically possible for discussion to take place concerning the introduction of controls on such migration, a political process which was expedited by the 'legitimator' of the disturbances in Nottingham and London in 1958.

The year 1962 saw the passage of legislation concerning Commonwealth migrants (Commonwealth Immigrants: Amendments to the 1948 Act) under which future immigrants needed permission, in the form of a work permit from the Ministry of Labour in Great Britain, before they could enter the country. There were three qualities of 'ticket', proposed by the then Conservative government. The Labour opposition at that time indicated that the law would be seen as racist. The law drew a line between those who were born in the United Kingdom or resident there and those who were resident in the independent countries of the Commonwealth or in the Colonies. These latter no longer possessed an automatic right of entry to the United Kingdom for the purpose of either residence or work.

The underlying rationale of this legislation expressed the deep-rooted ideology of cultural superiority and assimilation, at that time unchallenged in dominant English social values. The justification was that for effective integration of those migrants who were already resident in the country, a stronger control of further migration had to be introduced. This ideology, in the school system as well as in the broader society, embraced cultural dominance and assimilation and a social closed-door. In this respect, it was very similar to the old Colonial ideology of the British Empire. The school, distinguished by its commitment to assimilation on the hierarchical terms of the dominant group, was characterised by the way it supported the building of cultural, economic and social barriers.

As an indication of this ideology, in 1963 the Ministry of Education published important guidance on immigrant children.[6] The response to the Southall 'immigrant schools' controversy was to ensure, as the then Minister of Education put it, that the burden should be thinner and more broadly spread. The choice of terminology is significant. This was central government's first published advice in response to increasing cultural pluralism and it ushered in the second phase with its emphasis on the education of immigrants.

Phase 2: the immigrant and ESL phase

With the success of the Labour Party in the national elections of 1964, a second phase of development in multicultural education was opened up with equally little concession to pluralism. The Report of the Commonwealth Immigrant Advisory Service expressed the continuity of the policy of assimilation with the clarification, that 'a national system cannot be expected to perpetuate the different values of immigrant groups'.[7] And yet this was precisely what the Dual System was doing for religious minorities and the private system for elite groups. Circular 7/65 made explicit reference to the goal of 'social integration'.[8] One can be forgiven for thinking that there was a clear case of the Medes and Persians!

This period is characterised by growing protestations of toleration and in some cases romanticising of the culture of immigrants as also by a slowly awakening insight into the fact that gradually the proportion of these migrants who would be British citizens by birth would increase. It coincides with the introduction of more widespread systems of comprehensive education, consequent on the publication of Circular 10/65[9] and a massive expansion of higher and teacher education. Resources were not the problem. On the other hand, the new Labour government (and most Labour local authorities) continued to support a policy of integration in the school system and of closed doors with regard to immigration, with a commitment to the idea that discrimination could not be tolerated. The 'outsiders' of English society would now be helped to assimilate into existing British society.

In the White Paper and in the first race relations legislation, dating from 1965 (Race Relations Act, 1965), the two poles of the Janus-faced policy can, again, be discerned. In the White Paper the number of migrants who would be allowed to settle in Great Britain was reduced from 20,000 to 8,000. On the other hand, the law contained provisions making it illegal to discriminate on the basis of race in hotels, cafes, public houses, cinemas, museums and public transport. The limits of pluralism were clearly set, however, and such spheres as housing, the labour market and the education system were not included.

The Act introduced, for the first time, the Race Relations Board which was entrusted with overseeing the carrying out of the law. In a case of alleged discrimination on the basis of race, appeal could be made to the Commission which had the responsibility to engage itself for conciliation. Only after the 'possibilities' of the Commission had been exploited, was appeal to law possible but, even then, it could only be done in the name of the Commission. Thus, the efficacy of the Board and the legislation was circumscribed and weakened. In the interests of humanity, a national committee was set up to oversee the welfare of immigrants.

In the same year the Department of Education and Science, which had been formed from the previous Ministry, published Circular 7/65, in which express permission and justification was given for a policy of the dispersal of so-called immigrant children, in order not to exceed a 'reasonable' quota of more than 33 per cent of immigrants per school.[10] Although by 1971 only eleven local education authorities had introduced such measures, alternative measures with a similar objective were introduced by other authorities.

In spite of the many flaws in this policy, as also in the underlying attitudes of this second period, it is possible to detect the first school-political recognition that special measures were necessary in education to take account of the growing diversity of cultures. Infant and junior reception centres were set up to provide an introductory education for those children without English as their mother-tongue. Many schools established departments of English as a second language and beginnings were made with new methods and materials.

Under Section 11 of the Local Government Act, 1966, it became possible for additional resources to be made available to the extent of 50 per cent grant (later increased to 75 per cent) to those local authorities who faced particular difficulties in responding to the needs of 'Commonwealth immigrants'. In the same year, the Schools Council initiated a large project, English for Immigrant Children, to improve English teaching and to counter the pressing lack of materials and in-service training opportunities for teachers.[11] The next year, finance became available for a project on teaching West Indian children.[12]

Officials and members of the dominant culture in society still regarded the problem as one of immigrants, and it was this conceptual approach which characterised the first modest steps towards the introduction in schools of a multicultural education which 'celebrated' pluralism. Feasts, customs, festivals, clothing and food of 'immigrants' began to be dealt with in non-prestigious sectors of the school curriculum on an isolated, *ad hoc*, inchoate and folkloric basis. The first tendencies towards a new ideology were visible in the Plowden Report of 1967 and particularly in its concept of *educational priority areas*, which identified urban areas of particular social and educational problems which would receive preferential treatment because of their disadvantage,[13] one of the criteria for the designation of which was the presence of a large number of children with English as a second language. Disadvantage began to be seen in the context of its social pathology and immigrant education began to be impregnated with the first seeds of a policy of equal educational opportunity, which became a very powerful ideology in the 1960s. A distant vision of pluralist education to replace the existing deficit-oriented, compensatory form began to come into focus, and important but modest bases for a policy of multicultural schooling were forged to replace existing monist policies, in spite of the implicit social policy of assimilation and an equally unexpressed school policy of cultural hegemony. Parallel to this, however, there were also powerful setbacks and the measure of the country's values was expressed in the reaction to two speeches in February and April 1968 by a leading Conservative politician in Southall and Birmingham. Xenophobia was widespread and token strikes in support were staged by thousands of workers.

In 1968, the 'Janus' face was seen again in the new law about British citizenship, which bolted the closed door against immigrants from the Old Commonwealth even more firmly than it had been before, and the Race Relations Act of 1968, introduced to express the other face of the dual policy. Under this legislation the Community Relations Commission was established to look after those needs and demands which would lead to harmonious relationships between the races. The execution of these provisions remained with the Race Relations Board, established under the Act of 1965. The counterpoise was the 1971 Immigration Act which introduced the most stringent controls yet on immigration.

With the Urban Aid Programme of 1969 the more comprehensive social approach enabled policy-makers to look at the problems of inner city areas holistically and not solely in the context of the 'problem' of the immigrants. With the publication in that year of DES Surveys 13 and 14,[14] there was a first explicit recognition by government that prejudice had to be *actively* countered, that schools had to participate in this process. But the emphasis was still on educating 'immigrants'. It was now the aim of the Department of Education and Science to develop an appropriate climate and to see the presence of immigrant children as a positive matter and an opportunity for new initiatives in curriculum development. Both surveys attempted to clarify the necessary measures and to formulate appropriate recommendations for the implications of cultural diversity.

In the report of the Parliamentary Select Committee on Race Relations and Immigration,[15] the 'Janus' policy mirrored the themes of the two surveys. But the two facets of the policy were beginning to coalesce. English language instruction was necessarily stressed but also the possibility was identified of the formulation of a multicultural curriculum, and there were recommendations about the necessity of a 'multicultural teacher education'. The new ideology of attempting to see the problem as a whole prompted the Schools Council to make known that it intended to fund a new project 'Education for a Multiracial Society', a landmark in the development of multicultural education, as a policy for all children.

Shortly afterwards, the first provisional report of the Schools Council's work in this area was published in the form of a Working Paper entitled *Multicultural Education: Need and Innovation*.[16] In 1974 the Centre for Information on Educational Disadvantage was established in Manchester and the term 'migrant' or 'immigrant' was discarded by the Department of Education and Science, which gradually recognised that a majority of so-called immigrant children were, in fact, British citizens. From that time no statistics were collected nationally on the basis of colour or race, although individual local education authorities have compiled them.

Meanwhile a number of broader developments had been taking place which began to impinge on the curriculum and its reflection of changing values and for a gradual widening of social concerns. In

1964, the Schools Council had been established and hundreds of teachers' centres set up. The expansion of higher education in the mid-1960s combined with this to provide the seedbed for important development projects. The Association for Teaching in the Social Sciences was founded in 1963 and the new 'social studies' began to emerge.[17] Preparations for the raising of the school leaving age led to a new emphasis on social and life skills, particularly for older adolescents, and integrated and unconventional approaches were being pioneered by a series of Schools Council Projects including the Humanities Project led by Professor Lawrence Stenhouse, which tackled the issue of teaching to improve race relations.[18] Although the 'Race Pack' which arose from this project was never published, the work continued and resulted in a more recent composite publication.[19]

Other factors too numerous to mention, from the establishment of the *Journal of Curriculum Studies* and a plethora of new publications and organisations, to structural changes such as the introduction of the middle school, betokened a rapid growth of concern with the social aspects of curriculum, community involvement and an apparently changing and more open view of education. A Working Party of the Community Relations Council and the Lecturers' Union, NATFHE, published recommendations on reforms in teacher education[20] – without substantial effects.

In the meantime, the Department of Education and Science executed a *volte face* on its policy of dispersal, recognising it as contravening the 1968 Act. In 1975 the *Bullock Report* was published with a recommendation that schools should adopt a positive attitude to bilingualism:[21] a provision strengthened, at least in theory, by the Common Market Regulation dated 25 July 1977 on the education of migrant children, which came into effect on 25 July 1981.[22] A copy of the Directive was circulated by the Department of Education and Science as part of Circular 5/81 on 31 July 1981:[23] by 1984, less than 2.2 per cent of eligible children were receiving instruction in their home language.[24]

Phase 3: deficit approaches

The passage of the Race Relations Act (1976) may be seen as inaugurating the third phase in the development of multicultural education in the United Kingdom. The Race Relations Board and the Community Relations Commission were both replaced by a single entity, the Commission for Racial Equality. The new Act also replaced the two Acts of 1965 and 1968. Both direct and indirect discrimination on the basis of colour, race, ethnicity or national derivation were made unlawful, including in the school system. Religious discrimination was not included. Integration was the new policy.

The publication of the Report of the Special Committee of the House of Commons on West Indians led to the establishment of the 'Rampton' Committee, which was given the task of looking at the issues involved in the education of minority groups and making recommendations to the government. Extreme controversy surrounded the work of this Committee and before publication[25] the Chairman and several members had resigned. The controversy centred, in particular, around the issue of the underachievement of West Indian children and how far this achievement was related to racism, family circumstances, general intelligence or other substantial factors.

Meanwhile, during 1979, Her Majesty's Inspectorate of Schools had been carrying out a series of inspections of seven comprehensive schools containing substantial numbers of pupils from ethnic minority groups. They recorded the somewhat gloomy findings that:

> . . . only a minority of the schools had examined any changes which might be necessary in their approaches to pastoral care and subject teaching arrangements as a whole . . . there was a lack of informed advice . . . schools need to take account of the possibility of discrimination . . . most [schools] were experiencing difficulty in establishing mutually informative and supportive relationships with ethnic minority families.[26]

A consultative document was published by the DES in 1980 establishing a framework for the school curriculum and indicating that ethnic minorities, or the presence of ethnic minorities, implied special needs in the formulation of the curriculum.[27] In a further government document on the curriculum, from March 1981, it was belatedly stated that the curriculum in the school must reflect the fact that British society had become multicultural.[28]

In this indirect and partly arcane way, official cognisance was taken and the first declaration made of the fact that government had begun to support an expressly multicultural policy. This policy remained, however, embryonic insofar as there were as yet no national goals, let alone guidelines, for the implementation of such a policy in either schools or teacher education. For the most part, it was for the individual teacher or school to put it into practice, having garnered the necessary skills and expertise on a predominantly autodidactic basis.

A consultative document on the education of children from

ethnic minority groups was published by the Department of Education and Science in response to the Rampton Report and Report of the House of Commons Select Committee for Home Affairs on Racial Disadvantage, both of which had made explicit recommendations on the development of multicultural education.[29] Yet the vast majority of teachers remained untouched by the recommendations due to inadequate in-service facilities and activities,[30] and because, as national surveys such as that conducted by Giles and Cherrington in 1981 indicated, initial teacher education had failed to articulate to the demands made of it two decades previously for appropriate account to be taken of Britain's newly perceived pluralism.[31] There were even indications of regression in policies and practices.[32] Some surveys seemed to indicate that only a very small number of teacher education institutions had introduced compulsory courses in multicultural education and that a majority of the staff in one such institution remained unconvinced of the multicultural society in which they were working. A publication by an eminent teacher educator recorded a doleful history of neglected opportunities and responses in teacher education.[33]

Authorities in the field were still mesmerised by the under-achievement of 'ethnic minority' children,[34] as the cause was sought in the victims. Teachers' associations such as the NUT and NATFHE were meanwhile striving to make a contribution to introducing a policy of multicultural education and achieving discussion about policy amongst teachers and lecturers in the public sector of higher education.[35]

Further disturbances and riots occurred in the summer of 1981 and caused momentary, national, 'tele-induced' concern. Yet this soon passed as the nation celebrated the Royal wedding and, by late 1981, the further development, perhaps even the fate of multicultural education, remained predominantly unclear. Moreover, British society faced an important legitimation crisis with the further decline of the economy and the mounting numbers of unemployed, not least in the ranks of ethnic minority communities.[36]

Phase 4: the beginnings of multicultural education

The year 1981 was a turning point in the mounting debate about multicultural education. As Craft points out, there were no fewer than four major reports on the subject[37] and numerous conferences, meetings and other publications. The year concluded with the publication of Lord Scarman's Report on the Brixton Riots which also contained further lessons for 'educators'.[38] Pluralism became acceptable.

Within the next few years significant developments took place towards the identification of a more theoretically valid and pedagogically well-founded multicultural education in the United Kingdom, embracing whole school policies, testing, assessment and examination processes and procedures, staff employment and development policies and the curriculum seen as both content and process. A beginning was made to learn from other countries' experiences, writing, research and strategies. The Schools Council took a lead in requesting all its subject boards to scrutinise their work in the context of a multicultural society and the need for examinations to reflect that society. A series of publications was set in train,[39] but the government announced that the Schools Council was to be abolished. The results of this work have, however, now all appeared.

At regional level many local authorities began to publish policy statements on multicultural education,[40] although as late as mid-1984 a substantial number had not done so. The first publications began to appear identifying whole curriculum strategies and policies to make the school curriculum more attentive to cultural diversity.[41]

A national programme for 'the training of teacher trainers' in multicultural education was launched, which, for the first time, offered an opportunity for staff involved in teacher education to update and upgrade their knowledge of what multicultural education implied for their own tasks. It attracted external funding from government and commercial enterprises.[42] The number of institutions involved continued to expand beyond the initial half dozen or so. In some aspects of its work, staff sought to break down the idea that someone had the answer and could tell teachers what to do. It tried therefore to reinforce the idea of the professional autonomy of the teacher and, in particular, that aspect of the teacher's activity which involved the exercise of professional judgement, looking at and studying actual evidence of practice. Rather than glossing over the dilemmas with which multicultural education faced teachers, some teacher educators now tried to identify explicitly and confront the dilemmas to enable the teachers to do likewise, although change in teacher education was not commensurate with the need.[43] Teachers themselves were increasingly seen as having to work out the resolution of their own priority dilemmas as appropriate in-service education slowly became available.

In the 1981 Labour Survey almost one and a half million of the approximately 12 million heads of households surveyed indicated that they were of foreign origin. Approximately 100,000 pupils between the ages of five and sixteen did not have English as their first language. Yet 2.2 per cent of such pupils received integrated tuition in the language and culture of origin. As late as 1983, no teacher education institution in the country was providing training to enable graduates in ethnic minority languages to teach them in school.[44]

Proposals for a 'common culture curriculum' which had become current during the 1970s began to be focussed onto the 'social cohesion' dimension of multicultural education.[45] Individual subjects received renewed scrutiny to see in what ways the two major foci of multicultural education – special needs and provision for all – could be better reflected.[46]

Phase 5: the anti-racist phase

Gradually, multicultural education came under fire from several political directions.[47] Some writers raised a searing critique of its predominantly palliative nature, whilst others saw it as dangerously radical. Increased emphasis began to be placed on the role of multicultural education in teaching for prejudice reduction and the abolition of racism. The racism of existing subjects began to be discussed,[48] and LEAs began to publish policy statements reflecting the new anti-racist emphasis.[49] Many local authority policy statements such as those for Berkshire and the Inner London Education Authority envisaged measures for prejudice and racism reduction and eradication as a central and integral part of education. This relay was then picked up in school policy statements such as those of Quintin Kynaston School in London.[50] Controversy arose about whether obligatory anti-racist workshops for all teachers was a strategy compatible with democratic practice in a free society.[51] In the public sector of higher education institutions of initial teacher education validated by the Council for National Academic Awards received multicultural guidelines for courses[52] and the National Association for Multiracial Education issued a radical admonition to a recalcitrant teacher education to change the way it trained teachers.[53] A significant publication on race relations in schools was published by the Department of Education and Science[54] and concluded that '. . . there was little reported evidence of consistent and successful practice aimed at tackling problems' and identified the need for policy statements '. . . to be based on a realistic appraisal of how, in practice, what is taught and learned can effectively challenge the ignorance and prejudice upon which racist attitudes and beliefs are built'. At the moment when multicultural education began to face education with a whole host of new dilemmas concerning priorities, it began to be off-sided by a more politicised and exclusive commitment to 'anti-racist teaching'.[55]

Suspicions and accusations of racism seemed to many to achieve confirmation when in late 1984 a Council for the Accreditation of Teacher Education was established without any representative from any ethnic minority community and, alone amongst the nations of the Council of Europe, the United Kingdom entered a note of reservation on the introduction of intercultural teacher education. Moreover, such suspicions received futher confirmation with the publication in late 1984 of a consultative document on the 5–16 Curriculum, which as its concession to pluralism noted that pupils should have the opportunity '. . . to become familiar with the broadly shared values of our society'.[56] Moreover, endorsement of allegations that elite and dominant groups continued to be un-committed to Britain as a multiracial and multicultural society, and the educational implications of that fact, was given by the publica-tion of a research report in the dying days of 1984, which showed that schools in the independent sector, by and large, rejected the need for multicultural education[57] – the very schools which were most successful in enabling their pupils to gain university en-trance![58] Cabinet Papers from 1954 released for publication at the beginning of 1985 showed quite clearly that the then Prime Minister had sought to exclude blacks from employment in the Civil Service and to stem black immigration.[59]

These and other events inevitably led many to the conclusion that much which passed as multicultural education by the beginning of 1985 was either an ineffective and insincere gloss or a politicised attempt to impose ideologies without due process of discourse. The publication of the elephantine and costly Swann Report in March 1985 did little to either resolve issues or indicate guidelines for action by teachers. Whilst more balanced than much publication at the time, it had many of the marked deficiencies of multicultural education indicated above.[60] The year continued with horrific civil disorder and riots in several centres.

Summary

Across the five phases of development of multicultural education in the post-war period it is possible to see some fundamental changes and some still existing deficits. There has been a movement *inter alia*:

– from neglect to emerging concern;
– from implicit policies to explicit policy statements;
– from additive approaches to curriculum to integral, holistic strategies;

- from passive objectives such as recognition, awareness, etc. to active ones such as acceptance and commitment;
- from exclusively cognitive to affective goals;
- from weak to stronger anti-discrimination legislation;
- from curricular to whole school approaches;
- from discriminatory to active anti-racist approaches;
- from personal deficit to structural disadvantage concepts.

Whilst, however, a viable multicultural edcucation cannot be advocated without a central core commitment to anti-racism, and although there is more widespread acknowledgment that a democratic society cannot be monist, there are continuing lacunae in provision such as the following:

- lack of conviction about the need for multicultural education among the elite and dominant groups in society;
- absence of national policy statements;
- continuing negative stereotypes and racist antipathy, even in areas where there are few blacks;[61]
- the existence of Christian schools for a multicredal society;
- the continued marginalisation of many ethnic minority children;
- a glaring gap between theory and practice;
- bias in testing and assessment procedures;
- continuing inadequacy of teacher education;
- relative lack of response by higher education;
- lack of development work on pedagogies for prejudice reduction;
- continuing lack of cognitive and affective expertise and therefore confidence amongst teachers;
- archaic epistemologies in schools, largely determined by elite institutions, themselves untouched by and unconvinced of the need for multicultural education.

Thus, if a balance has to be drawn in the development illustrated in outline in this chapter, it can only be that, in the response to cultural diversity, the significant developments which have not yet taken place outweigh those significant developments which have.[62]

Part Two

Policy and practice: assumptions and trends

Chapter 4

National and local authority responses: policies and assumptions

Introduction

In Part One of this book I have tried to show the way in which multicultural education achieved prominence, worldwide and in the United Kingdom, as the 1960s, 1970s and 1980s progressed. I have emphasised that, whilst this was a worldwide phenomenon and not restricted solely to the United Kingdom, the phasing, quality and substance of the responses to cultural pluralism inevitably varied in different Western societies. These differences arose from deep-rooted historical, cultural, constitutional and legal differences in the countries concerned as well as from different national intellectual styles. There was also wide diversity in the responses of politicians, administrators and educators. By the early 1980s, however, all had a more extended period behind them in which they had attempted to come to terms with their apprehension of the cultural pluralism of their society, and more specifically, issues of racism and sexism, in their educational provision, as in their wider social and legal systems and procedures. In this chapter, and against this background, I want to look more closely at the way in which multicultural education has developed, as reflected in official policy statements and reports at national and local levels, particularly in the United Kingdom, before I then focus more closely on institutional responses, actual and proposed, in Chapter 5.

Some official British documents

Perhaps the major turning point in the British development of multicultural education was heralded by the declaration by the Department of Education and Science in 1977 that:

Ours is now a multiracial and multicultural country and one in which traditional social patterns are breaking down. One central example of this is the disappearance of the old stereotypes of the sexes, based on a traditional division of labour between men and women. Most girls now expect to have jobs as well as to bring up a family . . .

and later . . .

the education appropriate to our imperial past cannot meet the requirements of a modern Britain.

As if endorsing the global context of multicultural education as advocated in this book, the paper continued:

Nor are young people sufficiently aware of the international interdependence of modern countries. Many of our most pressing problems can only be solved internationally . . . so our children need to be educated in international understanding as well.[1]

For me, and reaching back to Chapter 3 and the five-phase evolution which I proposed there, this heralded the beginning of phases three, four and five of that development: the commencement of multicultural education proper rather than assimilationist measures to respond to 'immigrant problems'. Of course, I am not suggesting a clear-cut demarcation. Nor am I inferring that there were not schools, authorities and even academics who had expressed a prior theoretical or practical commitment. But this was the first expression by national government of an unequivocal commitment to the multicultural nature of British society and an appropriate educational provision with racial, sex and international dimensions.

Two aims are of particular relevance:

1 To instil respect for moral values for other people and for oneself and tolerance of other races, religions and ways of life; and,
2 To help children to understand the world in which we live and the interdependence of nations.[2]

Although these aims and the document do not use the word 'anti-racist', it will be apparent that racism is incompatible with tolerance of other races, religions and ways of life. It might, therefore, be argued that this was an early identification of the need to adopt strategies in the aims of schools, seeking to correct for discrimination on the grounds of race, religion, sex and styles of life.

But action was sparse; few people realised the importance of the formulation at that time. Central government has certainly 'gone no further' since. However, publication of a further document, in

January 1980, offering a framework for the school curriculum contained a possible list of aims for school education with a more active formulation including:

To instil respect for religious and moral values and tolerance of other races, religions and ways of life.[3]

Once again this aim is incompatible with racism, and implicit within the aim is that schools have a responsibility to develop tolerance amongst members of different races, i.e. education to foster racial understanding and correct for racism, now often called anti-racist education.[4] The document published by the new administration in March 1981 accepted and commended these aims without further refinement, as did the *Curriculum 5–16* document published early in 1985.[5] The element of interdependence of individuals, groups and nations is still emphasised.

The document identifies what it calls three major issues for consideration by teachers in their curriculum planning and implementation and one of these major issues is described by the document to be the fact that 'our society has become a multicultural one and that there is now among pupils and parents a greater diversity of personal values'. It also refers to the need for equal treatment between men and women. The same document re-emphasises the need for the wider curriculum to incorporate, as one of its key elements and in the context of the multicultural aspects of Britain today and membership of the European communities, a developing understanding of the world, the place of children in it and how people live and work.[6]

An Inspectorate document from 1980 drew attention to the need for schools to consider the curricular implications of the racial and cultural diversity of contemporary society: 'Schools cannot be expected to be more successful than the rest of society in anticipating the future.' The document also advocated the study of the beliefs and ways of life of historical characters and of people and communities, who live today in other parts of the world. It pointed out that this was especially important in a country which is multicultural, advocating further the development of the child's interest and pride in his/her mother-tongue, good personal relations and the need for Britain's role overseas, today and formerly, to be included in the curriculum in a balanced and sensitive way, as a measure of helping children to understand their multicultural society. The document asserts the need for children to begin to learn something of the characteristic practice and beliefs of Christianity and of other major world faiths and the influence which these faiths have on the life and conduct of the believer.[7]

But these high-sounding declarations have to be tested against reality. Surveys, for instance, at that time, of local authority arrangements for the school curriculum revealed that almost one-third of local education authorities said that the question of promoting racial understanding was not a major 'problem'. Only one in ten indicated that they encouraged the appointment of teachers and other staff from ethnic minority communities.[8] Moreover, only about one in five local authorities specifically stated that all subjects in their schools were open equally to boys and girls. They cited the 'cultural attitude' of some ethnic communities as a reason why some pupils and parents were reluctant to take advantage of a wider range of opportunities than those hitherto associated with their traditional sex roles.[9]

To take account of the fact that some ethnic groups were excluded from legitimate and equal access to the common culture, a series of *ad hoc* curriculum initiatives had arisen, both in schools and institutions of higher education under the label 'Black studies', Asian studies, etc. Such initiatives were seen as necessary as long as the process of cultural exclusion continued. They provided little basis, however, for a holistic and coherent policy of multicultural education within the school curriculum. For, as the Parliamentary Select Committee points out, such initiatives may be a curricular ghetto, unless they are supported by complementary measures of a fundamental and holistic kind.[10]

A glance across the Atlantic

Indeed, compared with many initiatives across the Atlantic in the United States, dating from the mid to late 1970s, British initiatives of that period in the field seem distinctly immature, inadequate, underresourced and tentative. Let us look at one exemplary scheme: the intergroup education programme, adopted in Maryland in the mid-1970s. It represents a rounded, inclusive, and yet at the same time, more sensitive and well-grounded approach than British initiatives of a similar date. The state guidelines on intergroup education stated quite emphatically that all children had to be educated to live effectively in a multicultural society, and that, consequently, curricular and instructional materials could no longer be tolerated which, by distortion or omission, disregarded the history and contributions of cultural and ethnic minorities.[11] The document specifies a total package on intergroup education including:

1 An integrated curriculum throughout the whole of compulsory schooling;
2 Integration of Afro-American and other minority content into the curriculum, rather than separate supplementary units;

3 Provision for separate elective courses in Afro-American and other minority cultures, where local needs warrant this;
4 Guidelines for the selection of educational materials emphasising minority contributions;
5 The reduction of prejudice, misunderstanding and animosity in schools;
6 Recruitment of teachers who have taken courses on minority groups;
7 Retraining of teachers through workshops which emphasise positive attitudinal and behavioural changes;
8 Involvement in the programme of all administrative and supervisory personnel at both state and local levels;
9 The co-ordination of all agencies and instruments in the design, implementation, evaluation and, as necessary, modification of a multicultural programme for all schools.[12]

Perhaps the most important assumption underlying the programme is the recognition that multicultural education has to be developed not only on a holistic institutional basis, but also on a holistic system basis. These overall *characteristics* of intergroup education are then matched by the definition of *objectives* for intergroup education and calibrated as objectives for the student. Another interesting aspect of the programme is the way in which it recognises the need for a common curriculum for all children, but also that in certain localities special alternative components will also be necessary.

The early 1980s in Britain

The gap between the declared multicultural objectives and educational practice in the United Kingdom was very wide, seen against the yardstick of a number of reports, surveys and Parliamentary Select Committee Inquiries of the early 1980s. A Schools Council survey of all local authorities and a large number of secondary schools with few, if any, pupils from ethnic minority groups found that official assumptions about multicultural education having relevance for all schools, and for all children, had made little impact.[13] Indeed, not all agreed this should be attempted,[14] although a later survey of some 255 multiracial secondary schools, published in 1983, found a wide degree of acceptance by headteachers and heads of department of the responsibility for the school as a whole to ethnic diversity.[15]

However, caution is needed in the interpretation of the results of partial surveys, since the schools were all multiracial. A different survey, conducted in 1982 in an area of the North of England where there was little ethnic minority settlement, found that a majority of teachers still favoured integration. The majority also disagreed with the idea that separate educational and social provision should be made for ethnic minority groups.[16] So the assumption of the authors of the Schools Council Report, that the wider perspectives on multicultural education as an integral part of the curriculum was broadly representative of approaches then being adopted in a considerable number of secondary schools, may be only part of the story.[17]

Local authority policy developments

What is indisputable, however, is that the early 1980s saw a proliferation of policy statements on multicultural education from almost every area of the United Kingdom. The publication of a series of 'pioneer' policy statements by some local education authorities and schools, such as Birley High School in Manchester,[18] led other authorities and schools to feel that they also needed such documents, and their responsibilities under the 1976 Act gradually began to dawn.

Authorities were increasingly spurred by external forces, such as the appearance of the EEC Directive[19] and Circular 6/81, requesting local authorities to review their arrangements for the school curriculum and drawing attention to the fact that, in the Secretary of State's view, schools should have written aims and promising a review in two years[20] – and, of course, the Brixton riots and the publication of the Scarman Report, with its criticisms of educational provision by West Indian parents such as:

1 lack of discipline in schools;
2 the alleged failure of teachers to motivate West Indian pupils sufficiently . . . ;
3 lack of sufficient contact between parents and schools;
4 lack of understanding by teachers of the cultural background of black pupils; and
5 failure of curriculum sufficiently to recognise the value of the distinctive traditions of the various ethnic minorities.[21]

In a survey, conducted in 1982, of all local authorities in the United Kingdom, 44 per cent stated that they had policies or practice in the field and 28 per cent possessed not only a policy but also an accompanying set of practices.[22] Follow-up surveys indicated extensive activity, reflection on practice, change and projected development in a context of a wide diversity of practice.[23] This diversity was noted by the Swann Report as a source of confusion concerning the precise meaning or content of multicultural education.[24]

The reality of curriculum development on the ground was also very different from the high ideals expressed in documents. What little curriculum development there was, was additive and folkloric with very little provision for supporting teachers' initiatives. Multi-racial courses of institutions such as Bradford College were exceptional, and, in general, the enthusiastic cocoon was only just beginning to be cast aside, with local authorities recognising the need, not just for peripheral and additive curriculum development, but for fundamental measures based on the agreement and publication of specific policies and aims.

In the ILEA a general review of issues concerned with the provision of an education within a multiethnic society had begun in the late 1970s, and at about the same time Haringey began to take specialised measures to encourage appropriate curriculum development, producing what was probably the first wide-ranging 'policy' in this area. The Bradford Metropolitan Council Local Education Authority, an early pioneer in this field, had also strengthened its commitment to the development of multicultural curricula through the activities of the advisory service and the T.F. Davis Centre, as well as through the research project on mother-tongue teaching conducted jointly with the University of Bradford and Bradford College.

As local authorities began to take more vigorous and comprehensive initiatives, however, central government became more 'quiescent'. The multicultural dimension became less pronounced in successive government publications and the initiative at national level seemed increasingly left to the publication of the reports of specialised commissions such as the Rampton and later Swann Reports.[25]

In its programme for action, the Rampton Report had recommended that: 'The DES should, as part of its current review of curriculum arrangements, invite all LEAs to define their policy and commitment to multicultural education and to describe how this is put into effect in their schools'; and, 'Teachers should review their work to take full account of the multicultural nature of British society'.[26] The response came in a Consultative Document from the Department of Education and Science, stating that: '. . . The Secretary of State recognises that there are certain broad constraints on the issue by him of detailed guidance on the curriculum.'[27] In the light of subsequent developments, this statement may have evoked some surprise!

Thus, whilst more and more local education authorities were appointing specialist advisers for multicultural education to support the initiatives being taken by teachers at that time, Inspectorate surveys and Department of Education and Science publications on the curriculum were increasingly muted.

The multicultural content of the national surveys

This was markedly so in the series of surveys of Secondary Education, Primary Education, Middle Schools and Education 5-9, which appeared in the five years between 1978 and 1983. The first of these to appear was the one on primary education in England, which had one reference to the multiethnic society and no reference whatsoever to multicultural education. The reference to multicultural society appeared under the heading, 'Other Aspects of the Curriculum', in the bland statement:

> In the course of work on these and other matters children acquire information and learn to respond imaginatively to what they see, hear and otherwise experience.[28]

The following year the most extensive survey of state secondary education in England ever carried out appeared and it had two references to the multicultural society. The multicultural character of the curriculum was not a major dimension of the investigation, nor of the schedule used by the Inspectorate to collect information. It reported that reading specifically selected for ethnic minorities or, more generally, to reflect the fact that ours is a multicultural society was seen only in a small proportion of schools. School libraries only occasionally stocked English versions of contemporary writers, dealing with such problems as living in an unfamiliar environment, the move from village to city and family relationships in a time of change.[29] Little wonder then that the Inspectorate could report that:

> particularly at risk are those aspects of education which are not simply identified with particular specialist subjects – language development, reading skills at all levels of ability, health education, careers education, social and moral education are some obvious examples, and at a more general and no less important level in the preparation of all pupils for life in a multiracial society.[30]

Nor did the situation improve under the new administration. For example, the succeeding survey of First Schools, which comprised an illustrative survey of eighty schools, had no reference to multicultural education in its index, although there were a number of references to ethnic minority groups, centring around the language and religious dimensions of the curriculum or morning assembly. The Report comments tellingly:

> In most schools, some children were being helped to develop self-confidence, independence and awareness of their strengths and weaknesses in ways that also encouraged a better understanding of others and a concern for them – though unfortunately this did not include an appreciation of the beliefs and traditions of people of other ethnic backgrounds.

And later

> There were some children from ethnic minority groups in about half the schools in the survey; their presence was rarely taken into account in religious education.[31]

The report concludes:

> Indeed all schools, whether they include children from ethnic minorities or not, should prepare children for life in a multicultural society and help representatives of each culture to appreciate what others can bring to the community.[32]

The next survey, concerned with Middle Schools, appeared the following year. The Report was a more detailed piece of work than the First School Survey and included references to such important developments as microcomputers, the new Technical and Vocational Education Initiative (TVEI), technology, etc., but no reference appeared in its index either to multicultural education or multicultural society, or indeed to ethnic minorities. There was an acknowledgment, under a heading called 'Recent Developments' that:

> In particular, the multiracial nature of British society and often of the pupils in the schools ought to find reflection in the programme of work in ways that recognise differences of life style but confirm and emphasise a common heritage.[33]

But this was 'lumped together' with the quality of the environment, developments in microcomputers and work in craft, design and technology.

Official publications on multicultural and anti-racist education

Teachers who scrutinised these documents might well have been forgiven for thinking that there was no major commitment on the part of national government to life within a multiracial, multicultural and multicredal society, and for education to reflect that fact in its very fundamentals. But, when the major consultation document on the organisation and content of the 5–16 curriculum was published, in September 1984, the area of multicultural education was totally excluded. The nearest the references to the primary phase came to including it, was a statement that '. . . the skills and knowledge acquired in the primary phase should help pupils to learn to understand themselves, their relationships with others and the world around them'.[34]

It is true that during this period the Inspectorate had also published two modest documents: a survey of organisation and curriculum in seven multiethnic comprehensive schools, and the results of discussions with a small number of LEAs on race relations in schools. The first of these concluded:

> The awareness in the schools of the educational implications of a
> multiethnic school population varied greatly and only a minority
> of the schools had examined any changes which might be
> necessary in their approaches to pastoral care and subject
> teaching arrangements as a whole.[35]

And later and slightly ludicrously, in view of increasing evidence of discrimination and racial violence: 'Schools need to take account of the possibility of discrimination and provide their pupils with advice and information to enable them to cope more effectively with discrimination, if and when they meet it';[36] a very good example of providing instruction for the victim. The final paragraph of this Report contained the sentence: 'All 7 schools sought closer ties with the community they served, but most were experiencing difficulty in establishing mutually informative and supportive relationships with ethnic minority families.'[37]

A Report of the Scottish Inspectorate was both more informative and more instructive. For example, the report on the education of ethnic minorities in the Strathclyde region, published by HM Scottish Inspectorate in December 1983, placed multicultural education at the top of its list of recommendations and as the priority element in the provision of in-service training for teachers. It advocated that: 'Investigation should be undertaken to judge the extent to which curriculum, assessment, resources and staff deployment required to be modified for implementation of a policy on multicultural education.' It prudently recommended the initiation of pilot studies, the extension of the provision of resources, a greater emphasis on in-service training for teachers, rationalisation of the collection of information, the identification of a senior promoted member of staff with responsibility for provision for ethnic minorities and the co-ordination of multicultural education, the drawing up of regional and school guidelines and consideration of multicultural education in the context of whole school reviews of curriculum, assessment, procedures, resources and staff development.[38]

The first DES document on race relations

In mid 1984, the government's long-awaited first statement on race relations in schools appeared, and was described by one educational journal at the time as 'a tiptoe round the minefield'.[39] The press was critical and castigated the Inspectorate for not providing an investigation of what schools were actually doing in the field of race relations. The document provided some provisional and tentative guidelines that a good school or authority should ensure that:

1 incidents of racial discrimination are dealt with openly;
2 graffiti are removed quickly;
3 racist symbols on clothes or badges are forbidden;
4 an explicit statement on race relations is made by the schools;
5 discussions between staff including non-teaching staff, pupils, governors and parents' representatives lead to a whole school review;
6 there are staff, particularly senior staff, from ethnic minorities;
7 careful attention is given to the possibility of bias in the curriculum content and material; and,
8 the general ethos of the school supports the idea of respect for all pupils.[40]

It is not surprising that the Inspectors found little evidence of consistent and successful practice aimed at tackling race relations, in spite of the fact that it was generally agreed in the discussion that this was important. This sad catalogue of inactivity continued on the part of Central Government, in taking leadership to indicate its commitment, and the commitment that it feels schools should have, to the development of multicultural education and good race relations. During the same time, however, local education authorities and schools were attempting to tackle day-by-day difficulties of making professional decisions and planning professional provision for a multicultural, multiethnic and multicredal society, against a deteriorating background.

The situation of ethnic minorities in 1984

The third Policy Studies Institute survey found, for example, that black Britons were still at the bottom of the job and housing markets, because of the persistence of racial disadvantage and that, far from being solved by legislation and government initiatives aimed at overcoming them, racial inequalities had become more entrenched and self-sustaining. The report concluded that vigorous positive action was needed to overcome the persistence of racial inequality because the legislative framework had been shown to be inadequate on its own![41] It referred to the complex jumble of old and new inequalities, arising partly from direct racial discrimination but also partly from the fact that black people are disadvantaged by institutions taking no account of cultural differences. In the same month, an article in a government publication indicated clear evidence of racial discrimination against non-whites. Based on data from the 1981 Labour Force Survey, it found that, for the same level of qualification, there were marked differences in obtaining employment. For example, only 9 per cent of white men with 'O' levels were unemployed, whereas 25 per cent of West Indians and 18 per cent of Asians were. Whilst the survey accepts that there is an age-effect difference, the general conclusion is that blacks in Britain are twice as likely to be unemployed as whites.[42]

Then, too, there were continuing and persistent reports of harassment and violence towards members of visible minority communities in both local and national papers and 1985 began with a revelation of the way in which the Cabinet in early 1954 had deliberately sought to institute moves to stem black immigration and the way the then Prime Minister had sought ways of keeping blacks out of the Civil Service.[43] The continuing sexism of British education was endorsed by reports on infant education and on the access of girls to science and technology,[44] and a report from the Universities Central Council on Admissions (UCCA) indicated that the type of school attended had an important bearing on the chances of a place at university, even when the data was controlled for social class.[45] Finally, the Swann Report of March 1985 indicated the important and efficacious effects of racism, whilst acknowledging the role of social class in educational underachievement.

Inspectorate reports

Furthermore, reports of the Inspectorate on individual schools and other institutions provided evidence of mounting cultural and racial tension and animosity in schools. The inspection of one school, for example, found that pupils of Bangladeshi background were shunned by their classmates, that they were usually isolated in class from pupils from other backgrounds, that tension between the ethnic groups was a commonplace feature of the school's catchment area, and that this phenomenon had had its impact on relationships between the pupils in the school. In spite of the fact that this particular school had a statement on anti-racist policy in its staff handbook, members of staff from ethnic minority communities and a high level of staff awareness to racial hostility, Inspectors were able to criticise the inconsistency of the way in which teachers dealt with incidents of name-calling.[46]

Another report on a private high school for Muslim girls in Dewsbury, West Yorkshire, indicated that the pupils did their work kneeling at low, narrow benches and blackboards, rested somewhat precariously on mantel shelves, that thirty girls aged twelve to sixteen were taught in a two-storey terraced house with one lavatory and no hot water, and that classrooms were small and crowded. The report indicated that no facilities were found for practical work in art and craft, science, home economics and physical education, and that the premises, a house, were unsuitable for a school, and that recommendations made by fire officers eighteen months previously had been largely ignored. The girls spent about 36 per cent of their time on Islamic Studies and Urdu, staff taught up to 96 per cent of their time and there was no teacher with discernible qualifications for teaching mathematics, science, history, physical education, nor English to girls in the upper years. The then headmistress was the fourth in less than two years and was in her first year of teaching. There were, in addition, no music lessons.[47] Such private schools do not, of course, come under the aegis of local education authorities. Measured against the principles and basic ethic of a multicultural society and particularly the commitment to equality of educational opportunity for all races and sexes, none of these practices and situations are congruent with the ideals and aspirations of a multicultural society or an appropriate education system.

Moreover, in a review of the first six months of their published reports concerning 106 such reports in the first half of 1983, but commenting with regard to primary schools, the Inspectors noted: 'There is hardly any evidence of work which takes full account of our multiethnic society.'[48] And in their second such review, again commenting on primary schools they note: 'Some schools, particularly those serving a multiethnic community, draw upon the teachings and festivals of other religions too; but this is not common.'[49] In issues arising from both reviews, race relations and multicultural education are absent.

Local authority initiatives

Given, however, that there has been an almost total absence of vigorous central government initiatives to develop an education appropriate to the culturally pluralist society in which pupils are growing up in schools, the response at local authority level was both more expensive and helpful to teachers in schools if, on occasions, overenthusiastic in its commitment to apparently coercive measures. I should like, therefore, to look now at some of the local education authority policy statements which emerged in the late 1970s and early 1980s and provided a framework for teachers in state schools to begin to develop multicultural education. Two *caveats* are necessary before I commence this part of the chapter, however. The first is that surveys in late 1984 seemed to indicate quite clearly a lack of commitment on the part of independent and private schools to multicultural education. Elite groups in society, in other words, were still in pursuit of a commitment to cultural assimilation. And, second, in a survey of all education authorities in London and a sample of other authorities throughout the country, it emerged that, by late 1984, there were still a large number of local education authorities who had not worked out and issued a policy statement on either multicultural education or anti-racist education. Amongst these was a number of London boroughs.[50]

The opposite side of the coin was commitment, such as that expressed in the Inner London Education Authority Inspectorate *Aide-Memoire* on education in a multicultural society, which raises a series of questions deriving from a concern that all children should be offered equal opportunities for educational achievement and should be prepared for a positive role in a multiethnic society.[51] The document raises a series of questions to enable schools to consider the appropriateness of the school's policies and practices in providing educational opportunities for a multiethnic society and, as a yardstick, when reviewing particular aspects of the school's work in detail.

The document manifests a number of the overall commitments advocated in this book as central concerns of multicultural education, including:

1   A commitment to an overall, holistic school policy;
2   A commitment to equality of educational opportunity for all children;
3   The development of strategies to correct for racism;
4   A whole curriculum approach;
5   The importance of classroom strategies and resources to support the learning needs of pupils in a multiethnic society;
6   The need for teachers to know pupils' linguistic repertoires;
7   An acceptance of the importance of ethos and atmosphere in the school's commitment to multicultural education;

8   Recognition of the central importance of staff development
    and of parents and their communities;
9   The acceptance of the importance of careers education and the
    transition from school to work; and
10 The importance of mutual acculturation and interlearning with
    pupils.

Two documents from the City of Bradford Metropolitan Council
Directorate of Educational Services indicate the way in which
thinking in local authorities was moving very rapidly at this stage.
The first of these, Local Administrative Memorandum 2/82, concerned itself with education for a multicultural society and provision
for pupils from ethnic minority communities. It helpfully set down
those things which schools had to carry out, because they were
required by law or part of the Educational Services Committee and
Council policy, and it enunciated the major aims as being:

1   To seek ways of preparing all children and young people for life
    in a multicultural society;
2   To encounter racism and racist attitudes and the inequalities of
    discrimination which result from them;
3   To build on and develop the strengths of cultural and linguistic
    diversity; and
4   To respond sensitively to the special needs of minority groups.[52]

The document covers areas such as school and community, parental
rights including information to parents, assemblies, religious education, procedures for giving information to parents on assemblies
and religious education, religious festivals, attendance at places of
worship for religious instruction, special provision for Muslim
prayers and such political-cultural issues as school uniform, jewel-
lery, physical education, school meals, recording of names, etc.

Nor was the process dimension of innovation neglected. For the
publication of the memorandum was accompanied by a series of
meetings with headteachers and the encouragement for them to
meet regularly with their staff to discuss the administrative
memorandum. This memorandum was succeeded by a further one
giving greater detail and support to teachers concerning racialist
behaviour in schools. It sought to assist headteachers and teachers
to know how to identify racialist behaviour and to follow firm and
consistent procedures for responding immediately to incidents of
such behaviour and reporting them regularly to the local authority.
Its advice on responding to racialist behaviour indicated the need:

1   To deal with the alleged perpetrators of the racialist behaviour;
2   To aid and support the victim;

3   To lay down firm lines of responsibility for dealing with
    incidents;
4   To deal with the impact of the incident upon the school
    community.

It asked for all schools to prepare, within three months of the
publication of the memorandum, a written account of the practices
and disciplinary guidelines which the school intended to deploy as
part of its school policy to counter such behaviour.[53] The guidelines
which the local authority distributed to schools at that time as a
baseline for their own more detailed policy included general principles such as:

1   That racialist graffiti or slogans, whether on books or walls,
    should be removed immediately and damage repaired;
2   That racialist literature, badges or insignia should be confiscated
    on discovery;
3   That in the case of the activities of extremist political
    organisations directly inciting racial hatred within the school,
    the police and the appropriate member of the Directorate of
    Educational Services should be immediately informed;
4   That pupils responsible for racialist behaviour should be
    reported to the head and, if necessary, to their parents;
5   That pupils who refuse to desist from such behaviour should,
    with the involvement of their parents, be acquainted with the
    seriousness of what they are doing and, if necessary, suspended
    from schools;
6   That children who suffered from racialist behaviour should be
    informed of action taken and of the school's attitude to such
    behaviour;
7   That the headteacher should meet with, or write to, parents of
    such children to explain the action taken and to discuss the
    matter with them.[54]

Similar processes were under way in other authorities. In Birmingham, for example, in June 1981, the Education Committee
received a progress report and policy statement on the question of
education for a multicultural society. The report highlighted
developments which had taken place and restated the objectives of
education in a multicultural society, suggesting further initiatives.
Schools were asked to respond with regard to how they were achieving three objectives as follows:

1   Preparing all pupils for life in a multicultural society, building
    upon the strengths of cultural diversity;
2   Providing for the particular needs of children having regard to
    their ethnic, cultural and historical background; and

3   Being aware of and countering racialism and the discriminatory practices to which it gives rise.[55]

The document sets out the kinds of reponses which schools had begun to make, including extensive documentation, where all members of staff had made their individual comments and with the head providing a covering letter and philosophical framework. The establishment of staff working parties was also reported, to examine in depth the school's aims, objectives and practices and to review, not simply what they were teaching, that is the content, but also how they were teaching and why, i.e. the methodology and the philosophy. Examples are given of particular curricular areas where specific responses had been made. The Report has one or two *caveats*: it comments that some responses suggested that multicultural education was perceived as relating to immigrant pupils and as relevant and necessary only when sufficient black pupils on roll necessited changes in the curriculum; and that many schools were conscious of their lack of knowledge concerning the cultures of many pupils but were also acutely aware of its importance in the education process.[56]

Similar developments were also taking place in Brent, which had a long history of commitment to this field and had already appointed an adviser for multicultural education in November 1980. Based on a report from the multicultural adviser, the Director of Education had reported to the Education Committee in 1981 that multicultural education, existing in schools at that time, was limited in scope. In October of that year the council adopted a policy statement which recognised that the council's responsibilities extended beyond respect for the 1976 Race Relations Act to ensuring that discrimination and racialism did not hinder children and to defining and combating discriminatory practices. It expressed the council's fundamental and significantly changed commitment to a multicultural education, based on a concept of cultural pluralism and the recognition that all people's cultures are inherently equal.[57]

Jeffcoate, however, reports the example of the London Borough of Brent which, under its Labour-controlled council, is said to have announced in 1983 that, in the event of enough teachers not volunteering for racism awareness courses, it would consider making these compulsory, and that willingness to attend would in future be made a condition of all new appointments to the Borough's staff. He denounces such initiatives as an infringement of teachers' rights and as a threat to the autonomy of teachers and pupils, which evokes the spectres of indoctrination and totalitarianism. He also refers to illiberalism as being a feature of several of the more recently promulgated anti-racist guidelines and policy documents.[58] Discourse, freedom and persuasion are the instruments for the achievement of a multicultural society, for without them there would be no justice for anyone, but the misguided and counter-productive nature of coercive initiatives must be evident. For there are certain aspects of behaviour in a multicultural society which are anathema to, and incongruent with, the basic ethic of that society, which Jeffcoate has himself so eloquently advocated and identified.

Several authorities identified not only general policies but also the implications of policy in the form of general principles, whose implications are scrutinised through a checklist of questions, together with a description of supportive projects and measures, such as those recommended by Berkshire's advisory committee for multicultural education.[59]

Many of the more recent documents have tended to focus more sharply on the very important and, for a multicultural curriculum, indispensable area of racism, without neglecting broader issues of multicultural education, such as the linkage with human rights, development education and global education, sexism and classism in education. One example of a documentation series and policy statement is that produced by the Inner London Education Authority entitled 'Race, Sex and Class'.[60] This series of publications includes an overview of issues concerned with achievement, the introduction of multiethnic education into schools, a policy for equality on race, an anti-racist statement and guidelines, multi-ethnic education in further, higher and community education and a policy for sex equality.

The document concerning a policy for racial equality excludes a perspective emphasising mainly assimilation and considers the limitations of a perspective emphasising mainly cultural diversity. It expresses a firm commitment on the part of the authority to equality, whilst succeeding volumes identify anti-racist and anti-sexist guidelines for ILEA establishments. The race policy includes the fact that all schools and colleges will have, as a common element:

1 A clear unambiguous statement of opposition to any form of racism or racist behaviour;
2 A firm expression of all pupils' or students' rights to the best possible education;
3 A clear indication of what is not acceptable and the procedures, including sanctions, to deal with any transgressions;
4 An explanation of the way in which the school or college intends to develop practices which both tackle racism and create educational opportunities which make for a cohesive society

and a local school or college community in which diversity can flourish; and

5   An outline of the measures by which development will be monitored and evaluated.[61]

A partial overview of LEA policies in multiracial education, drawn up by an education officer of the Commission for Racial Equality, identifies the motivation for the new racial policies put forward by the LEAs, indicating that LEAs see their policies as responses to pluralism and cultural diversity, but also, not least, as deriving directly from their responsibilities for compliance with the Race Relations Act 1976, and particularly Section 71. He sees variations in the range of issues, discussed in local education authority policy statements, as dependent on local characteristics, with certain common core issues present in all policy statements, such as ESL, mother-tongue, curriculum development, Section 11 funds, teacher training, particularly in-service, and ethnic statistics. He points out areas which are rarely mentioned, such as positive action, resource allocation, FE and policy evaluation. In his view, three particular issues are areas of problem: namely, who shall be involved in the formulation of such policies; where the resources may emerge for implementation; and how the policy may be evaluated.[62]

Whilst his criticism that many of the statements are abstract and lack the details of implementation may be valid, equally many of the statements which have appeared since that time contain substantial details on the practical implications and procedures for their implementation. Of course, the extent to which such policy statements and implementation procedures have appeared has depended, to some extent, on how 'up-front' this particular issue has been seen to be, and this has often depended on the extent to which substantial members of ethnic minority communities were represented in the area of the local education authority. This is now no longer the case, and policies on multicultural education have appeared in such authorities as South Tyneside and Sunderland.[63]

The publication of Department of Education and Science, *Circular 8/83*,[64] in which the Secretary of State for Education and Science requests reports from LEAs concerning curriculum development policy and practice, has afforded an opportunity for many authorities to re-identify and re-examine their curriculum provision and practice within the context of their commitment to multicultural education,[65] although that dimension is not explicitly referred to in the Circular.

Drawing together the threads of this brief review of national and local responses to the development of multicultural education, a number of characteristics might be said to emerge, as follows:

1   Relative absence of initiative and commitment at national level;
2   Mounting activity by LEAs in the early 1980s in the form of the publication of policy statement and guidelines;
3   Wide diversity in the sophistication and content of guidelines;
4   Increasing recognition by all local education authorities of their responsibilities under the 1976 Act in the sections concerned with education;
5   An opportunity for local education authorities to include in their responses to Circular 6/81 and 3/83 their commitment to multicultural and anti-racist education;
6   Increasing sophistication in some authorities in weaving together local authority policy statements and initiatives, and procedures and resources with individual schools, making sure that schools draw up their own policies and procedures, clarify their practices against multicultural yardsticks and clearly define their attitudes and response to racist behaviour;[66]
7   Absence of appreciation of the relationship of multicultural education to human rights and global issues such as development education;
8   Frequent absence of the 'process' dimension of curriculum development and the need for discourse, not least with the community;
9   Occasional examples of lapses in professional discourse and, more frequently, community discourse.

By early 1985, there was clearly a great variety in practice across the country as a whole, and it was not always those areas where high proportions of ethnic minority communities, where the most balanced and democratic policies and procedures evolved. In some cases, local authorities, where there was not a high level of ethnic minority presence, had more time and space and felt themselves less subject to compelling social and political constraints which has enabled them to achieve the goal of a more balanced policy.[67] On the other hand, there were authorities which did not have policy statements, let alone practices in this area, and many schools where issues of racism and racial discrimination were still not on the agenda. Looking at the policy statements themselves in terms of their content, it is clear that there is a continuum from those authorities which still have no policy, through those which have developed a radical commitment to racism as the central platform of their policy to those which have attempted to achieve a broader perspective, including global dimensions.[68]

Summary

Before proceeding to the micro level of implementation of multicultural education and the responses from schools, it seems important to define and clarify certain principles which appear to underpin statements of national government and local authorities in the field of multicultural education, committed to freedom, justice and equality for all, regardless of their race, sex, creed or social class, including the following:

1 The global context of human rights within which children learn and live;
2 The cultural biography of their country, region and locality;
3 The overall policy of the authority with regard to employment, social services, housing, recreation and leisure, environmental health, planning, economic development, links with voluntary groups and such institutions as supplementary schools;
4 The way in which the policy of the Education Department relates to the authority's broader policies on issues such as cultural diversity, multiculturalism, racism and sexism;
5 The authority's explicit policy statement on equality of educational opportunity regardless of race, sex, creed or social class;
6 The curricular implications of that policy;
7 The resource and staffing implications of a policy of equality of educational opportunity for all in a context of cultural diversity;
8 Staff development dimensions; the implementation of such a policy;
9 Arrangements for monitoring, evaluating and reviewing policy;
10 Procedures for the involvement of professional, community, lay and administrative groups in that process;
11 Specific school guidelines on organisation, staffing, curriculum, assessment and community and parent relationships;
12 Guidelines for dialogue to produce policy statements, to implement them and to review critically implementation of policy through professional self-evaluation.

In the next chapter, I shall be looking, in greater detail, at the guidelines which schools might set down for dealing with more specific aspects of such policies, for example, the eradication of racial discrimination through curricular and organisational strategies and the advice proffered to teachers with regard to how to deal with manifestations of racism or sexism in their classrooms, before proceeding to outline parameters within which a multicultural, anti-racist, anti-sexist and 'anti-credist' curriculum may be developed which is congruent with a multicultural society and its fundamental principles.

Chapter 5

Curriculum planning, implementation and evaluation*

Introduction

In Chapter 4 I have tried to give an overview of the responses in the field of multicultural and anti-racist education which have been gradually unfolding at national and local authority levels in the United Kingdom since the mid-1970s. I have scrutinised selected policy statements and guidelines issued by those authorities, identifying their strengths and weaknesses and indicating continuing gaps. I have pointed in particular to the flaccid and inadequate response of national government in education, and I have suggested a number of principles which underlie such policy statements.

In this chapter, I want to draw on the work of schools in the United Kingdom and to examine the curricular and organisational character of some of the recent responses to multicultural education, discussing guidelines and criteria for culturally appropriate strategies of whole school development en route for multicultural education. I shall be placing particular emphasis on holistic management policies for multicultural schools, which are balanced, culture-fair and supportive of the teacher in 'dilemma resolution'. I shall also be underlining the need to combat actively covert, as well as structural and overt, individual racism, sexism, prejudice and social discrimination. Retrieving my previous work on the curriculum, I want to identify the basic concepts of the multicultural curriculum and to argue the need for a cohesive, interdisciplinary approach, with core and community dimensions. Finally, I want to indicate appropriate guiding principles and criteria for multiculturalism in education, which emphasise the changing nature of perceptions of the field and the need for constant discourse, review and evaluation, including self, collegial and community-critical reflection.

* Parts of this chapter were previously published in *Educational Review* and I am grateful to the editors for permission to reproduce them here.

Teachers in the van of developments

Firstly, however, let me say that it is teachers who have made the running in this country in the practical development of multicultural education. *Pace* the early surveys such as those conducted by Brittan for the NFER, which seemed to indicate that a majority of teachers in the study espoused assimilationist objectives for Britain as a multicultural society and the fact that only 43 per cent of the teachers supported the view that lessons on race relations should take place in schools,[1] it is clear that they and their associations have in fact contributed substantially to the development of multicultural curricula. This has happened both through the existing syndical organisations of teachers, such as the National Union of Teachers, and also through the establishment of special teacher groups and associations, to respond to the needs of a multicultural, anti-racist education.

For example, the All-London Teachers Against Racism and Fascism organisation (ALTARF) was founded at a rally in Central Hall, Westminster, in March 1978 and resulted in the publication, in 1978, of an early document on teaching and racism. This document took most of the subjects in the secondary curriculum and attempted to provide practical ideas and examples of anti-racist approaches, in addition to defining what multiculturalism meant and how multicultural education could contribute in practice to the fight against racism in schools.[2] In a brief resource section, the document points to the advantage of treating racism as an aspect of global issues such as development and underdevelopment, and as the product of history and colonialism.[3]

The National Union of Teachers was an early contributor to the development of a professional ethos conducive to multicultural education and anti-racist teaching. Not without earlier initiatives, and perhaps the odd false start, the Union Conference passed a resolution, as early as 1977, to the effect that:

> Conference recognises that teachers and schools have a major part to play in the development of a harmonious multiracial society and express alarm at the growth of racist activity in Great Britain which directs hatred and suspicion against ethnic minorities.[4]

The resolution also called upon the executive of the Union to give urgent consideration to means by which the Union at both national and local level might become fully involved in opposition to all expressions of intolerance and racial discrimination and to consider and develop multiracial education curricula.[5]

Teachers had also been centrally involved in the initiative that saw the establishment of the Association of Teachers for the Education of Pupils from Overseas (ATEPO), which later came to be called the National Association for Multiracial Education (NAME). It was also the National Union of Teachers, together with the National Foundation for Educational Research and NAME, that caused the Schools Council to launch a research project on multiracial education which eventuated in the publication of Schools Council Working Paper 50,[6] and produced the conclusion that

> . . . there appears to be a considerable majority of headteachers in all types of schools whether multiracial or not and whether in immigrant areas or not, and of Heads of Department in multiracial secondary schools who consider that one of their main aims should be to prepare pupils for life in a multiracial society.

And further, '. . . an encouraging proportion of teachers foresaw changes in their syllabuses . . .'. It also reported that there was almost no area of the curriculum which had not made a contribution to multiracial education.[7] Nor was the National Union of Teachers reticent to enter the fray and to attack pseudo-scientific theories of the relationship between race and achievement,[8] or in providing guidelines for teachers on racial stereotyping in textbooks and learning materials,[9] courageously giving a lead to its members by declaring: 'Racism overt or hidden is incompatible with membership of a caring profession and teachers should be prepared to lead by example.'[10]

From its foundation in 1978, the Assistant Masters and Mistresses Association (AMMA) planned to consider issues concerned with the development of multicultural education and, in September 1980, a special working party was set up to draft the Association's submission to the Rampton Committee. In March of 1981, the AMMA's Executive Committee approved submission to the Rampton Committee of the Association's policy and it was later published as a booklet.[11] This document made a clear commitment to the education of all pupils for life in a multicultural society and was later expanded and updated, revised and republished in amended form.[12]

Examples of schools' strategies

But individual teachers and schools were also busy defining their responses to these relatively new areas of challenge: incorporating in the curriculum the dynamic pluralism of British society; clarifying their responsibilities in policy and practice in the field of prejudice reduction and elimination; and evolving fair and balanced procedures for dealing with unacceptable behaviour such as racism. The Birley High School document, for example, defines multi-cultural education as a *whole curriculum* matter, involving an attitude to life, its aims being the *promotion of a positive self-image* and *of respect for attitudes and values of others*, as well as the *improvement of academic attainment*.[13] Whilst, for its day, this statement of commitment by a school to multicultural education is extremely comprehensive and remarkably sophisticated, it does not yet include commitment to what has now come to be called anti-racist and anti-sexist education, nor is there within the document a political sensitivity to the issues of the distribution of knowledge in society as part of the class and power structure which are so vigor-ously debated today.

A more recent and up-to-date school statement which adds these elements is that of Wyke Manor School in Bradford, adopted after an intensive period of staff development.[14] Basing its policies on the initial multicultural education policy statement of Bradford Metro-politan District Local Education Authority, and its administrative memorandum on racist behaviour in schools,[15] the school published its own statement and guidelines on *anti-racism and other forms of prejudice*. The statement begins by defining racism and acknow-ledging that British society is a racist, sexist and classist one. It continues with a declaration of the commitment of each and every member of Wyke Manor staff to pursue a policy of *equal opportun-ity in education* and related fields for all pupils, regardless of race, colour, sex, religion or class. It also affirms that this commitment necessarily implies making an effort to eradicate evil prejudices.[16]

Already we can see some of the major principles inherent in a good and effective school strategy on multicultural education as illustrated in Table 5.1.

Notwithstanding earlier precedents, from the beginning of the 1980s, many schools began to formulate not merely multicultural education policies but increasingly in Metropolitan London to develop anti-racist school policies. We are fortunate in having a description of the evaluation of one school's anti-racist policy where staff were asked to examine whether:

1 The fact that they were teaching in a multicultural institution should affect their attitudes and curriculum;
2 What should be their attitude to different cultures;
3 In what ways the school might be termed, as an institution, racist;
4 Whether racist incidents should be treated separately from other kinds of indiscipline; and
5 Whether, if there were any racial incidents, involving only pupils, they could or would come to the staff.

TABLE 5.1: *Some baseline principles for a school policy*

- a holistic approach involving the whole curriculum and facets of the school's life;
- publicly available, properly promulgated written policy;
- promotion of positive self-esteem (as an essential baseline for);
- respect for the legitimate attitudes and values of others; and
- the improvement of academic achievement;
- commitment to equality of opportunity for all regardless of race, sex, colour, religion or class;
- deployment of definitive management measures, including dealing with prejudiced behaviour such as racism;
- incorporation of prejudice reduction pedagogies and substance into the school curriculum;
- recognition of central role of staff development;
- organic growth of policy through professional and collegial discourse.

After a long process of discussion and deliberation, staff concluded that, although there was no overt racism, there were some covert racist practices connected with such items as: school meals; the presence of relatively few black teachers; ignorance of other cultures, unawareness of pressures facing black girls outside the school; the fact that the curriculum did not adequately reflect the value of cultural diversity; there were stereotypes and negative images of different ethnic groups in the school; the assemblies did not sufficiently emphasise other cultures and religions; teachers often used idioms that reflected attitudes; low expectations and differential treatment by staff of pupils from different sects and ethnic backgrounds.[17]

The policy identified a number of principles which the staff would follow in order to achieve racial harmony:

1 All pupils and staff should be treated with dignity and should feel that their particular culture was valued by the school;
2 All pupils should be given equal opportunities to develop their potential;
3 School life should reflect the different backgrounds of the pupils;
4 The curriculum should reflect the various cultures of Britain;
5 There should be open discussion about living in a multiethnic community and this should include discussion about the causes of racism;
6 All racial incidents and attacks, whether physical or verbal, should be dealt with according to the clear school policy;
7 Distribution of racist literature and the use of school premises by racist groups should not be allowed.[18]

Another school which moved early to a definition of general principles on the articulation and identification of both problems and remedies was the North Westminster Community School. In its statement of general principles, the school affirms that the school should offer a curriculum which prepares young people to take their place in a multicultural world and should ensure that all of them have an equal chance to make good use of the education which the school offers. Implicit in this is the principle that the school will, on every occasion, demonstrate within the community its opposition to racism and its commitment to foster positive attitudes towards our multicultural society.[19] The document proceeds from general principles to discussion of problems which pupils have concerning racism in a variety of different forms, including low expectations and undervaluing of their languages and cultures. It also examines the area of staff and staffing, the curriculum, resources, languages and dialects, ethos and atmosphere of the school, and makes a commitment to the continued existence of the multicultural working group as a means of continuing source of thought and information for future action.[20]

Another school which defined its policy on racist behaviour closely in a statement for its staff handbook was Quintin Kynaston School in London. This statement expresses a very firm commitment to demonstrate that the school regards all students as being of equal value, and that racism is diametrically opposed to that aim and must, therefore, be positively resisted by the school. The statement works from a consideration of this and other comprehensive school aims to the way in which the school must deal with knowledge about race, culture and racism, the need for vigilance on the part of staff and advice on the action which may be taken if unacceptable behaviour such as racism is manifested by children.[21]

Some individual contributions

Individual teachers, too, basing their proposals on their own classroom experience, attempted to define approaches to a multicultural curriculum. An early pioneer in this field was Jeffcoate, who has defined a multicultural curriculum as one reflecting the multicultural nature of both British society and the world and drawing on the experience of British racial minorities and cultures overseas.[22] He justifies the multicultural curriculum on four basic grounds, associated with:

– the endemic nature of racism and the need for the school to promote racial self-respect and interracial understanding;

– the right of minority groups to see their cultures positively and prominently represented in the curriculum;
– the traditional view of the school curriculum, that is, its function to present an accurate picture of society; and
– the function of a multicultural curriculum which will interest and challenge children more than one which is not reflective of cultural diversity.

He identifies five criteria for the selection of learning experiences, including the fact that the curriculum should:

1   Be international in its choice of content and global in its perspective;
2   Reflect the variety of social and ethnic groups in contemporary Britain in the visuals and information conveyed by children;
3   Convey accurate information about racial and cultural differences and similarities;
4   Present individuals from different British minority groups as individuals with every variety of human quality and attribute;
5   Allow other cultures and nations to have their own validity and be described in their own terms rather than in British or European terms and norms.

We now have a further group of 'principles' for multicultural education to add to the initial list in Table 5.1:

– the encouragement of and participation in community action;
– a curriculum reflective of the cultural diversity of the school population in Britain, including languages;
– the permeation of a world/global international view and of culture overseas into the school and its curriculum;
– scrutiny of resources and resource allocation of policies, including displays, visuals, books, etc.;
– appraisal of staffing policy; and
– recognition of the importance of the school ethos.

In addition to his graphic descriptions of classroom practice and initiatives and strategies to develop a multiracial curriculum, Jeffcoate was also one of the first in Britain to define and classify objectives for multiracial education in terms of two basic master aims, respect for others and respect for self.[23] Cohen and Manion have altered these aims to some degree, but they still remain one of the most ambitious and inclusive statements of objectives for a multicultural curriculum which has yet been devised.[24] Cohen and Manion's version addresses, in both domains, self and other, *cognitive knowledge, cognitive skills and affective attitudes, values and emotional sets* as shown in Table 5.2.

TABLE 5.2: *A classification of objectives in multiracial education* (Adapted from a formulation by Jeffcoate, amended by Cohen and Manion)[25]

---

1.   *RESPECT FOR OTHERS:*

1.1 *Cognitive (knowledge)*

All pupils should *know* and *understand*:
the basic facts of race and racial difference;
the customs, values and beliefs and achievements of the main cultures represented in the world, in Britain and in the local community;
why different groups have immigrated into Britain in the past and how the local community has come to acquire its present ethnic composition;
the interdependence of nations and cultures around the globe;
the international and national context of human and civil rights instruments

1.2 *Cognitive (skills)*

All pupils should *be able to*:
recognise racism and other forms of prejudice and discrimination and arrange their courses;
detect stereotyping and scapegoating in what they see, hear and read, and be able to devise appropriate counter-strategies;
evaluate their own and other cultures objectively against agreed and explicit national criteria.

1.3 *Affective (attitudes, values and emotional sets)*

All pupils should *accept*:
the unique value of each individual human being;
the underlying humanity and essential core values shared by all democratic societies;
the principles of equal rights and justice for all and value the achievements of other legitimate cultures and of nations abroad;
strangeness without feeling threatened;
that Britain is, always has been and always will be a multicultural society;
that no culture is ever static, and that constant mutual accommodation of all cultures, comprising an evolving multicultural society, is normal;
that prejudice and discrimination are as widespread as they are morally unacceptable in contemporary Britain and the historical, social and political economic causes which have given rise to them;
the damaging effect of prejudice and discrimination on all groups in society;

---

the process of multiple acculturation in a multicultural society and the legitimacy and acceptability of multiple loyalties within democratic society.

2. *RESPECT FOR SELF:*

2.1 *Cognitive (knowledge)*

All pupils should *know*:

the history, values and achievements of their own culture and what is distinctive about them;

the common values of British society and their own community.

2.2 *Cognitive (skills)*

All pupils should *be able to*:

communicate efficiently in English and, if English is not their mother-tongue, in their own mother-tongue;

relate creatively to members of other cultures;

master the other basic skills necessary for success at school;

formulate criteria for judgement and action, compatible with the values of a multicultural society;

analyse alternative value positions of different cultural groups;

contribute to conflict resolution by persuasion and rational discourse.

2.3 *Affective (attitudes, values and emotional sets)*

All pupils should have developed:

a positive self-image;

confidence in the sense of their own identity;

a feeling of comfort with cultural diversity and a willingness and ability to learn from others.

It will be apparent from Table 5.2 that objectives to achieve multicultural education must recognise the complex interrelationship of intellectual and emotional dimensions in human values and behaviour, whilst aiming for increased national competence and higher levels of mental functioning. But the objectives alone remain inert unless accompanied by principles of procedure, the ethical criteria and the considerations of learning styles which govern how they are put into practice.

A holistic strategic approach

I have proposed a procedure for identifying and clarifying the basic ethic of a multicultural society and the master aims, which must determine judgements, concerning the validity of curriculum content and teaching/learning strategies, together with the principles of procedure for implementation and criteria for the evaluation of such a curriculum.[26] I do not intend to repeat here what I have already written in great detail elsewhere, but an overview of the complexity involved in that process is reconstructed from that initial statement in Figure 5.1.[27]

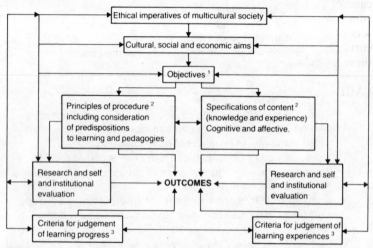

Notes

1 These will include overall objectives for the whole curriculum and paradigm objectives to guide and secure its multiculturalism and focus on prejudice reduction.

2 The school and the teacher are constantly monitoring and modifying the process by adapting the procedures and/or adding new content.

3 These include both pupils' and the teacher's evaluation of judgements.

Adapted from J. Lynch, *The Multicultural Curriculum*, London, Batsford, 1983.

FIGURE 5.1: *A possible model for constructing a multicultural curriculum*

Others, too, have developed an approach to the idea of a multi-cultural curriculum seeking to provide an *inclusive*, *comprehensive* and *holistic* plan for the way in which the curriculum, as it now exists, might be changed to reflect the multicultural nature of British society in the 1980s. Walkling, for example, raises the very difficult issues of what facets of any particular group's culture in a multicultural society should be included within a multicultural curriculum (a basic ethical issue of selection); whether there are fundamental, conceptual or procedural differences in the cognitive mode of different groups (affective teaching learning styles) and thus whether these should be included or not; and, thirdly, whether a multicultural curriculum should aim to confirm a child in its own way of life or provide him/her with the skills to achieve independence within a wider societal and global context. In clarifying these three questions, Walkling considers in turn *the substantive content, the procedures* and *the educational purposes* which might be involved.[28] Taking each of these areas, he then identifies two contrasting extremes in the case of *content*, tolerance or selection, in the case of *procedure*, relativism or absolutism and in the case of *educational purposes*, transition and transformation. These three sets of opposites, he argues, produce eight alternative styles of curricula, which might respond to a multicultural society along these three continua as shown in Table 5.3.

TABLE 5.3: *Styles of multicultural curricula (Walkling)*

1	Tolerant, absolutist, transmissionist;
2	Selective, absolutist, transmissionist;
3	Tolerant, relativist, transmissionist;
4	Selective, relativist, transmissionist;
5	Tolerant, absolutist, transformationist;
6	Selective, absolutist, transformationist;
7	Tolerant, relativist, tranformationist;
8	Selective, relativist, transformationist.

Walkling thus draws our attention to the complexity of the assumptions which need to be clarified before a multicultural curriculum can be constructed. Certainly, few people would hold to the view that all the values of all cultural groups in society can have a place within the curriculum. At its most simple, such a view would offend against the basic ethic of a multicultural society, respect for persons and their human rights, for it could offer endorsement to practices which are anathema to that ethic. A multicultural curriculum cannot support and endorse racist behaviour, nor the institutional racism of the majority; nor can it support the practice of some members of some ethnic minority communities of withdrawing girl pupils from school to contract arranged marriages abroad, below the age of legal consent and outside international covenant.

A multicultural society is not an 'anything goes' society and a multicultural curriculum can never include the whole cultural capital of all groups within society. The need, therefore, arises to identify detailed rational criteria, which can govern selection, so that it is just and fair to all. This need to select faces teachers in schools with painful dilemmas about what does 'go' within a multicultural society and what should be included within a multicultural curriculum and, equally importantly, what does not and should not!

The American educationist, James A. Banks, has formulated a series of broad guidelines for multicultural education which seek to identify and clarify underlying principles as a basis for decisions by teachers in their schools and classrooms about the shape and content of a systematic whole school approach to multicultural education. These guidelines include the normative elements as shown in Table 5.4.

TABLE 5.4: *Banks's guidelines for multicultural education*

1	Permeation of the total school environment by ethnic pluralism;
2	School policies and procedures which foster positive multiethnic interactions and understanding amongst students, teachers and other staff;
3	Reflection in the school staff of the ethnic pluralism of society;
4	Systematic, comprehensive, mandatory and continuing staff development programmes;
5	Inclusion of the learning styles of the students in the curriculum;
6	Provision of opportunities for students to develop a better sense of self;
7	Assistance with understanding the totality of the experiences of ethnic groups;
8	Awareness of the conflict between ideals and realities in human societies;
9	Exploration and clarification of the ethnic alternatives and options within society;
10	Promotion of values, attitudes and behaviours that support ethnic pluralism;
11	Development of decision-making abilities, social participation skills and sense of political efficacy as necessary bases for effective citizenship in an ethnically pluralist nation;
12	Fostering of skills for effective interpersonal and interethnic interactions;
13	Presentation of holistic views of ethnic groups as an integral part of the total school curriculum and comprehensive in scope and sequence;
14	Inclusion of the continuous study of the cultures, historical experience, social realities and existential conditions of ethnic groups, including a variety of racial compositions;
15	Interdisciplinary and multidisciplinary approaches to designing and implementing the multiethnic curriculum;
16	Use of comparative approaches in the study of ethnic groups and ethnicity;
17	Assistance to students to view and interpret events, situations and conflicts from diverse ethnic perspectives and points of view;
18	Conceptualisation and description of the development of society as a multidirectional society;

19 Provision of opportunities for students to participate in the
    aesthetic experience of various ethnic groups;
20 Fostering of the study of ethnic group languages as legitimate
    communication systems;
21 Maximum use of local community resources;
22 Assessment procedures reflecting ethnic cultures;
23 Ongoing systemic evaluations of the goals, methods and
    instructional materials used in teaching about ethnicity.[29]

Adapted from James A. Banks, Carlos E. Cortés, Geneva Gay, Richard L.
Garcia and Anna S. Ochoa, *Curriculum Guidelines for Multiethnic Education*, Washington, D.C., National Council for Social Studies, 1976.

The strength of Banks's position is that he sees personal identity arising out of the interaction of ethnic, national and global identifications.

To recapitulate, principles for the introduction and revival of multicultural education in school should include:

– the need for multicultural education to be continuous and
  coherent throughout the school life of the child and, therefore,
  carefully sequenced;
– the need for schools to foster positive ethnic interactions with
  significant others;
– the inclusion of a fundamental consideration of teaching/learning
  styles and their compatibility (see Chapter 7);
– the need to develop intercultural competence;
– the need to include the aesthetic dimension;
– the need to include an integral consideration of assessment (see
  Chapter 9);
– the need for ongoing self and institutional evaluation.

In an intelligent and readable contribution to this debate, Saunders, looking behind the objectives, has identified three major sources from which criteria may be derived for the selection of objectives and goals for education, for the choice of teaching methods and for the evaluation of the curriculum. These he refers to as:

1 the logic of knowledge;
2 the needs of children; and
3 the requirements of society for conservation or change.[30]

His comprehensive, diagrammatic representation of this approach to a multicultural curriculum identifies alternatives and clarifies his own view of the need for a *human rights-based multicultural education* which can respond to the three imperatives or criteria referred to above. He looks in detail at the accommodation problems, proposing planned strategies of change in order to overcome them, and identifying constraints such as those arising from institutional or personal racism.[31] His view of a curriculum based on *cultural reciprocity* and deriving from human rights is very similar to that advocated by Banks, and adds two further items, which I have included in Table 5.5.

Strategies for prejudice reduction and elimination

More recently, curriculum development initiatives in this field have returned to pastures first grazed in the United Kingdom by Stenhouse in the early 1970s and even earlier in the United States. Stenhouse's pioneer work in this field stretched back over many years before his untimely death in the early 1980s. Whilst some of his work remained unpublished and unacknowledged, in typically modest vein, he attempted towards the end of his life to identify a number of what he called researcher's speculations with regard to teaching about race relations. In particular, he asserted, *inter alia*, that:

1 Direct teaching about race relations will tend to have positive rather than negative affects upon interracial tolerance as compared with not teaching about race relations;

2 Schools should adopt strategies which accord with the context of teaching and the skill of the teachers involved;

3 Black pupils tend to have less marked racism and negative attitudes to other races than do white pupils;

4 Experience of the discussion of controversial issues in the light of evidence under a neutral chairman can lead to a position of open mindedness which transfers to new issues not previously tackled;

5 The effects of teaching about race relations to adolescents in schools are not likely to be persistent in the long term without reinforcement;

6 The influence of school and social context is not likely to reinforce interracial tolerance in the absence of actions or policies actively designed to do so;

7 When teaching about race relations meets the educational criteria of appeal to the judgement of those who are taught, as opposed to adopting the stance of brainwashing, a fairly substantial minority of those taught will, during teaching, shift attitude in an undesired direction;

8 The experience of the teacher in the classroom in the face of racism as expressed by some of the pupils is likely to be

TABLE 5.5: *List of items for inclusion in a school's strategy of multicultural education*

a publicly available, properly promulgated policy based on democratic premises

a holistic policy and approach

a basic ethic of respect for persons, their cultures and languages

equality of opportunity as a master aim

the promotion of academic development as well as positive self-esteem

explicit policies and measures for dealing with racism, etc.

curricular strategies for the achievement of prejudice reduction

recognition of the central role of staff development

organic growth through staff discourse and collegial decision-making

the design of a curriculum, reflective of cultural diversity in the school population and Britain, including languages and culture

a commitment to community action

the inclusion of a world (international, global) view, including major cultures overseas

the encouragement of high teacher expectations

staffing and staff development reflective of cultural diversity

appropriate resources, including displays, visuals, materials, books, etc.

the development of a multicultural ethos

continuing and sequenced implementation of a multicultural curriculum

the fostering of positive ethnic interactions

the appraisal of appropriate teaching/learning styles

the development of intercultural competence

the inclusion of comparative ethnic and interdisciplinary approaches

the inclusion of aesthetic dimensions

integral development of assessment and ongoing evaluation appropriate to cultural pluralism

a human and civil baseline, drawing on national and international instruments

the consideration of likely social and cultural constraints in the wider society

an acceptance of mutual acculturation of pupil and pupil, teacher and teacher and pupil and teacher sufficiently taxing to make it necessary to define explicitly the support and interest of figures of authority in the school and school system and to make provision for mutual support to be offered within a group of teachers sharing the problem.[32]

One of his co-workers, Nixon, identifies two approaches to racism awareness: a direct approach, which makes explicit reference to racism and explores specific instances of racist practice, relying heavily on small group discussion and role-play; and an indirect approach, through analogous situations or generalised themes and topics which may not make issues of racism explicit. Whilst recognising the severe limitations of the indirect approach, he suggests that this is better than nothing.[33] He acknowledges the importance of a global perspective such as that pioneered and advocated by Hicks[34] and, whilst recognising that no single, simple solution can be offered to the professional decisions facing individual schools and teachers, he pinpoints certain paired priorities which he advocates as part of a composite strategy. These are:

1 Racism awareness and teaching about diversity;
2 Experiential learning and the acquisition of facts and skills;
3 Contemporary and historical perspectives;
4 Local and global issues.[35]

Others have advocated more vigorous and sharply focussed approaches, in particular in the development of a curriculum that is concerned as a priority with racism awareness. In some of these proposals, the focus of racism awareness is so sharp that it excludes all other considerations such as, for example, sexism in the school system and the need to deal with issues of the curriculum for all pupils to prepare them for life in a multicultural society. Others seek to adopt more balanced approaches and strategies and to afford equality of opportunity. The infringement of the rights of minority children is sometimes ignored if it is perpetrated by minorities and racism is located in a highly restrictive way.

One proposal, advocated by Ruddell, suggests a gradual move from what he calls the 'kid-glove approach' to a harsh confrontation situation as appearing to have the highest chance of success. He includes within the strategies which he advocates talks, discussions and workshops, contact with ethnic minority adults, 'fairly strong white-to-white sessions in which participants are confronted with their racism', and 'fairly strong black reinforcement for the assertions made in the previous stage', including exposure to militant blacks who treat racism as universal in whites.[36]

The book accompanying the BBC series of television broadcasts on multicultural education also describes a workshop approach to racism awareness, in which the film, *Teacher Examine Thyself* is seen. In the film a group of West Yorkshire teachers are seen during 1980 at the first racism awareness workshop ever organised by an LEA as part of its own in-service training. The aims for the two-day session included:

1   To offer an opportunity to explore our own feelings and attitudes with regard to racism;
2   To gain an understanding of the nature and effects of institutional racism; and
3   To measure how we check institutional racism in ourselves and in our work.[37]

The work was based on American traditions and, in particular, a handbook for anti-racist training developed by Judy Katz at the University of Oklahoma.[38] Indeed, there has been a lot of work in this field conducted over many years in the United States and it might help us to detach slightly from the sometimes emotional, irrational and exclusive way in which this area has from time to time been presented in the United Kingdom, for understandable reasons, if we take a brief look across the Atlantic. For strategies to eliminate racism are central to my concept of multicultural education.

Multicultural education is an education appropriate to a multicultural society.[39] A multicultural society is one where there is a legitimately accepted diversity of cultural appurtenance, based on such dimensions as race, colour, language, creed, sex, class, region, etc. and committed to the basic ethic of 'respect for persons' (and their cultures, languages, etc.). By definition, an education founded on that imperative must provide for the development of a commitment to fundamental human rights, as defined by international and regional covenants and conventions,[40] as well as national legislation,[41] and, therefore, against racism, sexism, credism, etc. It must centrally foster, not just acceptance of, but social engagement for, human rights of which freedom from racist prejudice and action must be a central right. Thus, issues of human rights and teaching to correct for racism must be central to multicultural education, for how can you respect a person and his/her culture, yet nurture prejudice against him/her and deny him/her fundamental human rights, as enshrined in nationally and internationally binding declarations.

Racism: acquisition, reduction and elimination

So, to conclude this chapter, I want to look at what is meant by racism, theories of prejudice, and what we know about intervention strategies to correct for prejudice, of which racism is one virulent form. It goes without saying that racism does not occur in a social and cultural vacuum. It therefore seems important to clarify the concept of racism by defining it within the context of phenomena such as stereotyping and prejudice, as well as by locating it within the broader social, economic and political context of society. For any realistic definition must take account of the 'power-context' and 'resources-impact' of prejudice, i.e. its potential to become discrimination. That someone does not like us on irrational and false grounds we can learn to live with: to legislate against this would be difficult. It is the potential economic and behavioural consequences of that attitude of dislike, however, in abuse, hate, violence, lost opportunities, injured civil rights, jobs, etc. (i.e. the active form of prejudice that we call discrimination) that must concern anyone committed to human rights for all and justice in a multicultural society.

Merton has proposed a typology which distinguishes between prejudice and discrimination and indicates the way in which disadvantageous discrimination is not always directly related to individual, prejudiced attitudes. The typology consists of the following 'ideal' types:

1   the unprejudiced nondiscriminator;
2   the unprejudiced discriminator;
3   the prejudiced nondiscriminator; and
4   the prejudiced discriminator.[42]

It is, in other words, quite possible for those who are not themselves prejudiced (or to use a subset of prejudice – racist) to discriminate by not opposing, challenging, seeking to correct and alter either the prejudice (or racism) of other individuals or institutionalised racism. Moreover, as Hall has pointed out, racism does not necessarily rest on conscious intentions: it may derive from well-intentioned but false stereotypes and patronising attitudes.[43] Even more deeply embedded in the sedimentary strata of culture, it may be 'manifest' only in acts of indifference or omission.[44] It may become so much an integral but subliminal part of the taken-for-granted cultural profile of individuals, institutions and society that it may be powerfully influential yet unremarked, efficacious but unconscious, socially devastating but unintended. The individual (the institution and the system) may be powerful operants of prejudice and racism without even knowing it. Racism can be institutionalised and powerful, yet unfelt by those whom it silently poisons, imperceived except by those whom it disadvantages.

It is not, therefore, sufficient for multicultural education to educate against individual prejudice (racism); it must seek to generate *active* commitment and engagement for 'nonprejudiced nondis-crimination' as one of its consistent, major and central concerns, in order to overcome institutionalised racism and other forms of prejudice. But to achieve this goal we need to be clear about what we mean by the terms prejudice, stereotyping and discrimination and to see them in their structural (power) location. Tentative working definitions of racism, and the stereotyping which underlies it, might be provisionally formulated as follows:

Stereotyping is the classification of individuals and the
   attribution of characteristics to these individuals or groups on
   the basis of prejudiced, irrational and non-factual conceptions
   and information.
Racism (and prejudice) is a set of inflexible, institutional,
   personal and societal values, attitudes, behaviours and
   procedures which create or perpetuate privilege for one group
   of individuals and deprivation for another based on a racial
   (or other) cultural definition of groups and their members.
   (The active dimension of latent attitudes and values is
   discrimination.)

Of course, both of these definitions have their limitations, but taken together they focus our attention both on the individual dimension and on the 'power and resources' dimensions of pre-judice and their dynamic in society. If they may be seen in the context of individual (personal), organisational (institutional) and structural (societal) factors, however, they may also be susceptible to attenuation and erasure through similar kinds of initiative: in-dividual, expressly educational and broader social strategies. So let us try to trace the dynamic and ask how and through what media persons become prejudiced.

There are many different (and incomplete) theories of prejudice acquisition, including social structural (economic) and psycho-logical evaluations, summarised and partially appraised by Rose.[45] Simpson and Yinger [46] have sought to formulate a comprehensive theory of prejudice which incorporates evidence and theory from a number of sources around three major interacting factors which we may label for the purposes of a 'shorthand' summary as:

1 *personality requirements*;
2 *the structure of society*; and
3 *society's cultural heritage*.

In other words, it is not just internal personality factors which lead to prejudice (and racism) but the structure and culture of a society (or an organisation). A tentative definition of prejudice acquisition might, therefore be:

Prejudice acquisition is the complex process of socialisation by which an individual acquires the values, knowledge and attitudes which motivate him/her to treat other individuals and groups differently and unequally on the basis of their racial, ethnic and cultural appurtenances or composition.

Prejudice reduction approaches

I have provisionally defined prejudice and racism and indicated their relationship to their overt, active form, discrimination, referring briefly to the three media of prejudice acquisition and offering a tentative definition of that phenomenon. I now want to look at the central issue for education of prejudice (and racism) reduction and eradication.

Notwithstanding an extensive review of the research by Weissbach, Gaertner, Katz and Amir,[47] Banks has provided a useful summary of the research on approaches to prejudice reduction, dividing them into micro and macro approaches.[48] One of his major conclusions is that attempts at reform should address the total institution and system, including all major structural and curricular aspects. He trenchantly points out, '. . . it is imperative that the school not merely devise a few units or teaching strategies'. An *ad hoc*, 'one-off' cognitive blitz is thus unlikely to succeed and may in fact lead to regression. Rather, what is needed is a sophisticated multicultural curriculum, co-existential with the school life of the child, in which process will be as important as skills, systematically educating to correct for racism (and prejudice in general), including pedagogical strategies of continual reinforcement, and emphasising, as Banks proposes, the achievement of higher level mental functioning, such as concept attainment, value analysis, decision-making and social action.[49] Based on such an approach, we may provisionally define prejudice (and racism) reduction as:

Prejudice (and racism) reduction is a deliberate and ordered process which aims, by means of systematic and sustained educational or broader social strategies, policies and practices, at enabling individuals and groups to re-orient their values and attitudes, actions and behaviour, in such a way that their predisposition to prejudice is reduced, amended or eradicated.

The process may be applied to society as whole, a system such as education or an organisation such as a school, the very structure of society and the very core of its cultural transmission in family and school. But this is an enormous task, and it is important to understand its implications. Thus what is needed is an *interconnected* and *coherent strategy* aimed at *individual*, *institutional* and *structural* dimensions of society,[50] not some kind of simple 'one-shot' immunity to prejudice or racism, which would cure those who have it and immunise those who do not.[51] There is no magic panacea which will wreak overnight and wand-like some immediate transformation, or an antidote which may, once and for all, cure those who are bitten.

Looked at solely from the level of the school curriculum, the amount of previous work is very small. Not only has there been a paucity of prejudice reduction studies and experimental behaviour modification research, but there has been relatively little effective theory-building to pull together the child-rearing,[52] personality/organisation,[53] and social structural,[54] theoretical work of a quarter-century ago and to focus it on current needs. Most of the recent generation of local authority policy statements address a proxy for prejudice reduction strategies. The responsibility for actualisation is left with teachers: a 'misplacement' phenomenon remarked on by Dorn and Troyna before the publication of most of these recent statements.[55]

A number of widely dispersed and isolated attempts have been made to match change strategies to the causes of racism by means of a typology,[56] to develop teaching strategies and pedagogical principles,[57] to develop pre-school strategies, activities and experiences,[58] to teach and achieve change through drama,[59] to diminish prejudice by initiating children into discourse,[60] to teach through folk culture and role-playing,[61] through values clarification,[62] through simulation games[63] and not least by the development of packs, resources, new curricula and examinations and teacher education programmes,[64] including strategies to assist teachers to study their own practice.[65] Some important principles emerge from this work. Moreover, the 'terrain' of the multicultural curriculum in the core of its epistemology, in its purposes and in its teaching/learning strategies is subject to overlap and multiple occupancy with other important areas of concern such as human rights education, developmental education, environmental education, global education, social and life skills, etc.,[66] which means that substantial and complementary ground work has already been covered by others.

Notwithstanding the five levels of contradictions and ambiguities advanced by Kowalczewski as besetting teachers in relation to race and education, in the fields of:

– terminology and research in assessment;
– in their own defensive stance *vis-à-vis* their own racism;
– in the lack of overall central guidance;
– in the lack of any articulated theoretically valid knowledge; and
– in the role of the school in combating racism;[67]

some of which were detected in an in-service evaluation,[68] progress has been achieved in identifying tentative hypotheses for the curriculum,[69] its shape[70] and pedagogies[71] as well as in formulating propositions for teacher development.[72] There is an acknowledgment that racial awareness of self and others and the development of ethnic identity are well established by the time a child begins school. Thus, notwithstanding the need for broader societal initiatives, including pre-school and parent education, the school must begin, from its very first day with the child, to educate to counter prejudice and to ensure that the child is comfortable with racial and broader cultural diversity.

In a review of developmental principles for multicultural education derived from social research, Gay points out,[73] as do others, that racial biases and ethnic prejudices are inversely correlated with cognitive sophistication, moral development, social perspective-taking and receptivity toward ethnic and cultural pluralism. Thus, the school has to aim for the higher stages of cognitive and moral functioning, consistently and continually across all epistemological areas throughout the school-span of the child, across the learning areas of dispositions and values, competences, skills and abilities, learning and thinking techniques, interpersonal relations and social action and practical competences.[74]

Summary

Drawing together the various contributions which have been made by authors from distinctively different backgrounds and disciplines to the theme of the development of a multicultural curriculum and, bearing in mind the progress indicated at the beginning of this chapter, it might be useful now to identify a few principles which emerge from the work described in this chapter. Each person will make his or her own list, but for me, such principles would include the following:

1 Whilst there is no simple, single solution to the problem of developing a multicultural curriculum which is committed to human rights and aimed at correcting for abuses such as prejudice, racism, sexism and discrimination, both covert and overt, it is clear that piecemeal and *ad hoc* short-term approaches are likely to be unsatisfactory, ineffective and even counterproductive.

2 Arising out of this, several authors, practitioners and educators have identified the need for a composite, holistic, multidisciplinary, sequenced and continuous approach to the

development of a multicultural curriculum which can take account of the existing epistemology of the school, what we know about the learning styles of pupils, professional competence and knowledge in the field at this moment in time, and the fact that the curriculum, like an iceberg, is more hidden than seen.

3 Developing a multicultural curriculum is a task for all members of the institution, staff in particular working collegially, but also through what Banks called a process of *multiple acculturation* with the pupils, the parents and the wider community.

4 The development of a multicultural curriculum demands a continuing process of trial and error, and teacher and collegial evaluation of professional practice, in which biases and inadequacies may be identified with confidence and modified with support. This demands a climate of mutual acceptance and respect with which more recently advocated approaches to racism awareness may be incompatible.

5 If regression is not to take place, the commitment to a multicultural curriculum has to begin with the child's first day in school and continue, in the context of broader societal initiatives, to its last day.

6 The development of an ethos, which will facilitate a learning environment conducive to understanding and valuing all cultural groups, must be a central tenet of the management system within the institution and a central goal of a multicultural curriculum.

7 A multidimensional approach to attitude change, including contact with various ethnic groups, literature, simulation drama, role-playing, games and play, audio-visual materials, visits and vicarious experiences is much more likely to succeed than a unidimensional approach.

8 The school needs not only to declare but also to demonstrate its commitment to a society in which economic, political and social rights of individuals and groups should be respected, and not exploited by dominant power groups in society.

9 Staff development is at the core of the development of a multicultural curriculum. It should aim to encourage the growth of the professional and personal respect of teachers for themselves and for all members of the community as being human beings of equal worth, and enable teachers to evaluate the effects of their personal and professional behaviour, its impact on others and their human rights and dignity.

10 Approaches advocating the evocation of guilt through the stereotypical representation of one racial group as racist, are

unlikely to pass the criterion of commonsense, logical rationality.

11   A multicultural curriculum is only one part of the whole array of measures adopted as part of a whole school strategy for the implementation of a multicultural education, attentive to the human rights and dignity of all individuals, the need for tolerance and support for legitimate cultural difference and commitment to a democratic society in which conflicts are resolved through discourse and persuasion rather than coercion.

12   The commitment to multicultural education needs to be seen as part of a global commitment to human rights and interdependence.

13   Coalitions, conceptual and process, need to be sought with development and environmental education and education for peace.[75]

14   It is unlikely that closed and coercive procedures, representing a close approximation to indoctrination rather than education, are likely to be acceptable or to succeed.

15   Teaching approaches as well as staff development approaches will need to accept the fact that individuals and groups have the right in a democratic society to differ legitimately from one another, and that such differences denote neither inferiority nor superiority, neither prejudice nor open-mindedness *per se*.

16   Both in staff development and in strategies for the implementation of a multicultural curriculum the procedures will need to be attentive to normal procedures within a democratic society, where support for constructive social and institutional change may be levied, provided that the legitimate rights of individuals and groups and, in particular, minorities, are respected.

17   Such principles underlying a school policy will need to be closely interrelated and dovetailed with the principles identified at the end of Chapter Four for the development of authority-wide and national commitments to multicultural education;

18   The whole process should be subject to an inbuilt and integral process of continuing evaluation of policy and practice, involving all members of the school community and collegial decision-making, as well as the governing body, and, as appropriate, the wider community.

19   There should be an explicit, promulgated statement, freely available to all, setting out the policy, procedures and sanctions in cases of anti-social behaviour such as racism.[76]

The policy and principles will also need to take into account what we know about children learning and the diversity of values, attitudes, cognitive styles, experiences and manifold cultural presuppositions with which children come to school. This theme of the need for healthy pedagogical variety is at the core of what I have to say in Chapter 7. Before that, however, we also need to note the important role of parents and the community in developing multi-cultural education and the need for teachers to 'sell it to them' and to discuss and negotiate it with them. This theme of the central role of discourse with parents and the community is at the heart of what I have to say in the next chapter.

Chapter 6

School, parents and the community

Introduction

In Chapter 5, I have tried to give a brief acount of what schools and individuals have begun to achieve in the definition and delivery of multicultural education in school. I have 'pulled out' the underlying principles and assembled them into a provisional and tentative checklist for schools to consider, and then I have tried to integrate these with a specific area of curriculum commitment: prejudice reduction and elimination. In the process I have emphasised the need for holistic strategies and for discourse, both collegial and with pupils, parents and the wider community.

In this chapter, I want to retrieve the theme of discourse, which I first introduced in Part One of this book, and which I have identified consistently as the only viable basis for the development of multicultural education within a democratic society. Such discourse must reach beyond the school to include parents and the wider community in the delivery of a negotiated educational provision. I want, therefore, to look more closely at some of the issues of the interaction of the formal school with its own community and others, and to build an overview of ways in which parents and the wider community can be involved in the school, referring to the important role of supplementary schools, and the current policy of central and local government towards them, as well as the need for the school to co-operate with other agencies, such as welfare, social and religious organisations. I shall be emphasising the importance of family support for children's learning throughout the chapter.

Alterable and non-alterable variables

Firstly, however, it is important to state quite plainly that the teacher is not omnipotent. There are limitations to what the teacher can achieve, even with outreach activities into the local community. Moreover, in the pupil's learning environment, there are aspects which the teacher can easily change, there are others which can only be changed with difficulty and some which only broader political action can change.

Ryan and Greenfield have listed the main variables in school experience which affect pupil's performance as background and correlated factors, such as pupil characteristics, e.g. individual abilities and motivation, previous learning and experience, age, etc.; school characteristics, e.g. school facilities; school services, e.g. counselling, psychological and welfare; school programmes, administration and professional development; their variety and extent, school climate and leadership, home/school relations, remedial and special programmes; classrooms – their size, the number of pupils and leadership; teacher characteristics, e.g. training and length of service, the personality, the intelligence, the abilities and attitudes; and learning related experiences in the school environment. This no doubt incomplete list of factors represents an interactive and complex network, surrounding the teacher and pupil in the learning context.[1] So, differences in pupil performance are unlikely to be attributable to any one variable. Research conducted in the United Kingdom, and reported in 1979, identified such matters as the style of contact between pupils and teachers, attitudes to punctuality, marking, etc., the use of praise and encouragement by the teacher, the appropriateness of the teacher's qualifications and experience, and peer group reinforcement in the development of learning.[2] Some of these variables are more alterable and others are fairly stable or static.

The long-term work and research of Benjamin Bloom and his colleagues at the University of Chicago has sought to summarise those variables which are susceptible to alteration and those which are, relatively speaking, less susceptible. Under those variables, which they regard as being relatively more alterable, are listed areas, such as the quality of teaching, the use of time by pupils, the use of time by teachers, the cognitive characteristics of the learners, the affective characteristics of the learners, the rate of learning and, crucially for this chapter, home environment.[3]

Of course, it is not quite so simple as some variables being alterable and others non-alterable. For some variables have a stronger effect on learning than others and some are more susceptible to alteration than others. For this reason, Walberg has listed the variables in order of the size of the effect,[4] and Bloom has attempted to quantify further the effect of the size.[5] Whilst it is clear that some variables will be more accessible and susceptible to change in some societies than in others, placed in a hierarchy according to their effect-size, the following factors emerged as the strongest: changes in tutorial instruction, reinforcement techniques, feedback correctives through mastery learning, cues and explanations, student classroom participation, student time on task, improved reading and study skills, co-operative learning, homework, grading, classroom morale, initial cognitive prerequisites and home environment intervention.

Under home intervention, Bloom highlights those factors which provide out-of-school support from the home or peer group, such as the work habits of the family, the academic guidance and support given to the pupil, the stimulation available to explore ideas, events and the wider environment, opportunities for developing language use, the academic expectation of parents and the availability of a variety of extra-curricular activities.[6]

The gradual recognition of home-school partnership

In the United Kingdom the complex influence of the home and parental roles and attitudes on school achievement has been extensively researched. In 1954, for example, the Central Advisory Council's report stressed the fundamental influence of the home background of children,[7] and the Newsom Report of 1963 drew attention to the partnership between home and school, inherent in children learning successfully, and to the need for schools to know more about the home circumstances of children and for parents to know more of what goes on in the school. Like many reports after it, it recommended a strengthening of the links between home and school and the creation of new ones in difficult areas.[8]

The ways in which those who left the school early differed from those who did not was pinpointed by Schools Council's Enquiry 1 as being strongly related to home background. The existence of certain physical conditions and the lack of resources were also seen as unconducive to educational achievement, as was the lack of a tradition of extended education and the consequent imperfect understanding of the aims and methods of schools.[9] The pressure for dialogue mounted during the 1960s. At the primary level the Plowden Report endorsed the vital importance of partnership between home and school if children's learning endeavours were to be maximally effective. Its concern, it said, was with the whole person and therefore the whole family.[10]

With the foundation of the Home/School Council in 1970, and the Advisory Centre for Education in Cambridge in 1963, the scene was set for further emphasis on the important role of parents and teachers in partnership, in supporting the achievement of children in schools. A Schools Council research report from that date emphasised that most experienced teachers realised the vital role played by the home in successful child education, but that they sometimes failed to recognise the influential role that they themselves can play in determining the attitude of parents to the education of their children. More specifically, it emphasised that a great deal more could be done to integrate the school more firmly with the local community and involve it in the curriculum. Consequently, it argued, the curriculum itself could be more closely involved with the environment in which children had grown up.[11] All of these findings are relevant here.

Addressing the needs of children from ethnic minority communities, the Bullock Report emphasised that the role of members of the minority communities themselves was vital. It commented that the participation of the parent was gradually increasing: '. . . many primary schools worked hard to encourage parents to exercise a role in the life of the school and a number have gone further than seeing this in terms of performing some kind of service'.

It reported that parents acted as escorts on journeys and in environmental studies outside school, in the school library, in the games period and in home studies areas. In all these situations they were involved in the learning process. It emphasised the scope for many more such initiatives, but stated: 'it is no use pretending that the parent can slip easily into the learning situation. There are adjustments to be made and sensitivities on both sides to be respected'. And later, picking up the theme of ethnic minority community involvement in schools, the Report commented: 'There are good arguments for a more sustained and systematic service linking home and school, especially in the areas of intensive immigrant settlement.'[12] Whilst the aborted and anodyne recommendations of the Taylor Report are now largely overtaken,[13] teachers in schools were reported as being unaware in many cases of the bicultural capital of children from ethnic minority backgrounds and of developing coping strategies which enabled them to ignore and avoid ethnic minority children.[14]

In spite of the developments described above, a survey of local authorities, conducted as part of the Department of Education and Science curriculum review in 1977, published in 1979, indicated that only one in five local authorities were developing ways of encouraging parental and community involvement in provision for non-English-speaking pupils, including devices such as the use of home/school liaison teachers, the provision of English language classes for adults (especially parents) and the distribution of information about the school system in mother-tongues.[15] In the same document it was reported that some three-tenths of the local authorities had formulated no overall policy, nor given any general guidance to their schools, on the extent to which the information in school records should be made available to other parties, presumably including parents.[16] Earlier, the document reported that almost one-third of the authorities commented that they did not view the promotion of racial understandings as a major problem in their schools. Only a quarter of the authorities mentioned arrangements for co-operation with the local community relations councils or similar bodies and only one in six responses indicated that the authority was developing ways of involving parents from immigrant groups, including the appointment of home/school liaison teachers.[17]

In a report based on a survey of seven multiethnic comprehensive schools, the Inspectorate drew attention to the fact that whilst all schools were convinced of the importance of the quality of relationship between the school and the wider community, their attempts to involve the local community in the life of the school had not met with success. They comment that those schools where links into the community had been established felt themselves more confident in dealing with issues of prejudice, discrimination, racial tolerance and unequal representation. Only four of the schools had parent/teacher associations.[18]

A later HMI document based on a summary of discussions of meetings in five local education authorities concerned with race relations in schools indicated amongst schools' responses a conviction that the education welfare service could contribute in linking home, school and community, and cited ways in which schools had shown themselves sensitive to the needs of ethnic minority group parents, such as by having an interpreter present at parents' evenings, or having parents' evenings both in the afternoon and in the evening for those unable, or unwilling, to come out in the evening.[19]

The passage of the 1980 Education Act compelled schools and local education authorities to publish specific information for parents, but the modest statutory requirements published by the Secretary of State often remained unobserved. The Rampton Report commented on the wide gulf in trust and understanding between schools and West Indian parents and suggested that one way of overcoming this was to involve West Indian parents in the government of schools.[20] A similar finding was registered by the Home Affairs Committee of the House of Commons which, acknowledging that some authorities made a particular effort to include parent governors from ethnic minority communities, commented that they were conspicuous by their absence in several of the cities visited.[21] The Committee strongly advocated that the formal structures associated with the school, and particularly the governing body, should reflect the community it serves. It urged the Secretary of State to use his power under Sections 2 and 3 of the Education Act 1980, with particular regard to the extent to which ethnic minority parents were represented on governing bodies.

The under-fives: early intervention

Significantly, in view of research which appeared in 1984, the Report also referred to the need for day nurseries, play groups and mother and toddler groups for members of ethnic minority communities as an unrivalled opportunity for overcoming at an early age some of the disadvantages associated with cultural and linguistic difference. The Committee noted that the Department of Education and Science accepted that the provision of nursery education facilities fell below the desirable level of provision and referred to the prevalence of unregistered child-minding, particularly for West Indian under-fives.[22] This comment was endorsed by the Scarman Report in what it said about the under-fives.

Research carried out over a twenty year period by the High Scope Foundation under its Director, Dr David Weikart, in the United States demonstrates the social benefits of such early programmes. In a longitudinal study of 123 black and economically disadvantaged children in Ypsilanti, Michigan, the project showed that disadvantaged black children who received pre-school education later performed better at school or college, were more law-abiding and earned more money than a control group that did not have pre-school education. It is interesting also to note that the study included not only a pre-school programme which involved nursery schooling with a one-to-five teacher/pupil ratio, but also one-and-a-half hours' *home visiting* every week.[23] The Director of the project asserted that a cost-benefit analysis of the programme and its results indicated that investment in the pre-school programme was a good investment for society, with a return on the initial investment equal to three-and-a-half times the cost of two years of pre-school and seven times the cost of one year of pre-school.

The situation in the United Kingdom

In the United Kingdom, a chilling blow to any cosy myth which might have developed about the relationship between home and school was administered by the 'events' of 1981. The Brixton riots occurred in April of that year, and the Scarman Report commented incisively:

> It is apparent from the evidence that the extent of contact between parents and schools varies considerably, but that black parents in particular are often, for whatever reason, apparently hesitant to take a full and active part in the schools. Unless they do so, however, teachers will remain unaware of the way they view the needs of their children and the effectiveness of the school system.

The report seems to emphasise the *mutual acculturation* needed for parents to appreciate what schools are trying to do for their children and for teachers to understand the parents' expectations.[24] In spite of all that had been done, Lord Scarman could only point to the need for a substantial improvement of communications between local authorities, teachers, parents, pupils, minority groups and the community in general.[25]

The Green Paper, published in May 1984, set out a new framework for parental influence at school in terms of both the composition of governors and their functions, proposing that, in future, parents, elected by their fellow parents at the school, should be given the right to form the majority of the governing body, in the case of a county or maintained special school. In the case of a voluntary controlled school, they would form the majority, counted together with the foundation governors. These proposals followed but departed from the recommendations of the Taylor Committee, referred to above.[26] Governing bodies would be responsible for the conduct of the school, exercising, in consultation with the head-teacher, a general oversight of the school's working methods. They would also assess how far it was achieving its aims and objectives, how far it was adjusting to changes in circumstances, how far it was appropriate to the expectation of staff and pupils, how well the school has capitalised on its strengths and tackled its weaknesses, and how effectively it has consulted parents on issues such as pupil discipline, behaviour and school uniform.

Tomlinson has surveyed the development and current state of home/school and parent/teacher relations in multicultural Britain. She acknowledges the progress of the last fifteen years in improving and updating what she calls the 'old-style' links, including parent-teacher meetings, written communication with homes, parent-teacher associations, etc., and adding to them new foci, including parental participation in decision-making.[27] She also points to other models, such as the school and family concordat proposed by MacBeth in his report on the European Community, involving a formalised contractual partnership of rights and obligations in the field for both parents and teachers,[28] and the statement by Parents' Associations in the EEC, identifying legitimate objectives for such organisations.[29]

An outline typology of phases of community involvement

Elsewhere, I have suggested the need to move through four major phases of community participation in the formal school system if we are to achieve greater discourse with parents and communities as part of the process of developing multicultural education. These four phases are:

1   The efficient provision of *information*, its collection and collation internally with the school and from the wider community, including the application of that information into the school, its curriculum and organisation, as well as inversely outwards towards the wider community. This implies greater adherence to the spirit of the 1980 Education Act and the implementation regulations and a willingness for interchange of that information.

2   Heightened *involvement* through consultation of parents, pupils and the wider community in decisions affecting them and their own children. I have referred to this phase as a transition and training phase where all parties are involved in rapid interlearning (including training for both parents and teachers) in the pursuit of new knowledge and skills.

3   Greater *participation* by the community in all modes of school life and at all levels, and a reciprocal movement by the school into the community. This I regard as the first stage of realistic, active and potent participation for it includes not only the right to information but also broader participation in teaching and the governance of the school by parents.

4   The fourth phase builds on and absorbs the previous three. It involves *co-determination or partnership* in decision-making (*discourse*) with the parents and the wider community across the range of issues which are of mutual concern. It implies an efficient interchange of information and influence on decisions and representatives in decision-making bodies to reflect the cultural composition of the school's catchment area.[30] It might include the contractual relationship referred to by Tomlinson.

I have defined *discourse* as a process of human communication based on the accepted equality of the parties concerned in negotiation and co-decision about real issues of power and access to resources in education and society. It is interesting to note that, although not as broad as my last category, there are several similarities between the fourth level of my typology and what Francis Morrell has written about the involvement of parents from ethnic minority groups:

> Such an approach maintains that black people must be fairly represented at all levels of management and government, that all established practices and procedures must be examined to ensure that they do not work to the advantage of white and the disadvantage of black people, and that there must be mutual respect and appreciation between all sectors of the community.[31]

Needless to say, we are not yet carrying out phase 1 of the typology fully: mutual and efficient exchange of information.

If, for example, we glance across the Atlantic again for a moment, we can see in so-called Public Law 94–142 on the education of all handicapped children, dating from 1975, the kinds of procedures which may be necessary to improve the mutual trust and confidence, so essential if parents and teachers are to work in real partnership to provide greater educational equality. The Law provides, for handicapped children, safeguards such as the confidentiality of records, which have to meet the certain standards. Parents have the right:

1. to review all information in their child's record;
2. to receive a reasonable lay interpretation of the information in that record;
3. to obtain copies of all information concerning their child;
4. to ask for any inaccurate information to be amended, and if the school and parents disagree about the accuracy of any information, to request a formal hearing. If the school and the parent cannot agree, then a non-agreement statement can be entered in the child's record to this effect. They have the right to demand that parental consent is obtained before any personal data on the child can be disclosed to anyone other than school officials;
5. to challenge specific school replacements formally and legally;
6. to challenge the use of standardised tests for placing minority children in special education classes and to take civil action, should they wish to question the placement of their child.[32]

A systems approach to the typology

It goes without saying that schools cannot involve themselves in effective discourse as a basis for implementing multicultural education unless they give full rein to the involvement of parents and the wider community. The question, therefore, remains how the school, committed to multicultural education, can be more open to the community and to parental influence. For this there are three basic requisites: firstly, a willingness on the part of teachers to recognise the crucial importance of parents to the community in developing multicultural education. Secondly, the development by teachers of the intercommunicative competence and skills to be able to make that communication equal and actual; and, thirdly, the identification of an overall programme for immediately boosting the level of trust between parents and teachers and ultimately for achieving the goal of equal discourse as a basis for children's education.

But developing such trust as a basis for a systematic programme is not an easy matter, and it requires hard, systematic, careful planning and the fostering and development of quite specific skills on the part of the teacher and, above all, a policy and agreement to collegial action on the part of all professionals within the school. Looked at in a systems approach manner, there are four stages to this process: definition of the policy; the development of the strategy; the implementation of the strategy; and the evaluation of the effects and feedback.

If we take the first major area across which interaction between parents and teachers takes place, it will probably be in the area of information exchange. A policy for such information exchange as part of an opening up of the school to parents and the community might involve the staff defining the multifarious ways in which an easier and more fluent information exchange can be achieved between parents and teachers. This might be achieved through the participation of parents of different backgrounds in successive festivals throughout the year; through the encouragement of a parent-teacher association; through parents' evenings or interviews or socials, home visits or problem-solving conferences; by observation on the part of the parents within the classroom or by the provision of specific homework or samples of work for children to take home; through films of children at work or by the sending of performance accounts such as report cards, or through informal notes. If it is a multilingual community, then the aim should be to include the languages of that community.

A multicultural school pursuing policies appropriate to its community will need to calibrate all possible means for the exchange of information, according to the cultural biography of the school, and to bear in mind that there are different kinds of information which parents are interested in obtaining: performance, yes certainly; but also the details of the process which their children are experiencing

113

and which, under the Universal Declaration of Human Rights, they, as parents, have a prior right to know about and decide on for their own children. Once this first phase has been tackled in a multi-dimensional but systematic way, the school may then move to higher levels of the typology in the development of wider and more secure parental access and ultimately to the fourth level of the typology and full discourse and participation in decisions.

One way of achieving equality of discourse is by recognising the fact that teachers are no longer the only source of valid knowledge, and that there are often occasions when parents possess expertise which is not available in the school. An early policy statement of the London Borough of Brent Education Committee makes this point in drawing the attention of teachers to the need for parental involvement in the social life of the school when it says:

> Parents should be encouraged to feel that they are welcome in the school and are participants in the educational process. They must be drawn into the schools through social functions and otherwise thus gaining an understanding of the school's functions and ethos so that they can more effectively discuss their children's progress with equanimity. Social events for parents should be held to cater for the various cultural interests.

TABLE 6.1: *A simple checklist of measures for parental involvement*

1 The avoidance of jargon in letters to parents;
2 The use of languages which are the most appropriate to parents for letters to parents;
3 Matching parents' evenings to parents' needs and not to the system;
4 Devising strategies for parents' evenings designed to cater for 100 per cent attendance;
5 Taking care with regard to the way in which non-attendance at parents' evenings is interpreted;
6 Reviewing the strategy in operation and considering alternative ones;
7 Making parent and teacher contact a regular matter, and not something which only takes place when problems occur;
8 The inception of home visiting and routine clinics in schools;
9 The identification of parents with particular expertise and knowledge who may be able to contribute to the resources of the school;
10 The use of suitably qualified parents as non-teaching resources; and
11 Making available a separate 'friendly' room for interviews.[34]

And later

> Parents possessing expertise not available in the school should
> be encouraged to come into the school and help in lessons. . . .
> Particularly in primary schools and possibly in secondary
> schools, there should be provision of one of more parents'
> rooms to provide an easy eating place and to encourage parental
> activities.[33]

In a later policy statement the London Borough of Brent Education
Committee sets out a checklist with regard to the implementation of
multicultural education in the schools, including a series of questions concerned with the involvement of parents, which I have
adapted as shown in Table 6.1.

Teachers need to review existing policies and agree a checklist of
those community issues to which they will need to be sensitive in
developing multicultural education, if they are not to make serious
blunders, including the issues listed in Table 6.2.

TABLE 6.2: *An initial checklist of community issues*

1	*Parental rights*
a	Information to parents;
b	Assemblies;
c	Religious education;
d	Religious festivals;
e	Attendance at places of worship for religious instruction;
f	Special provision for prayers by particular religious groups;
g	Rights of parents to withdraw children from lessons unless arrangements can be made to parents' satisfaction.
2	*Pupils' rights*
a	Issues of modesty;
b	Wearing of clothing with religious significance;
c	Dietary needs;
d	Curricular areas of particular sensitivity, such as health education, drama, physical education, games, gymnastics, swimming and dance; but also domestic science, biology and art;
e	Showering and changing for PE;
f	School uniform;
g	Wearing of items of religious significance, such as the Sikh kara and the Muslim towiz;
h	School meals and dietary customs including during times of fasting;
j	Recording of names, for which sensitive consultation may be necessary for practical as well as pedagogical issues;
k	Recording incidents of racialist behaviour, literature, graffiti and violence, abuse and insults.[35]

The report of a survey of Mirpuri parents in Saltley, Birmingham, from late 1984 by the Centre for the Study of Islam and Christian-Muslim Relations in Birmingham stated: 'The main problem facing the schools of the children is not a lack of interest on the part of Kashmiri parents, but the lack of facilities to promote contacts between home and school.'[36] Attendance of parents at parents' evenings was regular; no parents complained about the attitude of teachers towards them, although the parents tended to be overawed by them, and it concludes: '. . . one must stress the potential and room for improvement in relationships between school and home. The Kashmiri parents appear to be far more willing than is generally assumed, but the ball rests in the schools' court'.[37]

Supplementary schools

One of the major ways in which teachers may show their commitment to the involvement of the community in children's education is to find out more about and seek to develop links with the supplementary schools. There are basically three kinds of supplementary schools to be found in the United Kingdom at the present time: religious, cultural including language, and basic education, although there is some overlap.

The only major documentation of West Indian supplementary schools which is available to us is that produced by Stone in 1981. She has emphasised the way in which the schools could, and do, contribute to improving the academic work of large numbers of black British children, and saw them as an important means of redressing the failure of black children by the ordinary education system in concentrating on the development of trendy concepts, such as multicultural education and the development of a positive self-image.[38]

We are also fortunate in having one or two brief descriptions of the workings of such schools, including a brief record of Mell Chevannes.[39] Pointing to the apparent absence of a good relationship between black parents and the schools which their children attend, he comments that teachers are not suddenly going to alter the views which they have, particularly of West Indian parents, who, he asserts, are considered by teachers to be uninterested in their children's education. He argues that because a good parent/teacher relationship is important to pupils' learning, it is important that practical initiatives are taken to achieve this.

The school described by Chevannes operated for two nights every week from 7 to 9 with forty pupils on the register, all of whom were born in Wolverhampton and had parents who were born in Jamaica.

The ages of the pupils ranged from five to sixteen years and included both male and female student pupils. A curriculum was offered, including English language, mathematics and social studies, with a concentration mainly on English and mathematics. The pupils were taught in small groups of six to eight, according to their age, and the groups were named according to West Indian heroes such as Mary Seacole. The relationship included home visiting by staff and a parents' evening held every term, to both of which initiatives the response had been excellent. There were both black and white teachers involved. Chevannes sets down a series of criteria concerning the kinds of teachers whose involvement the project would welcome, including those:

1   Who possess the willingness and commitment to identify with the pupils and to empathise with their daily experiences.
2   Who can help the pupils to develop a positive attitude towards themselves, particularly with regard to their physical characteristics: skin colour, and texture, bone structure, eye colour, mouth and lip size, nose shape, hair growth and hair texture – and their ethnicity.
3   Who, above all, can help the pupils to face the most racialist classroom and teacher, with a determined will to work hard and to achieve the best within the restricted educational system.
4   Who are prepared to accept that West Indian and Asian pupils experience prejudice and discrimination in this society and that the pupils' statements of these practices are not unwarranted but genuine and deep-felt.
5   Who are willing to support the pupils when they express anxiety and distrust of whites and white institutions.
6   Who are prepared to recognise and accept that the pupils' parents are interested in what goes on at school.
7   Who are willing to recognise that there are pressures of child care, patterns of work, pressures of finance, and fear of a predominantly white teacher-audience that militate against parental attendance at school.
8   Who expect high standards of educational achievement from the pupils in their charge and who are not prepared to accept low standards just because children are black and/or working class.
9   Who demonstrate competence and enthusiasm and intense commitment to learning in their own discipline and classroom practice.
10 Who, though possibly strongly socialist and politically committed to justice and anti-racialism, are not bloated with

117

> abstract political rhetoric and seeking to impose narrow
> sectarian views upon their pupils. The religious
> fundamentalism of many West Indian families is likely to make
> such teachers unempathetic and unacceptable.[40]

A survey by Nagra of Asian supplementary schools in Coventry indicates rather different aims, including enabling children to communicate with their parents and other members of their own community by teaching them their own language, helping to give the children a clear sense of identity, assisting them to understand and participate more fully in their particular social and cultural environment, and transmitting religion and culture.[41]

Nixon gives an interesting example of such a school in Coventry, the Islamic Studies School, where the Hillfields Gujerati Muslim Society organised weekday and evening classes for fifty students between the ages of five and fourteen, offering tuition to both boys and girls in religious education and Urdu.[42]

A major survey is also now available by Ming Tsow of part-time Chinese language classes. The objectives of these schools were seen as:

– enabling children to learn about their own cultural background; and
– enabling them to communicate with their parents.

The parents of attenders saw the main task as being to enable their children to retain their cultural identity. Classes were mainly held on weekends although a number took place on weekdays, particularly Wednesday, and most children attended classes for two hours a week. She notes that there was very little contact between teachers from other language classes or from mainstream schools.[43] She comments that individual schools and educational institutions should be aware of the linguistic diversity of their clients and should examine their own role in relation to these community demands, needs and their response to such efforts of community education. The development of community links could begin by bringing the everyday school teachers together with the voluntary class teachers to extend experiences.[44]

A report from the House of Commons, Home Affairs Committee, based on the first major survey of the 100,000 Chinese, indicates that they constitute the third largest ethnic minority community in the United Kingdom, and that many still use Hong Kong for their medical treatment and their children's education. Amongst seventy-seven recommendations are those to publicise public services, increase specific Chinese facilities and to 'cross the language barrier'.[45]

It is apparent that there are widely differing motivations for the establishment of supplementary schools and for aspirations on the part of some ethnic minority parents and some of their community leaders for separate schools. The motivation in some cases is to overcome the disadvantage which the normal school system is seen as perpetrating against black children. In other cases, it is to perpetuate the culture of the parents and the community, to acquaint young people with the language and religious backgrounds of their parents and community and thus to enable them to communicate more easily with those parents and that community. It is inevitable, with widely varying motivations for supplementary schools, that there are sometimes clashes of values and objectives between the state school system and the supplementary schools. Some kinds of supplementary schools may even overburden children as a result of supplementary evening and weekend study and there is little doubt that the existence side by side of state and supplementary schools can raise considerable dilemmas for teachers.[46] Differing objectives, values, world views, methods of teaching, approaches to education and relationships between teacher and taught may demand of teachers extreme tact and understanding and the negotiation of principles which will enable them to make professional decisions concerning what is, in their judgement, best for the child in the state school system. A multicultural society is not an anything goes society, and decisions have to be made about what is legitimate and permissible and what is illegitimate and non-permissible within a multicultural society. For these decisions to be valid, more intensive discourse is necessary for negotiation and shared decisions about criteria appropriate to a multicultural society.

Some language issues

Strongly related to the issue of supplementary schools is the question of language. We have already seen how some supplementary schools are organised explicitly in order to enable parents to offer their children a means of learning the home language and thus of communicating more effectively both with their parents and the wider ethnic minority community.

The central importance of language issues to multicultural education has been emphasised by a number of writers, whether the focus is on standard English, non-standard English, mother-tongue teaching, bilingualism or the provision of modern languages. Edwards, for example, urges that linguistic diversity should be looked on as a classroom resource rather than as a problem, and she describes a strict insistence on standard English as both impractical

119

and counterproductive whilst, at the same time, seeing nothing incompatible between tolerance of other languages and dialects in education and the fostering of standard English.[47]

A policy statement, issued by the National Association for Multi-racial Education in the early 1980s, for example, focussed on the issue of mother-tongue teaching as being one of the most important aspects of language learning and teaching for many ethnic minority community pupils and their parents. It emphasised the need for urgent action to be taken:

- to ensure the use of ethnic minority languages in schools, their encouragement and promotion;
- to involve parents, relatives and friends of minority pupils to the fullest extent in the work of the schools and to provide for communication with them in their respective languages;
- to provide for the teaching of minority languages within the normal school curriculum.[48]

These reasonable recommendations must be seen against the very extensive literature and research and development work which has been conducted abroad, particularly in the United States and Canada, and the meagre situation on the ground in the United Kingdom. For of those who would be entitled to such language provision in the United Kingdom, by early 1984, less than 2 per cent were obtaining it.[49] The overall tally of development work is also scant with two major projects sponsored by the European Community and conducted in the United Kingdom, one in Bradford from 1976 to 1980 and a Schools Council mother-tongue project from April 1981 to April 1984.[50] Rosen conducted a survey of the language of inner city pupils from October 1978 to June 1981[51] and almost contemporaneously the Department of Education and Science funded the Mother-Tongue and English Teaching for Young Asian Children Project, launched and conducted jointly by the City of Bradford Metropolitan Council Directorate of Education, Bradford College and the University of Bradford.[52]

Finally, the Linguistic Minorities Project (LMP), funded by the Department of Education and Science and located at the University of London Institute of Education under the direction of Dr V.S. Kahn, lasted from September 1979 to April 1983.[53] There were four major components to the work of the LMP and four major instruments were developed: the Schools Languages Survey, the Secondary Pupils Survey, the Mother-Tongue Teaching Directory Survey and the Adult Language Use Survey. The latter was conducted in close collaboration with the National Council for Mother-Tongue Teaching. The Schools Language Survey concluded that in one of the areas, almost a third, and in another almost one in five of the pupils surveyed, could be described as being bilingual pupils insofar as they were recorded by their teachers as speaking at least one language at home other than English. In the Mother-Tongue Teaching Survey, conducted in three areas, Coventry, Bradford and Haringay, the team found 106 ethnic minority language classes in one area, 183 in another and 143 in another, with the earliest dating from 1904, and quite a number dating from the mid-1950s, with the vast predominance of South Asian language classes having been founded within the last ten years.[54]

This provision is parallel to the main school system and discussion about mother-tongue teaching and bilingualism within the school system has tended to focus on the issue of transitional mother-tongue teaching rather than language maintenance issues. Yet a survey, carried out in 1981, showed that most Asian parents wanted their children to learn their mother-tongue to examination level in school. In a survey of 312 Gujarati- and Punjabi-speaking parents in Leicester, 95 per cent thought it important for their children to know an Asian language, and 60 per cent said they wanted them to take it to 'O' level standard and as one of their examination subjects. Of the children surveyed, a majority could speak their mother-tongue, although only 18 per cent could read and write it. On the other hand, mother-tongue was used in 92 per cent of homes with 74 per cent mostly using it when speaking to their children. As far as entertainment was concerned, films, books and newspapers in the Asian languages were more popular than those in English.[55]

In another survey, Joly reports that 'the mother-tongue issue is the most burning one'. In this case, she argues that community 'mother-tongue' is a misnomer insofar as none of the parents interviewed expressed the wish that their mother-tongue (a dialect of Punjabi) be taught in the schools. Yet they are reported as being generally in favour of having Urdu taught in the schools. Urdu is the official language of Pakistan, but it is also the written and literary language, whereas Joly comments that the language spoken by the people from Mirpur is not generally written.[56] The overwhelming majority of families interviewed in her survey not only wanted their children to learn Urdu, but had arranged for their children to study Urdu in the mosque or in a house, taught by a relative or friend who took small groups of children for a fee.

In a statement on this issue, published in 1982, the Commission for Racial Equality strongly criticised the government for its failure to encourage the teaching of ethnic minority languages in schools, and it called for a proper provision in schools for teaching ethnic minority languages as a standard part of the modern languages curriculum.[57] The statement also urged the Department of Education and Science to issue a circular to all education authorities, encouraging them to teach minority languages to examination level in mainstream schools and to help voluntary organisations with funds from Section 11 of the Local Government Act of 1966. The reality is, however, different.

In a survey of local authorities the Commission discovered that less than half contributed towards the upkeep of voluntary mother-tongue classes, that only forty of those who replied supplied premises and twenty of those charged rent, possibly in contravention of EEC regulations. In all, 175 schools were used by 110 different voluntary groups, speaking sixteen languages, although only three education authorities were recorded as employing teachers to take pupils to exam level in subjects such as Gujarati and Urdu.

Major initiatives in this area have been at supra-national level, rather than at a national level, with the exception of Welsh in Wales and Gaelic in Scotland. The regulation, published by the Council of the European Communities in 1977, has had relatively little effect,[58] and it took the Department of Education and Science four years just to publish it as a Circular to local authorities! Moreover, a survey of the training of teachers for ethnic minority languages, conducted in 1981, found that no institution of teacher education in the whole country provided training to enable graduates in ethnic minority languages such as modern Greek or Gujarati to teach them in a school. Of those who were participating in B.Ed. courses, 75 per cent were studying French, whilst only a small minority were studying German and an even smaller minority in a single institution were working on Asian languages.[59]

So the debate in the United Kingdom has tended to remain at a very modest level, centring on such issues as whether the teaching of mother-tongue would adversely affect the learning of English, whilst other countries have been developing major initiatives in the field of bilingual education. In Sweden, for example, full provision is made, as of right, for over 90 per cent of children covering approximately sixty languages and home language is included in compulsory school instruction, applying to the teaching of more than one hundred very different languages.[60] In Canada also, there has been research both on additive and subtractive bilingual policies, with immersion programmes being established in the 1970s with the aim of teaching native English speakers French in the early years of schooling – programmes which are said to be becoming ever more popular amongst the middle-class, English-speaking population. In the United States, the teaching of mother-tongue in schools has had both substantial legal and financial support, including the existence for a number of years now of the National Clearinghouse for Bilingual Education.

Whilst it is beyond the scope of this chapter to deal in detail with the hundreds of studies which have been conducted of bilingual education in the United States, it is instructive to quote from the results of one report, prepared at the request of the White House Regulatory Analysis and Review Group for an assessment of the effectiveness of transitional bilingual education. The Report covers an extensive range of valid literature within the field, and comments: 'We believe the literature makes a compelling case that special programmes in schools can improve the achievement of language-minority children.'[61]

Summary

Pulling together the three strands of this chapter, and recapitulating briefly, I have drawn on material supporting the central importance of the development of home/school and teacher/parent relationships, including the involvement of the wider community in the continued effectiveness of schools, emphasising the importance of negotiation and discourse in arriving at a legitimated curriculum for a multicultural society. Having identified an initial typology, I have linked this with two specific areas of current major concern: supplementary schools and mother-tongue teaching. I have emphasised that interlearning by both parents and teachers is a prerequisite for improvement.

I have tried to illustrate very simply in Figure 6.1 the interrelationship between these three issues and the crucial role which, it seems to me, they should play in achieving discourse for multicultural education.

Demands for supplementary schooling and for mother-tongue

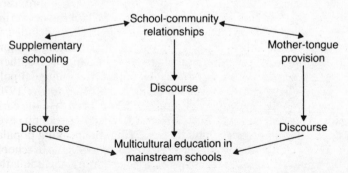

FIGURE 6.1: *Three major issues in school community discourse for multicultural education*

provision represent wholly legitimate demands of cultural minorities within a multicultural society. If these legitimate demands are rejected, ignored or neglected, then it will be more difficult to legitimate multicultural education within mainstream schools. Equally, unless effective dialogue exists between the school and the community, the discourse essential to the legitimation of mainstream schooling will be flawed and may be damaged to the extent that the ethnic minority communities and their children are alienated from mainstream schooling and increasingly, therefore, demand their own separate and parallel provision.

Coercive measures cannot solve this legitimation crisis for the school and only discourse can identify the areas of conflict, and the negotiated means to their resolution. That discourse demands the opening up of greater communication and negotiation between the school and the community across a range of issues which will enable the community to support the school and the achievement of children within that school, rather than fighting against it. Equally, it will be impossible for the teacher to choose appropriate teaching/learning strategies in the classroom appropriate to the values, cognitive styles and concepts of reward of the children, if he/she is not in potent dialogue with the community. That need for the teacher to match the culture of the child and the pedagogy of the classroom as part of an interactive process is the theme of my next chapter.

Part Three

Children and teachers: potential and achievement

Chapter 7

Children and learning

Introduction

In the preceding chapter I have sought to comment on three major issues, which are a fundamental part of the dialogue essential to multicultural education. These were the issues of school community relationships, supplementary schooling, and bilingualism and mother-tongue teaching. It will be apparent from what I have said in that chapter that children come to school with all kinds of different cultural and social values and predispositions to learning and that the teacher needs to learn of these in order to fulfil his/her educational functions – to do the job.

In Chapter 5 I have argued that the cultural context must inform and imbue the policies of schools and the content of what they teach. But a curriculum is more than a mere collection of content, on whatever basis it may have been assembled. It is also the materials, equipment, grouping patterns, displays and other aspects of the school which are all expressive of particular cultural values. Above all, it is a complex, subtle and usually unspoken series of interrelationships between all members of the school and between them and their community. In this chapter, therefore, I want to take one aspect – but an important aspect – of these relationships, namely that involved in the teaching/learning context, and examine it in the light of the fact that, in a pluralist society, children come to school with different cultural biographies from each other and from the teachers. These differing cultural biographies – cognitive styles – have a substantial influence on learning and attainment, and it is essential that teachers build them into their pedagogical strategies, as part of a sensitive, interactive, developmental, *iterative* process of mutual acculturation with their pupils. I shall explain what I mean by that phrase shortly.

The ways in which children conceptualise and think vary,

according to the process of acculturation and socialisation in which they have grown up before they came to school. Attitudes to learning, to books, to cultural artefacts, to sex roles, to rewards, to themselves and to many other matters, may already be very well-developed by the time they first cross the school threshold. I do not want to infer that they are static or unchanging during the school career of the child, let alone that they are unalterable: merely that they are already well-developed and have to be reckoned with in teaching. In this chapter, therefore, I want to look briefly at the area of differing cognitive styles, attitudes and values, and to advocate the need for the teacher, insofar as it is possible, to take these into account in the teaching/learning strategies deployed in the school and in the class-room.

One major caveat, however, is necessary before we commence consideration of these issues. I have hesitated more before writing this chapter than before any other in the book. This is because it is very difficult to discuss the issue of cognitive styles without running the risk of stereotyping and, in some cases, generating from such a consideration fixed and sometimes low expectations of children's performance based on their group appurtenance. This does not, in any sense, mean that the teacher should not attempt to take into account differing cognitive styles and value previous learning, but that the teacher must be circumspect, balanced, sensitive and, above all, reflexive towards the use which he or she makes of such considerations. He/she should remember that diversity within cultures is as normal a phenomenon as it most surely is across them. Another important matter which it seems fundamental to empha-sise is that when we speak of cognitive styles, we are referring to the differing ways in which individuals *process* information. It is *not* a matter of their ability or of the information itself but of *how* that information is processed.

Further, the amount of work which has been carried out in this field is, relatively-speaking, sparse. Certainly, the interface between multicultural education and cultural factors in learning and instruc-tion is not very substantial compared, for example, to the mass of literature on the relationship between socio-economic status and educational achievement.

Firstly, however, let me emphasise the importance of consistent and shared values and standards. Although the work of Rutter indicates an interdependent cluster of factors, which together promote a good school ethos, among these are pupil-pupil and pupil-teacher cohesion, a strong academic emphasis, high teacher expectations, an emphasis on positive rewards and consistent and shared values,[1] such shared values cannot be assumed to exist *a priori*. They have to be worked towards gradually and there will always be certain areas of values where teachers will need to take account of other powerful sources of socialisation, such as the family, religious and linguistic grouping and the community.

In one sense there is nothing new in this, insofar as teachers have been exhorted for many years now to take into account the child's background and to start from where the child is. Taking into account the background of the children has, of course, implied recognition of the linkage between cognitive style and the fact that all parents do not raise (socialise) their children in the same way. Moreover, as Goodenough has indicated, we all develop some degree of multicultural competence.[2] What multicultural education brings to this context is a realisation that the spectrum of cognitive styles within any classroom may be very much wider than most teachers have hitherto assumed or experienced. However, one major lacuna in the field of multicultural education so far has been that, whilst a number of reports, documents, organisations and individuals have emphasised the way in which the curriculum content should celebrate cultural diversity and be based on the assumption that Britain is a multiracial and multicultural society with different ethnic groups making valued contributions, there has been very little discussion of the way in which teaching/learning strategies should also reflect that cultural diversity.

Let me explain. Looked at in a slightly oversimplified way, what happens is that the tasks required by the teacher are subject to a process of mediation and interpretation within the child before the child gives a response. The response which is given by the child will be influenced by the functional cognitive process which takes place. The functional cognitive system involved in that process will, in turn, have been influenced by the cognitive biography, including values, of that child, which it has absorbed by a similar process since birth.[3] And that biography, in turn, will have been influenced by the process of socialisation and acculturation which has surrounded the child's development. Looked at in that light, it becomes very important for the teacher to adopt strategies which will enable all children and the learning processes of all children to have equal expression within the classroom and school.

Two major dimensions of cognitive style which are referred to in the predominantly American literature on this matter are those of field dependence/independence and verbal/visual modes.

Some dimensions of cognitive styles

What exists in the literature on cultural diversity and cognitive styles has tended to focus on issues variously described as field-independence and field-dependence, non-verbal communications, kinesics and context, including time and space, locus of control, motivation and values. I want to look at some of the literature associated with these and see if we can glean anything which might help us in teaching in multicultural classrooms and schools.

Let us look at just one example, the writings of Donaldson. In these he shows how children, who may not be able to solve a problem in an unfamiliar situation, can solve a logically identical problem expressed in terms of objects and relationships with which they are familiar.[4] A teacher, not knowing this, might merely assume lack of ability, rather than adopting a different more culturally compatible strategy. Equally, Cole *et al.* represent the view that what differs between cultures is not the quality of thought processes, but the content and premises of thought and the conditions and situations which evoke thinking: pupils' skills at tasks differ with their own culture's emphasis on these tasks and thus also their previous experience with these and/or similar tasks.[5] Equally, and bearing in mind the work of Doyle and his admonition with regard to the complexity of classroom life and the processes concurrently active there, it is important to emphasise that pupils develop a differential, interpretive competence in 'understanding the kind of response to instructions or learning tasks that they think the teacher is seeking and which they assume he or she will reward'.[6]

But this effort on the part of pupils demands a reciprocal effort on the part of teachers: to match culturally the pedagogical strategy. Here the evidence is not encouraging. One interesting recent study, for example, found that the problem of teaching/learning matching was one which teachers found most difficult and that, of a large number of infant level teachers surveyed, only an approximately 40 per cent match was achieved of tasks to pupils' attainments.[7] And the researchers report that teachers are not very efficient in diagnosing what children have learned or failed to learn and, crucially for the theme of this chapter, why.

The Scarman Report in the United Kingdom caught something of the flavour of this when it said:

> Unless they [parents] do so [take a full and active part in the schools] however, teachers will remain unaware of the way they view the needs of their children and the effectiveness of the school system . . . only if parents and schools can be brought closer together will parents appreciate what schools are trying to do for their children and teachers understand the parents' expectations.[8]

This latter point about teachers understanding parents' expectations underlines what was said in the previous chapter about the need for discourse between parents and teachers, not just for community reasons, but also for sound pedagogical reasons within the classroom, for it is one avenue of access to details about the cognitive styles, values and attitudes which have surrounded the children during their early socialisation.

Although most of the work in this area has been produced in the United States, it is relevant to consider whether it has implications for the pedagogical strategies which teachers in multicultural classrooms in this country should adopt. In their study of Jewish, Chinese, Black and Puerto Rican children, Stodolsky and Lesser discovered distinctive cognitive patterns that differentiated one group from another. They adopted four measures, verbal, reasoning, number and space, and found that whilst social class influenced the level of students' scores, regardless of social class, each ethnic group maintained its own relative set of abilities. This indicates perhaps, they suggest, the development of different intellectual abilities by different cultural groups.[9] They conclude that their study indicates that groups differ in their relative standing on different functions. Each fosters the development of a different pattern of abilities. It should be noted that they are not asserting that these differences are innate or genotype – quite the reverse. They are specifically pointing to the socialisation process which is different in different family and broader cultural group backgrounds, within which priority for the achievement of different tasks is differentially rewarded. When you think of it carefully, it seems to reinforce commonsense, namely that different people have different priorities. They value different abilities and skills, as well as cultural artefacts and styles. This does not in any sense mean that some are superior and some are inferior, merely that they are different and that they result in a different pattern of cognitive learning abilities and processes on the part of children when they come to schools.

For a nation which has been committed to a unidimensional concept of intelligence for a period of over fifty years, it is important to emphasise that everything points at the moment to human intelligence being organised vertically as a number of facilities rather than as a single ability or set of abilities. As Gardner's recent work endorses, human beings are capable of uneven achievement in several relatively self-contained domains and this is the reason why IQ tests show a false picture of individual talent, for they do not test or lock on to the full range of abilities which we possess,[10] a topic which I develop further in Chapter 9.

Cognitive styles might be very loosely termed ways of perceiving and calibrating objects and concepts in the external world and according to Kogan they are both numerous and complex.[11] The idea of cognitive styles, as it has been developed by Witkin, is argued by Bagley to have considerable importance for practitioners in education, 'since such styles influence the learning of social material, the effects of reinforcement, the use of mediators in learning, cue salience, teacher's instructional style, etc.'[12] He quotes the work of Laosa, arguing that understanding cognitive styles may be particularly important for teachers working in the field of multi-cultural education.[13]

Bagley reports that the British Advisory Committee on Race Relations Research recommended in 1975 that research should be initiated in order to attempt to establish whether different ethnic groups had different cognitive styles, but that, in spite of that initiative, little relevant research of this kind had been carried out in Britain. Bagley states: 'In Britain there is only a handful of studies which have looked at this issue.'[14]

Ghuman, for example, investigated field dependence among primary school children and found that field dependence/independence had no significant correlation with sex differences, but that middle-class children tended to be significantly more field independent than working-class children.[15] In a later study with older children attending one comprehensive school and comparing three groups, white, Asian and West Indian, there were no statistically significant differences.[16] Perhaps the most ambitious study which has been undertaken in Britain is that by Machtiger of a sample of London infant school children, where she found that cognitive style was strongly correlated with proficiency in reading, perceptual motor performance, aspects of linguisitic competence, ego strength and attitudes towards self.[17]

In the United States, Ramirez and Casteñada found a consistent difference in field independence/field dependence, between mainstream monolingual youth and Chicago youth, with the former being significantly more field independent.[18]

Vasquez argues that whilst one cognitive style is not inherently superior to the other for there is no consistent correlation with IQ, children who are field independent tend to achieve consistently better. The reason seems to be that the cognitive style of field independent students is more nearly matched by the cognitive style of the 'typical' teacher and that this 'cognitive fit' affords students a considerable advantage in the classroom.[19] He points out that there are other dimensions of cognitive styles which also merit attention, such as the analytic/descriptive and reflective/impulsive dimensions. This knowledge he sees as indispensable to the development of culturally sensitive approaches which can achieve equal learning opportunities in the classroom for all ethnic groups.[20] He strongly advocates that where children differ from one another along social class or cultural dimensions, different and varying motivational and reinforcement techniques are necessary if the teacher is to give equal opportunity to all children. He further points out that different social class and cultural backgrounds assure the existence in children of differences in value systems, and that motivation is dependent on the child's value system.

Thomas has recently summarised the available evidence on the intercultural perceptions and attitudes of school children, indicating the research evidence of early awareness of skin colour in young children, succeeded later in the child's development by the more complex categorisation necessary for ethnic differentiation. Whilst emphasising the incomplete nature of research into both intergroup and intragroup attitude formation, he describes how the feeling of belonging to a group intensifies so that the symbols and values of one's own group evoke positive feelings, such as attachment and pride, and the symbols and values of other groups may elicit negative feelings.[21] It is inevitable that this early socialisation will predispose children towards or against, totally or in part, some of the teacher's symbols and values. And the more similar the socialisation of the teacher and the child, the more likely there is to be sufficient overlap in their 'symbols and values' for them culturally to see 'eye-to-eye' on issues of learning, motivation and reward and, of course, vice versa. So the teacher has to reckon with some at least of the pupils in a multicultural classroom having less positive cultural orientation to the things which he/she values than others. And, as these values express themselves in the teaching/learning strategies employed by the teacher, he/she has to decide those value positions which are in conflict and essential and those value positions which are discardable without detriment and which will enhance the 'match' and therefore the learning of the child. This is a complex exercise in critical self-evaluation, for which staff development and collegial support are necessary.

Some implications for teachers

The need is for the teacher, accordingly, to try to orientate his/her reward strategies to the child's value system and, reflecting back to the theme of our last chapter, as Cahir argues, it is precisely because cognitive styles appear to be related in part to cultural differences and socialisation that every effort should be made to discuss with parents and community members their views on child-rearing and the education of children.[22] Needless to say, this is particularly important in the case of bilingual children and those whose home language is not English. Cahir suggests an initial checklist in order to enable teachers to think about their teaching strategies, including the following elements:

- the way in which the teacher indicates acceptance of pupils;
- the use of both words and actions to do so;
- the way in which the teacher indicates feelings, preferences, personal opinions in his/her role as a teacher and as an adult;
- how the teacher encourages co-operation, helpfulness, consideration and respect amongst all pupils;
- how the teacher communicates with pupils about their families and their community;
- how the teacher demonstrates understanding of the individual pupil's preferences and styles;
- how the teacher provides a model for pupils' different academic and social needs.[23]

In the United States, too, Nine-Curt has outlined certain cultural principles which, it is argued, should guide teachers and other school personnel in their teaching and professional work:

- being aware of and accepting their own ethnic, historical and cultural background, and the ethnic, historical and cultural background of others;
- being sensitive to their own particular communication behaviour (thus the importance of teacher self-evaluation, which I shall be dealing with in the next chapter);
- being sensitive to the communication behaviour of others;
- having the skill of switching cultural channels to establish an acceptable, non-offensive, productive relationship with students of other cultures;
- being open to communication systems which they may not have noticed before;
- practising one-to-one culturally specific personal relations with each student.[24]
- being open to new ways of thinking and behaving;
- being willing and able to 'unknow' something every day.[25]

The important thing, however, is to avoid stereotypic classifications, whilst at the same time allowing in teaching/learning strategies for important differences in the way in which children perceive, classify and calibrate information and their preferred modes of motivation, for example, whether oral, verbal or visual. I must, however, emphasise again that the concept of cognitive styles refers to an individual tendency and it is, therefore, not necessarily applicable to categories of student, although specific cognitive styles may be correlated with particular cultural groups or specific child-rearing practices.

Locus of control has also been a phrase which has been used to describe the extent to which individuals attribute their successes and failures to specific causes. For instance, if a person believes that his/her own actions determine the reinforcements that come to him/her, then he/she is described as being internally oriented with regard to locus of control. On the other hand, the 'external' person believes that his/her own actions are not the major determinant of the rewards or failings that he/she encounters in life. Put in a nutshell, Rotter describes locus of control as referring to the self-versus-environmental responsibility for an outcome.[26]

Research from the United States seems to indicate that children from lower socio-economic classes tend to score as 'externals' on locus of control tests, whilst middle-class pupils tend to score as 'internals'. Moreover, internality would seem to be associated with numerous traits which provide those possessing it with considerable advantages in learning situations, predominantly because they attribute causality to themselves. In other words, they think that their own destiny is in their own hands. This relationship between learning and locus of control has been examined by a number of writers in the United States. For example, the Coleman Report indicated that at all grade levels, Mexican American students' belief in their ability to control or influence their environment was the attitude most highly related to achievement.[27]

Locus of control is regarded as important because it affects learning in areas such as the ambition of the pupil and his or her dependence on others, the self-reliance and the extent to which pupils expect success and their orientation towards motivation, the intensity of their work, the emotional reaction to success or failure, their reactions to competition, their performance on tests, etc.[28]

Some 'coping' strategies for teachers

The implications for the classroom teacher within a multicultural classroom are evident. On the spectrum of locus of control between internality and externality there will be a large range within any multicultural classroom. As locus of control can affect not only the performance and particularly performance of assessments and tests, but also general achievement in competitive environments, teachers should attempt to begin to grade their work so that pupils may achieve success in the classroom, on a basis which will enable them to attribute that success to their own efforts. Praise and other forms of reinforcement should focus on that fact, so that gradually a pupil can achieve greater confidence in his or her ability to influence his/her own achievement and success.

Vasquez identifies four concepts or principles that may provide a

framework for building understanding of cause and effect relationships. The first of these is what he calls the sufficient condition, i.e.
that the cause has sufficient power to produce a given effect. The
second principle is that the pupils understand that without the cause
the actional result would not have occurred. The third principle is
the identification of the most likely cause from all of the other
possible causes. And the final principle is that the cause must
precede the effect in time. In their question and answer techniques,
Vasquez suggests, teachers may develop and enhance the extent to
which pupils can identify the relationship between cause and effect
and feel confidence at their own (the children's) influence over that
cause and, therefore, also their own responsibility for the effect.[29]

It is important to remember that culture is also introjected into
non verbal patterns of behaviour, where many of the basic mis-
understandings inherent in multicultural contexts often have their
origin. Birdwhistell even argues that non verbal behaviour not only
fills an important social integrative function, but that it has more
communicative value than verbal behaviour.[30] While Hall has
examined in detail the way in which humans from different cultures
use time and space, [31] and Key has given detailed consideration to
paralanguage, i.e. vocal but non-verbal behaviour.[32]

A number of points of departure emerge from such work as that
quoted above for the teaching strategies adopted by teachers. The
first is that insofar as it is possible it is important for those teaching
strategies to be able to offer a variety of children tasks in which they
can begin to feel success. As Barnes points out, recent work in
psychology has made it clear that coping with problems which are
part of a familiar context is very much easier than dealing with
analogous problems in unfamiliar contexts. Thus, a knowledge of
the cultural background and value systems from which the pupils
come achieves increasing importance, not just as an additional area
of knowledge for the teacher in developing multicultural education,
but as a crucial area of competence, upon which the teacher needs to
draw in order to develop appropriate teaching-learning strategies
for the variety of predispositions to learning which are in the multicultural classroom.[33] In this context the nine principles proposed by
Barnes and the tasks which he identifies, offering practice in applying some of the principles to the selection and ordering of activities
in the classroom, are of great relevance for teachers in multicultural
classrooms. For that reason, I am repeating the list of principles
here in the hope that the reader will refer to the original, more
detailed presentation for further assistance and guidance.

1 Pupils' abilities and knowledge;
2 Values and procedural principles;

3 Prerequisite concepts and skills;
4 Bite-sized increments;
5 Learning through simulation or the activity itself;
6 Varied activities;
7 Problems;
8 Discussion and writing, exploratory or presentational aids;
9 Familiar and unfamiliar experiences.[34]

There is an interesting account by Musgrave of the way in which, teaching in pre-independence Uganda, he had to alter his entire pedagogical approach in order to overcome the effects of the striking cognitive and conceptual disparities which he perceived between his British cultural background and that of his students.[35] So teachers can and do change their teaching/learning strategies to achieve greater match with their pupils and thus enhance their learning – both parties.

Another way of tackling this problem within the classroom is to introduce in the variety of methods of teaching adopted both peer tutoring and schemes whereby the pupils can take responsibility for other pupils' learning. In this work, all children are offered an opportunity for situational leadership and leadership resolves around the group with different children taking on responsibility for the direction in which the group's work proceeds.[36]

The other major area where teacher strategy can be reshaped to have an impact on achievement by pupils in the classroom is in the area of values and attitudes. In a comprehensive survey of research projects covering a fifteen-year period concerned with the education of pupils of West Indian background, Taylor asserts that the attitudes of teachers and hence probably their expectations were likely to be of considerable influence on the performance of children of West Indian origin in schools.[37] And she continues, slightly vaguely,

> It is somehow necessary for the school to find a way in which it can contribute to the process of instilling confidence in the pupil of West Indian origin and pride in his own ethnic group and yet also enable him to have a realistic appraisal of his position within society at large.[38]

The importance of the teacher's values is underlined by the fact that it is on the basis of those values that the teacher will decide on the extent to which particular forms of behaviour are rewarded and reinforced and the kinds of rewards which are given, with what effect. The story is apochryphal of teachers in the early 1940s in the mid-West of America giving alphabetic grades to indigent American Indian children, whose culture emphasises and values harmony, i.e. no differences among individuals, so that the 'best' pupils stopped working, so as not to be different.[39] Well, it may have been an accurate account of what happened or not, but the message is clear enough.

These processes of valuing particular patterns of behaviour and showing that process of valuing by the identification of particular rewards may be fundamentally different in different cultural groups. It is, therefore, important for the teacher to seek to adopt a process of 'conscientisation' with the patterns of behaviour which are valued in ethnic minority communities and to identify culturally congruent rewards.[40] Triandis has deployed a similar proposal, based on a large number of empirical studies. He suggests that for effective behaviour in a culturally different context, it is necessary to develop 'isomorphic attributions', similar to empathy, and that appropriate cross cultural training can lead to increments in cognitive complexity, to which field dependence/independence is attributed.[41] As Gay has argued, many children whose cultural values and identities are strongly rooted in their traditional ethnic heritage experience alienation and isolation in schools. She argues that such disaffection shows itself in situations of classroom management, where there are conflicting expectations between pupil and teacher about acceptable school behaviours, lack of interest in, or motivation by, mainstream instructional activities of a monolithic kind and thus low academic achievement.[42]

We are all familiar with the goodhearted teacher who says, 'I treat them all the same, no matter what the differences'. The problem with this strategy, as a basis for the teaching/learning situation in the classroom, is that some pupils' values and attitudes are more congruent with those of the teacher rather than those of other children. The inevitable consequence of this is that those pupils whose values and attitudes are more congruent with those of the teacher are the ones who are most likely to achieve success in the kinds of tasks which the teacher sets and are, therefore, to be rewarded. Moreover, the kinds of rewards which are allocated are more likely to be meaningful to those pupils whose values and attitudes are similar to those of the teacher than other pupils who may come from different backgrounds. The result is that ethnic minority pupils in many cases suffer a double disadvantage. Not only are they allocated inappropriate tasks, but if they should succeed, they are allocated inappropriate rewards. Such a conflict is likely to lead to frustration and alienation both for pupils and teachers. Teachers might be better advised to scrutinise their own values and to appraise which of their pedagogical strategies and reinforcement preferences are really necessary and appropriate and which can be discarded as artefacts of their own cultural biography. Some observers would argue that they should make the major adjustment in a multi-cultural classroom,[43] what I have referred to previously as mutual acculturation. For this, both detailed knowledge (see the previous chapter) of the cultural context is necessary, and collegial strategies of professional growth and development: an issue central to my next chapter.

Summary

Summarising this chapter, it seems important to emphasise that there is more to teaching multicultural education than injecting a culturally diverse content into the curriculum, even though that content rests on detailed and up-to-date knowledge of the cultural context of the school. Teachers also need to consider very carefully the teaching/learning strategies which they adopt and the policies for reward and reinforcement against the same cultural background and as a support for the equal educational opportunity of all children. Thus, in addition to the curricular facts about multi-cultural content, resources, media and learning environments, there needs to be a process of pedagogical matching with functional characteristics of pupils including their learning background, their interpretive competence, their motivation, the values and attitudes of the cultural background from which they come and, insofar as is possible, some understanding of what might be considered to be appropriate rewards and reinforcements.

The problem is to take into account these relevant functional characteristics without generating the basis for new stereotypes. But, basically, teachers need to remember that there are other factors in addition to ability which control and sometimes deter-mine learning and attainment and that, by dint of their very social-isation, many children are ill-adapted to the values and attitudes, tasks and rewards, priorities and indeed the general ethos of the school. Teachers can help children to overcome these disadvantages by trying to pull together the curricular facts and the student facts in formulating their instructional strategies, attempting to match the two and varying the pedagogical approach which they adopt, so as to include a multiplicity of different approaches and methods.

Amongst these different methods may be variable use of dif-ferent approaches including oral and visual, verbal and non-verbal stimuli, a broad selection of cultural artefacts, exemplars and con-tent, different learning experiences for the pupil including peer group tutoring, co-operative group learning and graduated ap-proaches to skill requirements, based on a diagnostic and reflexive progression by the child which emphasises and rewards success across a spectrum of different concepts of what reward might be. I have attempted to illustrate this process in Figure 7.1, and to indicate diagrammatically and I hope not too simplistically, the important role of such a matching process in attempting to achieve not only success orientation for all, but equality of educational opportunity for all.

At the risk of oversimplifying, a number of principles emerge from the considerations introduced briefly within this chapter. They might be identified as follows:

– the use of a diversity of content, materials and stimuli;
– the goal of increasing the sense of involvement of pupils in the school culture;
– strategies aimed at increasing self and ethnic image of child;

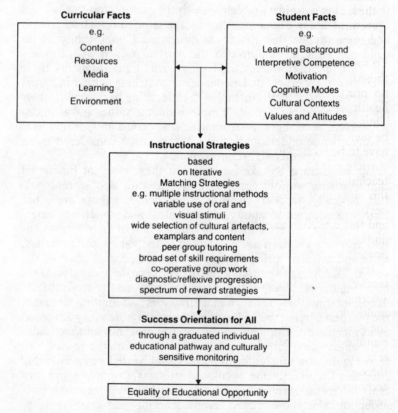

FIGURE 7.1: *Instructional strategies for multicultural classrooms: a model*

– acquisition of cultural experiences, values, beliefs and expectations of differing groups;
– the generation of a culturally receptive classroom and school atmosphere;
– the celebration of diversity in indirect teaching, e.g. display, etc. and in both verbal and non-verbal behaviour;
– introduction of pedagogical strategies to boost pupils' locus of control;
– providing for a variety of achievements in different modes;
– the adoption of a range of stimuli: oral, verbal and visual;
– the inclusion of peer group learning and co-operative group work;
– the use of multiple instructional methods;
– the adoption of an iterative matching strategy for lesson planning and implementation;
– the identification of and with pupils' values and attitudes;
– the institution of continual discourse with parents and community.

To some extent the concerns of this chapter have overlapped with those of the previous chapter, and deliberately so, for there can be no process of matching curricular and student facts without a healthy dialogue with the parents and the surrounding community. Thus, once again, the development of multicultural education has to be seen as a holistic process in which all of the pieces of the jigsaw have to be related to one another, before an effective multicultural curriculum can be designed. It may seem to some in discussing the teaching/learning strategies which have been briefly referred to in this chapter that iterative processes such as those advocated are beyond the scope of most teachers currently teaching in classrooms and this is where I have overlapped with my next chapter. For self and collegial evaluation are indispensable to an effective iterative process for teaching/learning strategy development.

It is for this reason that my next chapter is devoted to the issue of teachers improving their professional practice. Then, after considering the staff development which is essential to the launching of multicultural education, I proceed in Chapter 9 to look at some of the issues of testing, examinations and assessment which are symbiotic with the consideration of the multicultural curriculum, content and pedagogy with which I have been concerned in the last three chapters. In that chapter I shall again be referring to new techniques, such as those presently emerging, of computer adaptive teaching and testing, which offer a means of adopting a more effective iterative strategy towards both teaching and learning.

Chapter 8

Professional growth and development

Introduction

Chapters 5, 6 and 7 of this book have dealt respectively with the curriculum, community and pedagogical dimensions of multi-cultural education. In those chapters I have emphasised the need for systematic and deliberate change based on discourse if we are to construct an educational provision appropriate to a culturally pluralist democracy. In each case I have referred to the need for mutual acculturation to take place so that teachers and teachers, teachers and pupils, teachers, pupils, parents and the community are engaged in a reciprocal process of sharing – interlearning I have called it. It almost goes without saying that inherent in the strategies and developments which I have identified in those chapters is a massive agenda for professional change. Staff development is at the core of the introduction of any feasible and credible multicultural education and institutions will need to consider both carefully and corporately what is their own agenda for action. Each area, each school and each individual teacher, to some extent, will need different but overlapping expertise, knowledge and attitudes to enable him or her effectively to pursue a multicultural curriculum within the overall context of multicultural education.

In this chapter I want to consider some of the major needs in this area and how they may be responded to in the form of policies for professional growth and development, within the context of an overall agenda to correct for current excesses such as racism and prejudice and to achieve the goal of the introduction of multi-cultural education for all children.

To set the scene, let me quote a major piece of research into in-service provision conducted by a team led by Professor John Eggleston. They comment that '. . . many teachers have keenly felt professional needs to identify and develop new styles of teaching that are more appropriate for a multicultural society . . .'.[1] As indicated in Chapter 7, developing new styles of teaching is a very personal thing. So let us take a careful look at what it is that we may need to include in our 'multicultural staff development shopping list'.

Whilst I am not centrally concerned with the teachers' colleges in this chapter, I want to commence by garnering some idea of what may be implied in an institutional staff development policy to introduce multicultural education from the recent writings of individuals and organisations published in the United Kingdom and abroad, including policies for teacher education institutions. The year 1984, for example, saw the publication of two British documents which, although addressed to the teachers' colleges, may indicate to us some of the areas of competence, attitude and knowledge which may be necessary prerequisites for teachers in schools, wishing to introduce multicultural education.

Two British documents

The first document, published by the Council for National Academic Awards, sought to suggest principles in respect of multicultural and anti-racist education, together with a checklist of items for possible inclusion in courses.[2] The document calls for appreciation of the richness and variety present in Britain, and indeed worldwide, to be utilised in educational curricula at all levels. It advocates education for diversity and social and racial harmony which recognises the diversity and richness of cultural traditions and achievements amongst different people, together with a serious study of race relations, involving a commitment to both multicultural and anti-racist education. It demands a critical approach to the problem of how cultural bias, prejudice, racism and stereotyping in teaching materials may be developed and of how teachers may become more sensitive to the possible presence of unintentional racism in their own expectations, evaluations of, and attitudes to, ethnic minority pupils and students. The document is intentionally non-prescriptive but it provides a number of pointers towards necessary areas of staff development.

At the risk of doing injustice to the document, it may be said to reflect five major themes of this book;

1 The need to consider multicultural education against a global/ worldwide backcloth;
2 The requirement that racism and race relations should be seen as central to any effective multicultural education;

3   The need for a social and economic context to multicultural education;
4   The need to include not only curriculum and teaching method but also teaching materials in appraising pedagogical processes for bias and prejudice; and
5   The need to consider the diversity of legitimate cultural traditions and achievements amongst and within different ethnic and racial groups.

One might say that the major missing dimension within the document is the issue of social cohesion and the way in which multicultural education must contribute not only to maintenance and creative extension of cultural diversity, but also to continuing social stability with justice.

The second major document concerned with this issue, which appeared in the United Kingdom during the course of 1984, was the National Association for Multicultural Education statement on teacher education.[3] This document takes a more uncompromisingly anti-racist approach to the needs of teachers and teacher education, resting on the twin beliefs that all teachers in Britain should adopt an anti-racist approach throughout their professional activities, and that to do so effectively demands as full an understanding as possible of the context within which they work and of the educational, cultural, social, moral and political issues on which their decisions depend. The statement recommends the adoption of explicit policies and implementation strategies *vis-à-vis* a number of areas of institutional provision, including management, staffing, recruitment and assessment, provision of courses and staff development opportunities, course content and evaluation of resources.

To some extent, this document also provides a useful checklist for schools against which they may consider their own professional needs. The document calls not only for knowledge of the issues relating to equality in a multiracial society but also for the adoption of an anti-racist approach in classroom practice. At the risk of doing injustice to what is a document of some detail, it may be said that the document provides a fairly comprehensive agenda within which schools might reconsider their courses and practices and that, added to this, it calls for an explicit consideration by teachers of the context within which they work and the extent to which they have developed strategies for teaching which might be considered to be explicitly anti-racist.

Whilst both of these documents are a helpful beginning at setting a checklist of items to be considered for inclusion within a school's staff development policy and practice, they do not, as yet, identify the explicit competence and areas of knowledge which might be necessary in order to achieve those goals, nor the care needed in selecting implementation strategies.

Working 'dialogically' for professional growth

However good the policies and policy statements, it is the people who implement them who determine their effectiveness. Describing procedures and assumptions grounded in a Schools Council Project, involving five local education authorities in the North of England and involving a dialogical approach which entailed 'close-quarters' working with teachers to help them define their own requirements, Biott, Lynch and Robertson propose the following initial list of propositions about staff development:

1   the promotion of multicultural education involves a constant process of professional enquiry and development and the avoidance of ready-made answers;
2   this involves educators extending their own reference group and criteria for professional judgement or the development of new ones;
3   in this process, dialogue between professionals on a basis of equality and between professional, lay and administrative personnel, on the same basis, is indispensable and seminal;
4   criteria generated for judging processes in one part of the country may be inappropriate in other parts of the country;
5   whilst it is desirable that there should be overall policy objectives, nationally, in LEAs and in schools, these latter need to be 'worked up' *in situ* and the actual implementation needs to be fostered, nurtured and monitored at classroom level;
6   the dilemmas which multicultural education evokes for individual schools should be much more widely discussed;
7   the ideas of people who have 'found the answers to problems' of implementation should be tested through enquiry for their appropriateness in each setting;
8   accounts of actual enquiry in one setting may be a rich resource for discussion groups in their writings;
9   any approach will inevitably have a high level of provisionality and needs to be subject to constant monitoring and dialogue;
10 the professional activities most likely to lead to growth will be those in which the teachers themselves have defined their own tasks, on a basis of partnership with others;
11 educators need to bear in mind the lessons of other 'apparent' innovations generating activity without real change;

12   above all, introducing real multicultural education into a
     school is more likely to be part of subtle and organic
     professional growth rather than a grafting on of completely
     new resources;
13   activities which do not appeal to the professional judgement of
     teachers are unlikely to incur their support.[4]

An example from Canada

Less comprehensive and related to shorter-term goals, the City of
North York Board of Education in Canada set up a series of seminars
on racism awareness for teachers from two families of schools, part of
whose learning task was to present similar workshops in their own
school and plan the professional development of the staff in that
school across an academic year. The seminars sought to involve staff
by:

– providing input from everyday experiences;
– requiring pre-reading of selected texts;
– requesting participants to keep a 'reflection journal';
– encouraging and equipping participants to observe aspects of
  race relations in their schools;
– requiring syndicate work, including presentation by participants;
– preparing participants for a pilot racism awareness workshop to
  their own staff;
– expecting participants to plan out the professional development
  for the staff in their schools for one academic year.[5]

The course not only itemised the expected benefits for participants – a very important consideration at times of tight staffing
ratios – but also a list of organising or gridding principles which are
worth repeating in full:

1   Racist behaviour is not natural – it is learned.
2   Racism is produced both by belief systems and social structures.
    It is not simply a matter of changing attitudes or changing social
    structures. Rather, what is required is the recognition of the
    relationship between both, knowledge about the interests which
    racism serves, and practices by both institutions and individuals
    to promote equality.
3   Racist behaviour has both a cognitive and an effective
    dimension. Any exploration of racism must allow for the
    expression of both ideas and feelings about the subject.
4   Educators respond best to initiatives in Race Relations when
    they are directly applied to classroom practice.
5   Educators find in-service programs most rewarding when their

experience as practitioners is taken into account and not trivialised.

6 Educators are likely to make changes in their sphere of influence when there is a support system within the school to provide encouragement and feedback.[6]

Some proposals from the USA

Gay has identified a number of baselines for areas of staff development content for multicultural education, such as:

1 Basic information about ethnic and cultural pluralism;
2 Knowledge acquisition and values clarification about ethnic groups and their cultures;
3 How to combat racism;
4 Linguistic knowledge of black students in its historic, economic, cultural and political contextuality;
5 Competences for perceiving, believing, evaluating and behaving in different cultural contexts;
6 Skill development in translating multicultural knowledge into programmes, practices, habits and behaviours of classroom instruction;
7 Competences in making educational objectives, curriculum content, learning activities, meaningful to the experiential backgrounds and frames of reference of all students;
8 Skill in achieving teaching and learning style congruency; and
9 Psychology and sociology of ethnicity including issues of human behaviour and learning.[7]

Even bearing in mind the absence of reference to mother-tongue teaching, to grouping issues, to issues of assessment and evaluation, and of relationships with parents and the wider community, the list proposed by Gay represents a 'tall order'. What Gay is advocating is not merely the achievement of cognitive gains but also of affective objectives that will reflect in the skills and attitudes of teachers, and will, in turn, be reflected in the interaction between individuals and groups in the teaching/learning situation in the classroom and outside, in the school and wider community. Gay also points to the current situation where most teachers (and other members of Western societies) live in a situation of ethnic encapsulation.

In a later paper, and drawing on traditions of competency-based teacher education, Gay seeks to set an agenda for teacher staff development for the introduction of multicultural education by identifying five major areas of competence as follows:

1   Knowledge, including not only cognitive understanding but also knowledge of the cultural context within which a teacher works and of the ethnic biography of his/her community and the broader society;
2   Performance, including the specification of teaching in instructional behaviour and attitudes and the rearticulation of teaching/learning styles and experiences in order for those of the teacher and the pupil to be more culturally congruent;
3   Consequential, including identifying student behaviours which might be expected to result from the teacher adopting the performance behaviours identified above. In this way, a means of evaluation would be available for the teacher to gauge the effectiveness of his or her own performance;
4   Affective, including the attitudes to be demonstrated by educators, for it is only in the actual demonstration of attitudes that an institution can gauge whether, in fact, it is a policy of multicultural education in practice as well as in theory and 'in policy'. This is crucially important for the development of an appropriate ethos within the school, where in overt behaviour, as also in secret conversation, there is a commitment to the introduction of multicultural anti-racist education;
5   Exploratory or Expressive, involving the ways in which, through experience, teachers might acquire the appropriate background of values, attitudes and competences, for example, through more interethnic contact.[8]

An initial typology

Taking the contributions of Gay and other writers within this field, I have proposed a typology of staff development needs for teacher education, if an effective multicultural and anti-racist teacher education is to be introduced.[9] This could be adapted so as to provide the outline for an institutional policy for teacher development for the introduction of multicultural education to address the following six areas:

1   *The Cultural or Contextual*. This would include such items as the development of a heterogeneous staff and student body, interethnic contacts, fostering interethnic friendships and professional and personal associations and links with supplementary schools.
2   *The Moral/Affective*. This is concerned with the development of an ethos for multicultural, anti-racist education in the school, and involves the collegial preparation of a list of criteria against which the institution's functioning can be judged and the

commitment to multiculturalism, in the private sphere of non-offical discussions and conversations, as well as in more public contexts, may be judged.

3   *The Cognitive*. This is the area of knowledge of sexism, racism and race relations, the bases of prejudice acquisition and reduction and the knowledge of the cultural map of the context within which the teacher is working, which is essential to the personal and professional functioning of individual teachers. It includes issues such as the impact and importance of teaching/learning styles and locus of control and language studies.

4   *The Pedagogical Performance*. This refers to the specific teaching and instructional behaviours and professional attitudes which will be essential if multicultural education is to be developed for all members of the school community, teachers, pupils and parents.

5   *The Consequential*. This defines the behaviour and attitudes that one would expect from the pupils and staff if the moral and affective ethos of the school represented commitment to multicultural education.

6   *The Experiential*. This area draws our attention to the fact that new competences are not solely developed by cognitive means but that experiential means are often necessary in order to gain insights into the situation in which many members of ethnic minority communities are currently located. Thus a teacher might be seconded to a community relations council for a while, or to some other community body.

Some initial principles

In the development of such a policy three basic principles are very important to bear in mind. The first of these is that not all schools need the same staff development; secondly, not all teachers have the same staff development needs; and thirdly, unidirectional strategies are very unlikely to yield improvement. Such issues have been addressed by Banks when he considers the school as a social system and cultural environment where mutual acculturation takes place, that is, both teachers and the students assimilate some of the views, values, perceptions and the ethos of each other as they interact across the teaching and learning activity. Looked at this way, part of the experiential dimension of the staff development is in fact the very process of sensitively interacting with the pupils. Emphasising the need to formulate and initiate change strategies that will address the reform of the total school environment as a prerequisite to the successful implementation of multicultural education, Banks also comments that not all teachers of any race or ethnic groups or social class background will benefit from identical training approaches and models, but that it is necessary to take into account the cultural experiences, personality and levels of knowledge of the individual.[10]

In his earlier work, Banks has already identified a typology of the stages of ethnicity through which individuals would have to climb from ethnic psychological captivity to a goal where the individual has reflective and positive ethnic, national and global identifications, and the knowledge, skills and commitment needed to function within his/her own culture, nation and world, or globalism and global competency. In between these two are four intermediate stages: ethnic encapsulation, ethnic identity clarification, biethnicity, multiethnicity and reflective nationalism. He puts forward the view that only teachers who have reached stage three, cultural or ethnic identity clarification, are in a position to be able to benefit from powerful affective techniques such as anti-racist teaching.[11]

The importance of Banks's work is less the fact that he has developed a provisional typology of stages of ethnic 'enlightenment', but that he has accepted the fact that different training strategies are necessary for different people, and that their own culture and social background, as well as their level of competence and knowledge in multicultural education and in multiculturalism generally, need to be taken into account before the strategies which are appropriate for them can be fully identified.

The importance of discourse and democratic procedures

But, as we all know, the 'how' is just as important as the 'what'. So is there any evidence about how we can best go about it? Using the well-known conceptualisation of planned organisational change strategies: empirical-rational, power-coercive, and normative-reeducative, Grant emphasises the limited effect of the first two and the importance of the third if the normative culture which guides people to their actions, personal attitudes, cognitive modes and overt behaviour is to be changed.[12] Slightly reformulating Grant's work, one can identify several inherent principles for the implementation of staff development as indicated in Table 8.1.

If we add these to our previous points, the generation of staff development policy for multicultural education becomes both a much more complex and a much more interactive enterprise than that which has been identified by some recent attempts to impose on all teachers' attendance at anti-racist workshops. This is not to deny the importance of democratic, racism reduction training for teachers,

TABLE 8.1: *Principles for multicultural staff development*[13]

1 For normative reeducative change to be effective, a framework of empirical-rational and power-coercive measures is necessary but not sufficient (e.g. research, legislation, etc.);

2 While strategies for information provision and correction of misinformation are necessary, it must be recognised that the 'problems' may lie in the attitudes, values, norms and external and internal relationships of clients;

3 The effective use of new knowledge, therefore, requires the elimination or, at the very least, attenuation of negative attitudes and pathological norms from the teacher's repertoire of beliefs and values;

4 Only normative-reeducative change can achieve fundamental value, meaning and habit reorientation;

5 Democratic discourse is an indispensable part of such a change strategy entailing what Stenhouse called 'appeal to the judgement of participants', involvement of the participants in working out the change programme themselves and in its implementation and evaluation;

6 Planned change relating to cultural pluralism demands mutual and collaborative effort and dialogue, aimed at openly defining and resolving problems and bringing into consciousness nonconscious elements. This involves support and participation by other dimensions of the pluralistic culture;

7 The resources, concepts and methods of a variety of behavioural sciences, used selectively, relevantly and appropriately, will be necessary assistance to the implementation of programmes of change;

8 Participants in such a planned and systematic normative-reeducative programme of change may travel through three major and overlapping phases: awareness and recognition; acceptance and appreciation; and affirmation and full commitment. (Baker, in a similar model for the training of teachers, proposes a sequence ranging from the acquisition of knowledge, through the development of an appropriate philosophy to the implementation of multicultural education, and this might be seen as the parallel cognitive and pedagogical dimension to Grant's mainly affective illustration.[14]) Not all will reach their goal;

9 For the above a 'whole-institution' approach is required.[15]

but to indicate that there may be certain pre-stages through which teachers have to go before they are fully able to benefit from more detailed policies and procedures for prejudice reduction, and that such workshops must be open for discourse and participation. For the same *caveats* have to be borne in mind as those which were referred to in Chapter 5, namely that within a democracy discourse, including dialogue and persuasion, are the means to achieve progress, rather than coercion which may, in any case, result in the alienation of the individual. This process involves open learning situations rather than closed ones and appeal to the judgement, both professional and personal, of the individuals participating in such a staff development enterprise. There are many examples of such approaches.

One school's approach

We are very fortunate in having one or two descriptions of how particular schools 'went multicultural'. Carlton Duncan, Headmaster of Wyke Manor School in Bradford, for example, has given an account of how he led his school from a monocultural to a multicultural approach to educating all children to their maximum by following both micro and macro strategies for a staff with little or no previous experience in the field.[16] Adopting both an organic approach, through committees and working parties, preparation and position papers by staff, etc., as well as the injection of outside expertise through a programme of visiting speakers and intensive discussions between visiting consultants and each faculty in his school, Duncan gradually expanded and developed the expertise and confidence of his staff to address the introduction of a multicultural curriculum, whose aims and objectives had emerged from professional debate in the school. He set up a system to monitor effectiveness in addressing these specific aims and objectives, and involved both governors of the school and parents in the process, by informing, presenting papers and seeking approval and support.[17]

Willey states that the strategy of setting up working parties was a common practice reported to the Schools Council survey as a kind of focus for initiating and monitoring debate amongst staff, which he regards as sometimes evoking suspicion and antagonism.[18] Although he acknowledges the complexity of the process and its difficulty, however, his exclusive emphasis on staff self-examination and examination of the school's practices as the only means of achieving positive responses to diversity is too narrow, as is demonstrated by Duncan's approach, which included wider expert inputs, links and dialogue with parents, consultancy and networking approaches, and a process of political legitimation, without which such efforts will founder or remain parochial in their effect and their conception. All these processes are part of the normative-reeducative process emphasising discourse, dialogue, negotiation and agreement of policy procedures and principles before implementation.

The teacher as evaluator

A similar emphasis is advocated by Nixon, who draws on the tradition within the field of curriculum studies emanating from the work of Stenhouse and emphasising the central role of the teacher as a researcher in which systematic self-study and the study of the work of other teachers through classroom research procedures is central. He rightly sees this activity conducted within its social and political context as a patent means to the identification of the principles which need to underlie practice, including those of negotiation of access, boundary, release and confidentiality.[19]

Combating racism as part of staff development

In Chapter 5 I emphasised the symbiotic relationship between curriculum implementation and evaluation. If multicultural education is to be successfully implemented, it will be necessary for the teacher to undertake a deliberate, planned and systematic study of his/her own practice, as part of an overall programme of evaluation. For, in order to 'equalise' treatment of pupils, it is necessary for the teacher to have both as accurate a picture as possible of his/her behaviour in the classroom and cultural knowledge of the children. In this way, it is possible not only to gauge learning outcomes, but to relate these to issues such as whether feedback from pupil's behaviour is representative and the extent to which tasks, cues and encouragement are effectively matched to the different cognitive styles and value systems which inevitably exist in a multicultural classroom: the iterative process described in my previous chapter.

Evaluation is concerned with observable outcomes, their detection and assessment, for these outcomes provide the evidence for decisions and, as appropriate, change in future teaching/learning situations and strategies. They may include:

- the performance of the teacher;
- the learning gains of the children;
- the utilisation of appropriate 'culture fair' content;
- the use of culturally suitable resources, including from the cultural backgrounds of the children;
- the equality of participation of children in classroom activities;
- the extent to which different cognitive styles are accommodated in the teaching/learning strategies;
- the cultural appropriateness of record systems;
- the movement in field independence of pupils;
- the evenness of success of motivation strategies, etc.

Whatever the focus, it is important to consider ways in which evidence may be collected. The instruments of evaluation may include one or more of the following:
- audio recordings of classroom work;
- self-analysis protocol is completed after lessons – perhaps for discussion with 'sympathetic' colleagues;
- intervisiting arrangements in the same school whereby two or more colleagues sit in on and appraise each other's lessons;
- intervisiting with other schools;
- examinations, formal or informal, written, visual or oral;
- ad hoc tests and sampling of pupils' work;
- marking and correcting strategies;
- use of objective tests;
- study of video recordings of segments of teacher, individual or group teaching and learning;
- listening to pupils;
- study of transcript of lessons or discussions.[20]

The intervisiting technique is a particularly useful medium for non-threatening enhancement and extension of professional skills such as those required in multicultural teaching. Two or more colleagues may sit in on each other's lessons and prepare a protocol which is then the subject of discussion between 'evaluator' and 'evaluated' on a mutual basis. It is an efficacious means to extend the criteria for professional judgement as part of the overall process of discourse. Its purpose is to improve the self-confidence and self-critical capacity of the teacher.

Of course, as Alexander reminds us, extending and upgrading professional competence as part of systematic self and institutional evaluation may encompass a number of interrelated decisions about:

- The purpose of the evaluation (aims and objectives);
- The aspects to be evaluated (focus);
- The means of collecting evidence (methods);
- The criteria for judgement (yardsticks);
- By whom, how and with what, it will be conducted (organisation);
- To whom the results will be available and under what conditions of confidentiality;
- The corrective action to be taken and the way (action).[21]

Elliott draws our attention to two aspects of evaluation in particular which are crucial to multicultural education:

- the need to have not just formalistic checklists but guidelines concerning the process of evaluation; and

- the need to have not just formalistic checklists but guidelines opinions which teachers have of themselves as part of a thoroughgoing process of research.[22]

His description of action research involves the kinds of information-gathering techniques which can be utilised, how they can be organised and applied both to individual schools, networks and systematic levels of education. It provides a clear and helpful guide for teachers. Thus, it is important that the evaluation of multicultural education is seen as part of a coherent, well-thought-out policy of staff development, at personal and institutional levels, for without it multicultural education will stagnate.[23]

Another programme, designed by the cross-cultural communication centre in Toronto, is concerned with combating racism in the workplace. It takes the experiences and understandings of workplace racism as the initial basis of the course. The course was constructed on the assumption that participants must recognise and come to terms with their own relative privilege *vis-à-vis* Third World peoples, and the effect of that privilege on their relations with others, and especially visible minorities.[24]

Any such strategy for the development of in-service provision for teachers in this area will also need to reckon with the current existence of stereotypes and the need to enable those stereotypes to be unlearned. There is already a certain amount of material on the market which can assist in this process, such as the series of filmstrips from the Council on Interracial Books for Children in New York,[25] which, although they may be intended for use in schools, are also of value in the development of appropriate strategies of staff development, and the Life Styles Project, initiated and developed at the University of Nottingham.[26]

A prerequisite to the launching of an appropriate staff development process for schools is the existence of a comprehensive, practice-oriented policy which can identify principles, enunciate guidelines for action and identify procedures in areas such as dealing with and handling racial and ethnic incidents. The policy will need to come about by dint of two major processes, namely the scanning of institutional and personal needs and the interfacing of this process with discourse and interaction with the community. By community, the immediate context of the school is meant, but, as I have pointed out on many occasions in this book, account will also need to be taken of the macro-global context with which the school exists and which provides certain prerequisite principles to which the school must adhere, as also the background of legislation and policy provided by national and local education authorities.

This should ensure that any policy on multicultural and anti-racist education will be firmly embedded in the recognition of international and universal human rights to which all citizens are entitled. Such a process will need to recognise the desirable existence of a process of mutual acculturation through which individuals, both teachers and pupils as well as the wider community, learn from each other and articulate their values, attitudes and knowledge of their cultural and social context. Above all, any such policy for staff development will need to take into account the centrality of race relations and the requirement for the unlearning of existing stereotypes. In the short term, a survival pack with regard to racial and ethnic incidents in schools and classrooms will need to be generated and implemented. The school will need to make an explicit commitment to condemning and refusing to tolerate any expression of racial or ethnic bias in any form by its students, staff or other members and identifying what action should be taken if racist behaviour occurs.[27]

Summary

Pulling together the strands of this chapter, we are in a position to identify a number of 'provisional' guiding principles which may facilitate the preparation, by each school, of its own staff development policy for the implementation of multicultural education and to correct for racism and sexism as follows:

1   There should be a comprehensive practice-oriented, policy statement on multicultural education, including sexism and race relations, which identifies principles, guidelines and implementation procedures;
2   Practical implementation will need to be preceded by a scanning of institutional and personal needs and the drawing up of a cultural map of the institution;
3   Any policy needs to be embedded within the broader context of human rights to which all children and adults are entitled;
4   Both the policy and the scanning will need to take place on the basis of interaction and discourse and to eschew coercion;
5   The community needs to be deeply involved in the whole process;
6   The process needs to allow for mutual acculturation;
7   The programme needs to be developmental and move from awareness to the generation of a commitment to social actioning and personal and professional development;
8   The policy needs to start from where each teacher is, recognising individual needs and differing competences;
9   The programme needs to be continual and developmental: it

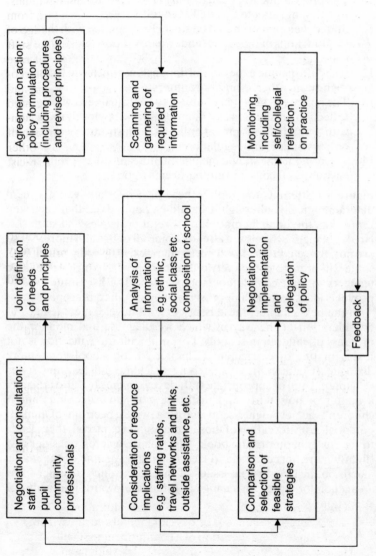

FIGURE 8.1: *Initiating staff development at school level*

should identify longer-term goals and more immediate
objectives, including the process of self and collegial
evaluation of professional practice;

10 The programme will need to aim at high levels of mental
functioning: affective as well as cognitive;

11 Staff development should be strongly integrated with the work
and functions of the school and, wherever possible, it should be
collegial;

12 It should include experiential dimensions which will facilitate
'significant other' ethnic encounters;

13 The policy will need to be subject to continual review,
reflection, evaluation and monitoring and be closely integrated
with the staff development policy of the institution, carried out
on a systematic and regular basis;

14 The programme should include 'significant-other' professional
encounters facilitating mutual acculturation.

Figure 8.1 attempts to simplify these principles and express them
diagrammatically, although it should be pointed out that each step
represents the implementation of several principles and subtasks.
No doubt many schools are already doing all of this and more. Some
are not. Some educators will prefer alternative 'guiding principles',
some will prefer a completely different approach which will enable
teachers to start completely from scratch. The list is intended to
provoke ideas rather than prescribe panacea-like precepts.

In the next chapter, these issues of staff development lead us to
consideration of the way in which we diagnose and monitor the
progress of children in schools. For, multicultural education is not
just a matter of curriculum (Chapter 5), of school community
dialogue (Chapter 6), of matching teaching and learning styles
(Chapter 7) and of appropriate staff development. It is also crucially
a matter of how fairly and justly we can make decisions about
children's achievement, seen across a wide spectrum of human
potential. Consideration of these 'educational controls', then, leads
to the final chapter of the book, Chapter 10, where I consider in a
slightly more speculative and free-ranging way some of the major
macro-political and social issues of this book which together form
an agenda for a pressing change of direction towards multicultural
education.

Chapter 9

Assessment and the multicultural school: practice and promise

Introduction

In this chapter I want to describe briefly the reasons for the growth of assessment (including testing and examinations) in education, consider the claim to objectivity of current systems and argue the lack of comparability and equity in contemporary content and processes of external examination with regard to social class, sex and ethnic dimensions in particular. I then want to discuss the appropriateness of profile approaches to assessment in the multicultural school, refer briefly to issues of record-keeping and progression, and finally set down some tentative guidelines for teachers to consider, criticise and amend in pursuit of a fairer system of assessment, record-keeping and progression-recording, appropriate to a multicultural school.[1]

The historical development

Looked at historically and traditionally, the major function of assessment in education has been to act as a means of selection and placement both within the formal educational system and, in support of the means of production, in the economic sector too. To coin a phrase, the implicit theory could be described as 'graded grains make for better economic placement and better economic placement leads to better economic performance'. The corollary of this economic function at the political level has been that schools and their curriculum have needed to be 'policed' in order that the structure of society could reproduce itself through a well-defined hierarchy of knowledge. As industrial society has progressed, the selection, and thus the cultural 'policing', has needed to become ever more refined and extensive: a development which in

159

democratic states, needs complex means of explanation and justification, what the sociologists call legitimation, to make it acceptable to the bulk of the population.

The development of 'objective' tests has been one major way in which such selection procedures have been legitimated. Mercer, for example, points out that Binet's original 1905 instrument was developed in order to select children for educationally subnormal schools.[2] Most items dealt with skills and information which, it was believed, all French children had an equal opportunity to acquire. Let us call this the *societal curriculum*.[3] She relates how, when the original Binet scale was modifed in 1916 by L.M. Terman, it similarly involved question content which reflected the dominant anglocultural group in the United States. Because girls had scored higher than boys, when the 1916 version of the Stanford Binet test was revised in 1937 by Terman and Merrill, it was amended to fit in with their assumption that boys and girls had equal intelligence. In order to achieve this, they reduced the number of verbal test items in which girls did better and introduced more non-verbal tests where the reverse was the case. The interesting thing about this is that they did not alter the scale in order to accommodate to the different performance (or inherent equal ability?) of other groups and to respond to other discrepancies such as those between rural and urban young people, between young people from different socioeconomic groups such as the professional and working classes and those from different racial groups.

The bias in the early testing movement has also been pinpointed by others. Verma, for example, writes of the 'strong elitist and racist values of the testers and the way in which their tests reflected the common element of their culture and their model of a successful individual'.[4] Addressing the use of the Wechsler scale, Kagan has cogently shown the way in which *a person's score reflects the probability that he has been exposed to the information requested* and points out that if the Wechsler scales were given to children in a number of developing countries, the majority would be classified as 'mentally retarded'.[5]

The growth of the myth of objectivity

In spite of early criticism and more conclusive recent proof of cultural bias, however, the myth developed, both in the United States and elsewhere, that these tests were, in some way, 'objective', and that they somehow measured an isolable genetic component in intelligence. This was the strong conviction of such people as Goddard and Terman in the United States and Sir Cyril Burt in this country. The history is not a happy one, as we are now aware after the exposé published in *The Sunday Times* in October 1976 (subsequent to Princeton Professor Leon Kamin's work), which set in motion a series of revelations of 'the most sensational scientific fraud this century'.

By that time, the damage had been done and Burt, the first educational psychologist appointed to a school board anywhere in the world (in London, 1913) and Professor (in his latter years Emeritus) of the University of London from 1931 to 1971, had wielded enormous influence on education in this country and abroad. The bonus is that there is now widespread scepticism of psychological testing and of the validity and reliability of such tests. Moreover, in spite of the widespread belief that objective intelligence tests assess innate, i.e. inherited, intelligence, it is now increasingly accepted that both school achievement tests and intelligence tests measure that which has been learned, i.e. the child's acculturation to *the existing school curriculum*, on the one hand, and to a 'valued' selection from *the societal curriculum* on the other. The 'physics envy' of such tests and their pretensions to scientific objectivity and the errors and injustices in the way that they may 'mismeasure' man have been graphically portrayed by Gould as a warning to all who use tests.[6]

The Jensen controversy

The myth of objectivity dies hard and Jensen's 1969 committed assertion of the inferiority in intelligence of blacks proposed, at a time of heated controversy about desegregation in the USA, that differences in intelligence tests scores were four-fifths attributable to heredity and one-fifth to environment and that, since blacks scored 15 points less than whites, it followed that 80 per cent of 15 points difference between blacks and whites is caused by genetic factors. The work brought out into the open once again the issues surrounding race and intelligence and the alleged objectivity (and thus the reliability and validity) of such tests.[7] An interesting hypothesis, it was put forward almost with the aura of consolidated dogma. It was followed shortly after by the British psychologist Hans Eysenck's contribution concerned with the education of black children in Britain.[8]

The core and controversial contention is that there is a relationship between race and intelligence not, let it be noted, whether performance on intelligence tests is partially influenced by genetic, i.e. inherited, factors and characteristics, about which there is more general and continuing dispute. The problem is that, of course and inevitably, any intelligence test depends on the communicative competence and culture of the person being tested and that cultural competence, in turn, must inevitably depend on what children have inherited from their parents and upon the economic, social and cultural context within which the person has grown and learned: their *societal curriculum*.

But there can be no such thing as culture-free learning, nor indeed, for that matter, a culture-free test, for any test must reflect knowledge and the ability to communicate that knowledge, i.e. culture, however that is defined. That such knowledge is dependent on cultural exposure, the motivation to learn, the independence of the individual in that situation and 'minor' items such as the acquired test-taking skills of the individual and even the 'race' of the tester,[9] are apparent. Thus testers who avow 'objectivity' and assert that they are testing intelligence are in fact confusing intelligence with knowledge of a specific curriculum and non-race-specific hereditary characteristics.

It remains only to say that it is important to consider the work of Eysenck, Jensen and others on its scientific merits. It has proved a useful and powerful spur to the reconsideration of issues concerned with race, intelligence and heredity, and brought the issues of racism in education out of the filing cabinet into the arena of educational debate. Several fairly cool and balanced appraisals of the evidence have been made, coming to the inevitable conclusion that the evidence for any relationship between race and 'intelligence' is weak, flawed and incomplete.[10] And if the evidence does not support the hypotheses, then it would be scientifically and intellectually untenable to act in educational or indeed other matters as though it were proven. For the moment, perhaps forever then, there is no proven association between race and intelligence.

The paradox in all this is that traditionally tests have controlled for age, and as we saw earlier, some tests have even been amended in order to attempt to take account of the sex variable, but they do not usually control for socio-cultural differences, and therein lies the problem for a pluralist society if any such test is ever to have any kind of normative validity. For a pluralist society has a plurality of *societal curricula*, and to attempt to classify children from the perspective of only one inevitably leads to apparent 'underachievement' because of the cultural bias.

I have given this historical cameo, not to indicate the perfidiousness of people who construct and use tests, let alone of psychologists in general, but rather to indicate my view that so-called 'objective' intelligence tests measure a particular *societal curriculum* expressive of particular socio-cultural values and assumptions just as achievement tests in schools measure a *school curriculum*. I am not denying that achievement in society is the result of interaction between what we are born with i.e. our inherited biography and the cultural, social and economic environment which interacts with our biography as we move through life. Nor do I reject the claim that one major function of the school in any society is and must probably remain the selection function. The important thing within a pluralist, democratic society (and also incidentally to some extent in some rather authoritarian societies) is that the system of selection itself has to be legitimated by persuading the populace at large of the equality of educational opportunity within which it is bedded. The equation, if you like, has to be: selection + equality = legitimation. Any reasonable interpretation of tests, their development, and interpretation must acknowledge them as seriously culturally biased.

Formal examinations

So much for the tests, but how equal are the kinds of examinations we use? In comparison with the dozens and dozens of standard tests currently in use, there are approximately 25,000 syllabuses in secondary school examinations at 'O' and 'A' level and CSE.[11] Not without 'honourable' precursors in the nineteenth century,[12] these latter examinations derive from the long tradition which was initiated with the establishment in 1917 of the School Certificate and continued with the replacement of that School Certificate in 1951 by 'O' and 'A' level examinations of the General Certificate of Education, which were aimed for the top 20 per cent of the ability range, whatever that might mean. Then in 1965 the CSE, Certificate of Secondary Education, was introduced, aiming at a further 20 per cent of the ability age-range and in 1972 the Certificate of Extended Education (CEE) was then inaugurated. In 1984, there were in England and Wales, eight GCE examining boards, six of which were associated with universities, thirteen regional CSE boards and three different modes and many different mixtures. For a single board, there might well be as many as 1,000 syllabuses. How fair are these examinations? Does one child have as much chance as another regardless of board, subject, marker, paper, region, sex, class and race?

The twin issues of comparability and equality

One of the major criteria for equality in examinations is comparability: an equivalent grade in the same subjects for different boards should have roughly the same worth and measure similar matter. But with the number of boards, the large variety of syllabuses and the methods of assessment, is this possible? Does the variety of subject matter vie against such comparability? Can the choice of subject, of question, militate against it? Does the heterogeneity of candidates influence it? Can it be said that the human error of markers and moderators makes present procedures less than perfectly reliable and infallible? How does the complexity of the subject matter, and the examination questions set, work for comparability? Does this make examiner disagreement more likely? Does the number of candidates influence this as well? Above all, does the 'final grade' reflect the probability that the candidate has been exposed to the information required and the 'single grade system' adequately reflect the multidimensional and complex process which has taken place, in every child's school career, between extry and exit?

Let us look at a few examples. In 1970-1, 44 per cent of pupils left schools without any GCE or CSE qualifications but a decade later this had been reduced to approximately 14 per cent.[13] Had national intelligence or the efficiency of the school system increased so much in a decade? Then there is the continuing issue, for as long as they exist, of the divergence in achievement between the various examining bodies. For example, the boards which pass the highest proportion of their candidates are the Northern Ireland Board and the Oxford and Cambridge Boards, and it is no coincidence, I am sure, that these are the boards which have the highest proportion of independent and public school candidates taking their examinations, roughly 66 per cent and 89 per cent respectively.[14]

These divergencies often occur across subjects as well. In 1977 the Associated Examining Board passed approximately 46 per cent of its candidates in English language, whereas the Northern Ireland Board passed approximately 68 per cent. Internally, within an individual board, there is also divergence. The pass rate in 'O' level English language for the Associated Examining Board, syllabus I, for example, is 43 per cent but for mode 3, it is 74 per cent. Even areas such as question choice are seen to act as variables vying against equality and comparability, for '. . . the most able candidates are seen to attempt the easy questions . . .'.[15] Then, too, there is the opportunity which children have to learn specific content. In spite of the fact that the acquired test and examination-taking capability of a child and whether it has encountered the material previously must self-evidently have an effect on its score, the Assessment of Performance Unit concluded in 1983 that

. . . it is not feasible, within any realistic limits of time, manpower and financial resources, to collect information in the context of a national survey to describe the opportunities individual children have to learn the topics tested.[16]

The question inevitably arises, how are we controlling for that variable, and if not at all, how can we be sure that this is not the dominant variable in educational achievement? The answer is that we just do not know, that available knowledge is simply too inadequate, incomplete and faulty to permit firm conclusions that performance in examinations is solely the result of 'ability'.

There are also, of course, powerful sex and clientele variables, not to mention regional and social class disparities.[17] And if we then turn to the issue of equality of outcomes, we will find that the public schools, which educate less than 6 per cent of all school children, provide approximately 50 per cent of the entrants to Oxbridge. Moreover, Goacher's research on the use made of examination results indicates widespread confusion, misunderstanding, irrationality, arbitrariness, insensitivity and consequent inconsistency and misuse of the examination results by employers and tutors in higher education in a way which leads to serious injustice for many young people.[18] It will thus be clear that there are massive inbuilt divergencies with regard to school, sex, region, social class, examination board, subject mode, syllabus and examination, which substantially demolish any claim to objectivity, comparability and, therefore, equality. As Desmond Nuttall has asserted, 'Comparability is a myth'.[19] And if comparability, then so also is equality of opportunity.

The ethnic dimension

But are there similar divergencies with regard to the ethnic dimension? The first thing to say is that even if there were no ethnic differential *per se*, there would certainly be such a differential related to the differing socio-economic structures of the various ethnic groups. What I mean by this is, for example, that 40 per cent of whites are in some form of non-manual work whereas only 8 per cent of citizens of West Indian and Pakistani background are. For Indians the figure is 20 per cent and for African-Asians it is approximately 30 per cent.[20] We know that there is a strong relationship between social class and achievement and as there are more members of lower socio-economic groups in the ethnic minority communities, there will therefore be fewer higher achievers – even excluding, for the moment, consideration of more subtle forms of enforced disadvantage, such as racial discrimination. Where we find the co-ordinates for ethnicity and social class crossing each other, i.e. *ethclass*, there is clearly a substantial difference observable.[21]

Bernard Coard in his book, *How the West Indian Child is made Educationally Sub-Normal in the British School System*[22] has argued, admittedly in a polemical tract, that current modes of testing are culturally biased and inaccurate and that the selection procedures based on these must therefore be invalid. These contentions find some support in the work of Townsend[23] and, more recently, of Tomlinson.[24] Coard also contended that there were low teacher expectations founded on racial stereotypes and that, in case this was insufficient, there were also ethnocentric curricula and pedagogies with little teaching of the history, language and culture of minority groups. It is all a familiar tale to us now some twelve years after his book, although, as Tomlinson points out, the ESN dispute has now been broadened into 'disruptive unit issue' and the over-representation of some ethnic minority children in the *ad hoc* withdrawal facilities which grew up in the 1970s.

So is it appropriate to ask whether this influence of *ethclass* on achievement is still discernible? Or perhaps we should not be framing the question in that way, for such a formulation implies that there is some kind of culpability associated with belonging to a particular *ethclass*; that it is the *ethclass* which is the source of causation of low achievement, rather than the way in which the circumambient economic and social structure reacts on pupils from a particular *ethclass*. For the argument of Coard's book is that it is the structure and the system which 'bracket out' West Indian children and define them as low achievers or even ESN in such unacceptably large numbers, not their ability. It is thus in the locus of interaction between *ethclass* and system, across items such as definitions of achievement, valid knowledge and culture and human intercultural relationships that the solution of this 'problem' has to be sought. In other words, to blame the black child because s/he is discriminated against is not only manifestly unjust but because it is a false diagnosis, it is a good recipe for 'no-change' or the wrong change. So let us reformulate the question as one addressing the kind of correlation which exists between race and school achievement in the first instance and race and life chances in the second.

To answer the question about the ethnic dimension in examinations is very difficult. Since 1972, there has been a complete lack of national statistics on race and education, a fact which makes national, valid comparisons very difficult, if not impossible. Thus we are thrown back on isolated work where the samples are often small and, to some extent, unrepresentative and skewed. It is perhaps not surprising that the result of this is some rather contradictory results!

I shall not bore you with extensive details of these results, but merely indicate one or two of the typical findings.

Taylor in Newcastle, for example, reported higher levels of achievement and commitment in educational success amongst male Asian school leavers than amongst a matched sample of white males.[25] Taylor's findings have been replicated and largely confirmed by Driver and Ballard with a larger, mixed sample because of the criticisms which were made in particular of the data base of Taylor's original research.[26] Moreover, Brooks and Singh found in a sample of Asian school leavers of both sexes in Leicester in 1979 that Asian children fared worse than whites in 16 examinations, although because of factors such as low response rates the findings need treating with caution.[27] On the other hand, Little's analysis of the performance of Asian and Caribbean ILEA primary school children found that Asian children slightly underfunctioned in English language but performed at a similar standard to whites in mathematics and verbal reasoning, whilst children of West Indian background performed below whites in all areas.[28] Essen and Ghodsian also found in second generation immigrants that only 'West Indians' obtained lower scores.[29]

Driver, however, has challenged the conventional wisdom of underachievement of West Indian children.[30] He looked at school leavers from five schools between 1975 and 1977 and he compared 2,310 cases finding that in mathematics, English and science, West Indians did better than whites; white boys did better than white girls, but that West Indian girls were better than all other groups. The problem with Driver's work is that he did not control for social class! After what has been said above about the strong correlations between social class and achievement this omission must cast serious doubts on the validity of the results.

When the sample has included ethnically mixed samples of students matched for social class, the performance of pupils of West Indian background was found to be lower than that of all other groups,[31] and when broader strategies have been adopted to include developmental status, school achievements and post secondary outcomes, it would appear that West Indian lagged behind non-minority children from pre-school to adolescence to a marked degree.[32]

There are other studies, highlighting subtleties and intra-group distinctions based on such factors as language, religion, sex, birth-place of child or parents etc., which could be further elucidated. But Tomlinson, summarising thirty-three studies on this theme, found that twenty-six of them indicated that West Indian children scored lower than whites, or were over-represented in ESN schools or under-represented in the higher school streams.[33] For Asian children, twelve of nineteen studies show a lower score, or under-representation in higher streams or slightly fewer 'O' levels and CSE passes.

More recently, and restricting her work to twenty-nine studies involving children of Asian origin, Tomlinson[34] makes a number of trenchant points, which teachers would be wise to bear in mind, about comparisons between educational achievement of 'Asian' and white children:

1 Is the implicit assumption correct that such comparisons are fair and correct?
2 Do they allow for the heterogeneity of children of Asian origin?
3 Have they tended to neglect the social class dimension (referred to above)?

She concludes:

> The variables affecting educational performance are complex and the conclusions from the research studies simply do not allow for crude generalisations to be made comparing minority group educational performance.[35]

But, at a generalised level, we have a situation where existing studies, with all of their limitations, appear to show some ethnic minority children to be 'underachieving', but differentially so depending on such variables as sex, ethnic group and social class,[36] and such factors as whether they were born in Britain and, if not, how long they have been here. But what does 'underachievement', according to existing procedures and criteria, mean? Is this the fault of the system, the examinations and assessment procedures, the criteria; a function of the differential social class distribution of the population among the various racial and ethnic groups, home background, language problems, deep-rooted cultural traditions, etc.? In responding to this question, we are faced with two sets of 'facts': on the one hand, that there is no evidence of a genetic difference in intelligence among people of different races and, on the other hand, there appears to be a differential, but highly complex and for the moment inextricable picture of achievement at school according to ethnic background. The precise reasons for this cannot at this point be ascertained, for available information is too partial and faulty for firm conclusions. But that teachers have the task of giving all children equal opportunities is apparent, and for this they require better systems of assessment and examinations.

Differential life chances

The conclusion that there is differential school achievement among different ethnic groups really makes our question of the unevenness of life chances according to ethnic background superfluous. But let us persevere, for a moment, and ask about the employment opportunities of children of ethnic minority communities, including where they have similar qualifications. Unfortunately, here too, we encounter the problem of complex and sometimes confusing evidence, but once again with a strong indication that the causal relationship between race and unemployment is stronger than that between success in public examinations and employment.[37]

In general, we know that black people are disproportionately 'hit' by unemployment, which is not only significantly higher among black people than among the population generally but that it also rises faster when overall unemployment is soaring.[38] Among the young, the problem is even worse and a survey conducted in six major areas by the Commission for Racial Equality in June 1982 found that whereas white and Asian youths shared a similar rate of 40 per cent, the rate among Afro-Caribbeans was 60 per cent.[39] Nor does lack of qualifications appear to be an adequate explanation of high unemployment, for work by Smith and Campbell and Jones suggests that educational qualifications are irrelevant for recruitment to many jobs, that, in any case, a similar proportion of Asian and white school leavers have similar qualifications and that West Indian and Asian men have much the same risk of being unemployed, regardless of qualification.[40] An analysis published by the Department of Employment in 1984 confirmed this somewhat bleak situation more nationally and authoritatively. Drawing on data from the 1981 Labour Force Survey, it indicated quite unequivocally that blacks in Britain were twice as likely to be unemployed as whites and that only a small part of this difference was attributable to factors such as level of qualifications or age distribution in a particular ethnic group.[41] More specifically and with regard to those having the same qualification, it discovered only 9 per cent of white men with 'O' levels unemployed compared with 25 per cent of West Indians and 18 per cent of Asians. Thus, whilst confirming the generally lower level of qualification among non-white groups – only 1 per cent of West Indian men were found to have degrees compared with 14 per cent of Asians and 10 per cent of whites – even when ethnic minorities, and particularly youngsters, have equal qualifications, this clearly does not give them equality in the job market.

Setting job inequalities within both an historical and broader, contemporary social context a study published by an independent social policy research unit in 1984 found the job position of blacks in Britain little different from when these groups first arrived in the 1950s and 1960s with black people also living in worse housing than the quality of housing generally.[42] The disparity between white and black tenants of council housing had actually grown in the ten-year period 1974-84. The Report found that racial inequalities had become entrenched and self-sustaining, deriving partly from direct discrimination and partly from disadvantage caused because institutions took no account of cultural differences.

Thus, while advocates of multicultural education assert that curriculum reform and increased support for ethnic minority achievement will result in better life chances for black children,[43] the critics point to compelling arguments against such a direct causality.[44] Without discounting the importance of both inter-group and intra-group differences and of explanations of apparent educational underachievement related to sex and socio-economic and cultural factors, such as social class, religion, recency of arrival, child-rearing patterns, fluency and competence in English, family structures and traditions, the historical legacy of slavery, family discord and instability,[45] and, whilst eschewing simplistic generalisations embracing all ethnic minorities equally, and without ignoring powerful socio-economic status, regional and sex differentials, the most compelling and convincing rationale which emerges for racial inequality is one which is seen to advance racial prejudice and discrimination, not the educational failure of ethnic minority pupils, as the major reason why, in disproportionate numbers, some groups fail to achieve employment and thus suffer disproportionately poorer life chances than their white counterparts.[46]

A major issue: the myth of comparability and equality

We have, of necessity, come a little way from the major theme of this chapter, so let us return and ask what light the evidence summarised above throws on the crucial issues of assessment and examination in a multiracial society which are the central concern of the chapter? The first such issue is surely that our desire to measure accurately as part of the process of selection and economic placement within our society would appear to have seduced us into believing that we have achieved objectivity and equality. Nothing could be further from the truth for, as the evidence in the earlier part of this chapter indicates, we have achieved neither objectivity nor comparability but rather a system whereby the examination tail is vigorously wagging the curriculum dog on the road to 'self-fulfilling social-class (and ethnic?) destinies'.

One of the main reasons, for example, why multicultural curricula (and assessment procedures and examinations) have been slow to develop (and incidentally why it is premature to judge their impact) has been because Examination Boards have generally not measured their examinations against multicultural yardsticks, nor have teachers made their assessments in school multicultural. External examinations have, in general, had a sterile and restrictive effect on the development of curricula and have, until recently, remained largely uncorrected for adaptation to the multicultural and multiracial nature of our society and its members. Internal school assessment has remained, by and large, likewise inattentive.[47] Moreover, there would appear to be some evidence to suggest that examinations (and standardised tests) have actually had harmful effects on a majority of children, because only a few can achieve by them.[48]

The need, therefore, would appear to be for multicultural curricula, with examinations and assessment to match, all reflecting a pluralism of approaches and perspectives on individual children and their abilities and achievements. But how do we achieve this?

Work to reform assessment and examinations

Well, the results of initiatives taken by the Schools Council began to appear in late 1983 and early 1984. All subject boards had been asked to call their work and curricula to the bar of a public 'multicultural' accountability, and ten subject experts were commissioned, each to undertake a six-month study, with a view to reviewing existing 16+ examinations to see how far they meet or could be developed to meet the needs of a multicultural society.[49] All of these reports have made their appearance[50] and they began to make a useful contribution to the overall policy debate at the same time as discussions about the 16+ criteria generated by the GCE and CSE Boards' Joint Council for 16+ National Criteria were taking place. Criteria for the last five subjects were published by the council in November 1983 and a decision for a joint examination, the GCSE, was announced by the Secretary of State in mid-July. Whilst early comments by the Secretary of State for Education and Science, for example his reservations about attempts to give an explicitly multicultural dimension to the criteria for English, were not interpreted as indicating a sympathy with the need to match the criteria to a multicultural society, the importance of the Schools Council work in this field rests in the contribution it makes to the overall debate.

In early 1984, too, work came to fruition in the development of new tests, developed by the National Foundation for Educational research, *The Educational Abilities Scales*, which can give a far broader measure of pupils' abilities over a whole range of skills and can be used with third-year pupils in the secondary age range.[51] The five scales measure clerical aptitude, mechanical comprehension, symbolic reasoning, spatial reasoning and science reasoning, representing well-defined areas of cognitive ability. They are not intended to be diagnostic but to help teachers build up a broader information base for individual pupils at a time which is crucial in the provision of educational guidance.

Movements away from a single grade

A significant additional contribution to the overall debate has addressed the narrowness of the single mark syndrome and attempted to move to a description of performance which can have both *lateral* and *longitudinal* depth, i.e. a continuous system throughout the school life of the child which records not only achievement across a range of capacities, skills, areas of experience and fields of knowledge, but which also seeks to acknowledge the processes by which these are 'achieved'. Several Examining Boards have experimented with graded tests and, as a report on in-school achievement from the Welsh Inspectorate in 1983 comments:

> The analysis of course objectives has resulted in fuller and more descriptive methods of recording achievement; this and the pressure of school leaving certificates for all pupils is leading towards a fairly widespread adoption of some form of profile reporting.[52]

Suggestions in early 1984 by the Secretary of State that examinations should measure 'absolute', i.e. criterion-referenced rather than relative, i.e. norm-referenced, achievement were received as welcome indications of the chance for change,[53] although the distinction is not quite as simple as implied, for as a recent publication of the Assessment of Performance Unit indicates, selection of criteria may determine pass norms, but criteria cannot be derived from norms alone. Work deriving from the Munn and Dunning reports in Scotland and aimed at the development of grade-related criteria has shown the need for extensive development before implementation, while the 'slipperiness and complexity' of the 'norm-criterion' debate alerts us to the need for caution as much as to the opportunities for change.[54] The findings of the Schools Council Primary report that 'in that context of widespread use of standardised tests in primary schools, teachers' interpretations of results quoted on record are "still" fraught with difficulty . . .'[55] and the conclusions of a new guide to tests used in schools which found much testing highly questionable,[56] indicate the inaccuracy, provisionality and therefore potential for unfairness involved in even well-established forms of assessment.

Since the publication of pioneering work by the Scottish Council for Research in Education,[57] discussion of 'profiling' has become much more widespread. Both the Further Education Unit of the Department of Education and Science and the City and Guilds of London Institute published important contributions to the debate in 1982 and the following year work was proceeding on the presentation of a profile which would be acceptable to all schools in Wales,[58] the results of a Schools Council national review and of a subsequent action research project on the subject were published in 1983,[59] and a Schools Council report pointed to the inadequacy of the single 'big bang' system of examinations and emphasised the need to test a wide range of skills, to match assessment with teaching and learning and to develop a stronger link between curriculum and assessment.[60] The Secretary of State's further suggestion for a record of achievement for all school leavers may give scope for all pupils to leave school with a broader, more balanced and positive identikit of their records of achievement across their school lives.

Teachers attempting to develop methods of assessment attentive to multicultural criteria will also need to take into account the exponential development of information technology and its implications for their work. Already, developments in computer-aided profiling have been reported in the United Kingdom,[61] which may provide a wider range and greater subtlety of information as a basis for pupil-teacher counselling and guidance discussions than can be available through normal sources. Moreover, the development of computerised adaptive testing (CAT) may provide a more standardised, flexible, efficient and potentially less frustrating means of achieving an accurate assessment of examinees' ability than current practices can offer.[62]

Notwithstanding the difficulties documented by Goacher – particularly that teachers tend not to know their pupils well enough – the publication in November 1983 of the DES Policy Statement on Records of Achievement[63] could be taken as evidence of a growing conviction of the inadequacy of present assessment and examination systems within and without the school – and surprisingly of a widespread agreement across different sectors of education and training on the need for more continuous, inclusive and open means of recording pupil 'progression'. In response to increasing demands for greater openness, a number of local authorities have introduced 'open file' policies and many others are considering doing so, with profile reports seen as one powerful means of engaging in closer counselling dialogue with pupils and parents.[64]

Growth points for 'multicultural assessment'

The overriding need now is for the debate about multicultural education to be locked onto such issues as those above, for consideration of the issue of assessment against the needs of a multicultural society helps us to identify growth points from what already exists and is developing (but which may not be 'labelled' multicultural) to a more appropriate assessment and examinations deal for all pupils. The principal trends seem clear, and there would appear to be widespread activity pointing in the following directions:

1 Increasing recognition of the fallacy of the belief in the exactitude of current tests, assessment, examinations, and the need to replace them with multiple indicators which can be reviewed speedily, accurately and holistically. For any one measure can inevitably be misleading and unjust. (In this connection, too, there is growing understanding that not all facets of assessment need to be equally reliable in all their elements. There is a relationship between *reliability* which means that the more reversible a decision is, the less severe are the consequences of inevitably imperfect decisions.)

2 The need for a more comprehensive and continuous concept of the school curriculum, of achievement and educability, whereby the population may be kept open to and capable of learning throughout their school lives in a way which could have an immeasurable effect upon pupils' learning and development after school, and particularly in a world where, in some parts of the country, 80 per cent of them are likely to be unemployed for the foreseeable future.

3 The fact that the present public examinations do not reflect the whole school course nor the cultural diversity of our society; they are achievement tests which assess candidates' 'one-time' status in a fairly narrow range of subject knowledge, not how the child has reached it, the quality of the process or the breadth of its cultural and intercultural competence. The need, therefore, is for a broader, more comprehensive, balanced and positive profile system of assessment (and record-keeping) which can reflect a broader spectrum of capability and experience on the part of the pupil, including aspects of its parallel curriculum. Such assessment should be open to the pupils, who could include

their own comments on that assessment if they so wished.

4 A recognition that there must be greater openness and accountability to, and involvement of, parents and community; parental support has a powerful influence on achievement; there should be less secrecy, for example, concerning pupil records, which should be much more open to parents as should also the results of tests, examinations and psychiatric and other records.

5 The implications of developments in information technology for assessment within a multicultural school are far-reaching, and potentially revolutionary, with regard to accuracy, speed, culture-fairness and the achievement of a tolerable workload for teachers, but the staff development implications are relatively unexplored.

6 Certain revised technical criteria will need to be applied to all examinations and assessments whether internal or external. For example, all curricula for all subjects need to be critically scrutinised in order to test them for multiculturalism. The rubrics of examinations require careful reappraisal to ensure that examination questions are framed in a culture-fair way. Specific attempts should be made to include situations which are familiar to ethnic minority pupils as appropriate in examinations, so that all syllabuses must reflect the diversity of British cultures. In the selection of texts for literary style examinations, there should be a broad spectrum of values, life styles and content available, and all examinations and the attendant curricula must include a range of values and ways of life, including those of different ethnic and racial groups; in-school correction and marking must be positive and helpful, but honest about weaknesses.

7 Broad evaluation strategies, including assessment of the school and its performance by the community, must replace narrower assessment in schools.

Guidelines for multicultural assessment in schools

In spite of what has been said about the inadequacy of current assessment and examinations in schools, and the deficiency of current staff development in this field, teachers are continually faced with the need to assess their pupils: a child may join the system later than usual; the teacher is required to assess the pupil for placement in a group within the school or a unit outside it; a child returns from an extended stay with relatives abroad,[65] decisions have to be taken about the external examinations for which a child is to be entered;

assessments have to be made to monitor and assist the child's learning particularly in language, reading and mathematics where standardised testing is widespread, and to accompany its progression through one school and from one school to another; judgements have to be made to provide a springboard for the school leaver's even more difficult quest for employment. According to a recent survey, teachers are using tests more than they did a decade ago and certainly more pupils are taking public examinations.[66] Some mixture of standardised tests, teacher-produced assessments and external examinations combined with teacher observation and informed professional judgement is likely to be the experience of all pupils between entering and leaving school, although not all teachers are involved in all of these. How can the teacher in the multicultural school fulfil these tasks and be fair to the pupil, bearing in mind that no assessment is likely to be 100 per cent accurate or fair?

To some extent, the answer to this question derives from what has been written in previous chapters, concerning the nature and principles of multicultural education. To some further extent, the answer lies in the way in which professional judgement and common sense on the part of the teacher can balance knowledge of current inequalities based on sex, social class and ethnicity, without maladapting these as a basis for false stereotyping. The task is not easy, but teachers are increasingly aware of the way in which the stimuli they provide may inadvertently heighten sex and racial stereotyping. Fortunately, also, many teachers, schools and local authorities have already commenced pioneer work and several examining boards have extensive experience of such areas as graded testing, of the introduction of new subjects such as Asian and Caribbean studies and of providing examinations for candidates from differing cultural backgrounds. It is upon this previous work that I have relied to 'guide' the provisional guidelines for teachers with which I propose to conclude this chapter.[67]

Contextual guidelines

1 Any policy for assessment in a multicultural school needs to be firmly locked into a curriculum (seen as process, materials and organisation as well as content), which emphasises and expresses the centrality of the school's commitment to multicultural education, including teaching to correct for racism, within a school policy of equal opportunities. (See, in particular, Chapter 5.)

2 Grouping and referral policies are a part of this policy and must

be attentive to the same principles; teachers should seek to foster collaboration and co-operative as well as competitive qualities in pupils and to give credit for these in their view of the whole child.[68] (See Chapter 4.)

3   Likewise, management practices and the teachers' relationships with parents and the wider community must endorse, not just respect, active commitment to and support for the cultural pluralism of the school and society. (This inevitably involves close consultation – not just the distribution of information – about the details of policies such as those for 'naming' children, parental rights, mode of distribution of information required under the 1980 Education Act,[69] active involvement of parents in career, subject choice, examination entry and transfer decisions, access to records, etc.) (As outlined in Chapter 6.)

4   Teachers need to continually keep up-to-date concerning the experience of their pupils in family, peer group and community and to know the cultural profiles and strengths of those communities. Parental interest should be maximised to assist pupils in school and at home, and where home facilities for study are known to be poor, opportunities such as revision and homework clubs, etc. should be made available to pupils. (See Chapter 8.)

5   Judgements about pupils should, wherever possible, be collegially informed. Staff need to support each other so as to be able to critically and independently appraise each other's judgements.

6   Decisions about pupils should be prudently cautious and tentative, widely informed and express awareness of current sex-, social class- and ethnically-based inequalities without using these as the basis for harmful stereotyping.

7   Behavioural assessments should be provisional and, if possible, inclusive of knowledge of the pupil's behaviour outside school, in the family, neighbourhood, community, peer group, etc.

8   Decisions should be untainted by conscious or unconscious stereotyping and free from false and unsubstantiated concepts of innate ability based on ethnic, sex, social class and other cultural group appurtenance.

9   There needs to be a school policy on the use of standardised tests, their use and appropriateness. The values and underlying assumptions should be discussed collegially and their limitations fully and frankly discussed.

10 A major dimension of the school's staff development policy will need to address the raising of teachers' expectations, the

eradication of the effects of negative stereotypes and the acquisition of new skills in areas such as profiling, the implications of developments in information technology, etc. (See Chapter 8.)

Assessment and examination guidelines

1 Examinations and in-school assessment should be continually monitored against the criteria for a multicultural curriculum, including racial, social and class and sex bias; they should be more culturally diverse and there should be more examinations with particular cultural emphases. In the marking and correction of pupil's work, identification of weakness and errors needs to be seen as only the initial step leading to remediation. It is not an end in itself.

2 Parents and the wider community should be party to potent dialogue with regard to the methods and content of assessment.

3 Judgements by the school should, according to their gravity, be more provisional, open to challenge and redress by individuals and communities. They may often be very wide of the mark.[70]

4 Observational judgements should adhere to normal criteria for a good anecdotal record, e.g. accuracy, specificity of event, detail of the setting, clear separation of fact and interpretation, typicality of event, etc.[71]

5 Syllabuses and examination questions should accurately reflect the diversity of cultures in school and society, giving opportunity for a range of values, ways of life and cultures to achieve legitimate expression.

6 The rubric and language of examinations should be framed in as culture-fair a way as possible and teachers should be sensitive to the way in which the English language may reflect and promote racism and sexism.[72]

7 Assessment strategies should be expressive of a broader spectrum of forms of assessment, including project work and course work, and of a policy of evaluation of the school (and its departments, where appropriate) and its performance by the community, which should include the critical, principled and collegial evaluation of classroom practice to eliminate unintended bias. The results of external examinations should be regularly evaluated and their implications discussed collegially and with parents and the wider community.

8 Assessment should be seen as a multidimensional, cumulative and continually changing profile of the educational

achievement *and* experience of the child.

9 Particular care needs to be taken over the 'face validity', use and interpretation of the results of standardised tests. Teachers need to be aware of the framing assumptions, the purposes for which the test may be appropriate and the settings for which it was designed. On non-standardised tests, results should be converted to Z-scores.

10 Policies for record-keeping, openness of records and transfer of information from teacher to teacher and school to school, as appropriate, need to be firmly linked to the criteria for a multicultural curriculum, the policy guidelines for the assessment of teaching and learning in that context and 'good parental and community involvement practice'.

11 With the advent of more powerful microcomputers, schools need to construct bridges between their multicultural curriculum and assessment and their approaches to information technology.

Summary

In sum, every school has to seek to evaluate the academic and other successes of its pupils and its own effectiveness. But assessment and examinations can be inaccurate, unreliable, invalid, unfair and biased. Within a multicultural society, assessment and evaluation need to be reflective of the range of cultures in that society, continuous over the school-span of the child, progressive, multidimensional, cumulative, culturally sensitive, experiential, open and related not only to cognitive knowledge, but also to skills and abilities. Recording of such material as assessment scores and transmission of information likewise needs to meet these criteria, and to be more collegial, provisional and widely informed. Above all, and, as we have seen in this chapter, while assessment is both necessary and desirable, our present methods and procedures have not served all our children well. They were developed a long time before we realised how multicultural our society had become and they exhibit marked characteristics which can be, so to speak, racist, sexist and socially and culturally biased. Present assessment practices can poison the well of our cultural pluralism by injecting invalid and invidious judgements about some aspects of our multiculture and of the children for whom it is cultural home.

Teachers have a crucial and continual role in reforming current educational practice in the field of testing, assessment and examinations, so that they are fairer to all pupils, more helpful to all teachers and more accessible and understood by parents and the community. As a rule of thumb, teachers may wish to stop, before they think, before they test, before they decide what the results of that test mean and how they should be recorded and used.[73]

Part Four

Strategies for change

Chapter 10

Diversity, equity and cohesion: agenda for action

Throughout this book, I have emphasised the interplay of three major factors in the implementation of multicultural education, and as a means to the resolution of dilemmas in pluralist societies: democratic freedom, discourse and equity and justice. These factors embody the need for democratic pluralist societies to allow not only for tolerance of difference, but for celebration of that difference in conditions where dialogue is possible. The task for advocates of multicultural education is thus to plan and implement educational systems and programmes that will enable the maintenance, development and renewal of political cohesion and the peaceful and creative reform of the social and economic order, including its value assumptions, its structures of organisation and of knowledge, within a contextual commitment to equity and social justice for all. This task calls for a balance between stability and change. There can be little doubt that the intertwined commitments to continued cohesion, to celebration of difference and to equity, represent major dilemmas, not only for teachers, but also for society at large. It is, however, in the very existence and generation of dilemmas that democratic societies find their momentum to peaceful and creative change and reform, through processes of persuasion and discourse.

In this, the final chapter of the book, I want to set down a basic agenda which I consider to be essential if these three objectives are to be pursued and multicultural education for all our children introduced swiftly and effectively into the education system. I want to centre my remarks around three major areas which have already been identified within this book for another purpose, but which I should now like to briefly retrieve as the organisers of a pressing agenda for reform. These three areas are human rights, educational development and personal and professional growth.

Human rights

I have reiterated frequently from the beginning of this book that the central importance of any commitment to multicultural education must be seen in a wider regional and global context. It goes without saying, therefore, that any commitment to human rights as being a prime mover for multicultural education rests on the basis of *mutuality*. The North/South report [1] and the consequent publication of the further report of the Brandt Commission [2] have alerted us to the fragile interdependence of all human beings on 'Spaceship Earth' and the responsibility, which we have, for each other's human rights. For this reason, the commitment to human rights as a core area of multicultural education involves the advocacy and enforcement of those human rights, not only for ourselves and co-citizens, but also and perhaps more so, for aliens in our society and our fellow human beings abroad. There can be no artificial frontier in the commitment to the basic ethic of multicultural education, namely respect for persons. And the mutuality which derives from the principle, as well as from the international instruments referred to in Chapter 2, enforces on us a much broader view of multicultural education, than that which has usually been advanced so far.

Having said that, it is essential that each nation affords to its citizens, in addition to a commitment to international covenants, conventions and agreements, their own national charter of rights and freedoms. In the United Kingdom the Constitutional Reform Centre, formed in 1985, has pressed for the incorporation of the European Convention of Human rights into British Law, and these efforts have attracted the support of members of Parliament from all major parties and persons from all walks of life, including education. Certainly, the very volume of cases filed against the United Kingdom and the number, in which the cases have been found admissible (twice as many as against any other state in Europe), would seem to indicate, at a purely pragmatic level, the need for easier, more direct and less expensive means, whereby individuals may prevent infringements of (or indeed unwarranted alterations to) their basic human rights.

More directly in the field of education, such a charter of rights and freedoms would provide an essential moral baseline upon which schools could rest their socialisation of children, and which would provide a central and indispensable core for their curricula, practices and procedures. It would also provide a sharp cutting-edge for professional judgement to resolve current dilemmas for teachers. Such a document would, furthermore, furnish an identification of those commonalities which comprise the covenant, to which all full members of society would be expected to subscribe for themselves and their fellow citizens. In this sense, such a charter would provide signposts, directions and guidelines for the identification of core common aims and content areas for the school curriculum, seen as both substance and process of any education, appropriate to a democratic pluralist society in whatever kind of educational institution, whether public or private, state or religious, formal or non-formal, voluntary or compulsory pre-school or post-school, i.e. for a multicultural education common for all, which yet does not stifle diversity.

It hardly needs repeating that an explicit element within such a charter of rights and freedoms must be the liberty of the individual to live his or her life free from discrimination based on race, sex, ethnicity, colour, creed or handicap. Such fundamental rights will need further enforcement in specific legislation and instrumental regulations, not least in schools, and the radical reform of current mechanisms for enforcement by individuals and groups. Present systems are too complex, circumspect and costly for the majority of ordinary citizens to seek easy redress for the infringement of their rights, and therefore injustice often goes unchallenged and un-redressed.

But as I have argued earlier in this text, whilst legal and constitutional norms are essential, and mechanisms for their enforcement indispensable, norms of custom, of practice and of general morality must also be addressed if individual citizens in their daily lives are to be protected from the scourge of discrimination on their backs. Here, what Althusser, the French social philosopher, calls the state ideological apparatuses have an important role to play in generating a societal ethos which can outlaw discrimination and banish prejudice. Explicit codes of practice are essential prerequisites to the implementation of any policy, attentive to human rights in such structures as the mass media and education.

The policies and the codes of practice will need to address not only the employment and participation of all cultural groups, but also the content of that which is broadcast or taught. Religious and other organisations committed to a specific world view have a particular responsibility in this respect, for they cannot enjoy the freedom of worship and expression which a democracy must endorse and protect and, at the same time, denigrate members of other religious or philosophical groupings in their basic tenets. If discourse is essential to democracy, then, equally, openness is essential to discourse and that openness in turn rules out a secret and selfish commitment to sectoral interests, whether they be economic, social or cultural.

In many Western societies of the 1980s and in the United Kingdom in particular, justice and legitimate success in society owe more to birth, race and sex than they do to talent or any concept of equity. A democratic society cannot legitimate such a situation long-term, after which the only alternatives are coercive enforcement of a situation, anathema to the very values implicit in democracy, or on the other hand, discourse to alleviate injustice and banish discrimination. The time has come for a serious discourse to dismantle the privileges of birth, race and sex which scar Western democratic societies. Minorities must be brought into more equal discourse about the principles which regulate society. In this task, the education system has a central role to play and teachers are in the van of this pursuit of human progress.

There are two further issues in this pursuit of human rights and equality for all, the resolution of which are crucial prerequisites to the health of democratic society: enhanced entitlement and language policy.

In the case of the first, it goes without saying that there are contrary imaginations. It is evident, for example, that in some circumstances affirmative action may infringe the right to equality, as the case of Bakke v Regents of the University of California highlighted in the United States. Moreover, as Glazer's insightful essay 'Who's available?'[3] so eloquently shows, the labyrinthine complexity, some would argue impossibility, of deciding the pool of talent available for a particular job category, makes it well nigh impossible to decide what a correct and just share of particular jobs might mean. Furthermore, in justice, scope has to be retained for individual and private decisions about vocational choice which may mean a differential representation of particular groups in different occupations. Again, not all members of all ethnic groups are disadvantaged, nor is disadvantage the exclusive prerogative of certain ethnic groups. Would the human rights of individual members of a group be breached by a potentially stereotypical representation of all as having the same needs? Some groups and individuals, too, are 'disadvantaged' by the very fact of their membership of a particular cultural group: sex is often a more powerful discriminant for inequality than ethnicity, religion, race or cultural group. Yet there is clearly neither moral superiority nor automatic entitlement attached to minority, or indeed, majority status *per se*. In legal terms there are human rights but not minority rights in the strict sense, and, therefore, the best defence of minority rights may ultimately rest in the advocacy and securing of individual rights.[4] If social harmony in a democratic society demands equality for all, it also demands justice for all. Thus in the ladder of life it may be both more pragmatic politically and more just socially to retain uniform standards, whilst enhancing entitlement for those who have been historically disadvantaged and discriminated against.

But these matters are not easy to discuss, let alone to resolve with justice, and there is always a counterargument. To many, even the discussion of the options referred to above may appear unpalatable, for they would use the slogan of equality to exclude discourse about the detailed realities of its implementation. In the highly charged, sometimes almost hysterical, atmosphere of Britain in the 1970s and 1980s, it has not been possible to raise such 'taboo' issues for discourse without running the gauntlet of being labelled. Yet it is persuasion and discourse which are the means to progress in democracy, not confrontational, strident and irrational rhetoric. The time has come for a more urgent and open national debate, bearing in mind that others have also had to face similar dilemmas.

On the other side of the affirmative action debate is the fact of deepening inequality in British society in the 1980s, to the point where dialogue, persuasion and discourse are made increasingly difficult. The searing injustice of racism and sexism stalks the land and is unseen by leading groups in society. There is no doubt that the human rights of many members of visible minority groups are daily infringed by violence, harassment and exclusion from their rightful participation in the full benefits of democratic life. An unrepresentative chamber of nominated dignitaries symbolises the old aristocratic, one-faith privilege of a nation long ago, rather than reflecting the multiethnic, multicredal, multiracial and multicultural composition of the diverse society we all now inhabit. If not yet ready for mature democracy at the highest level, what a golden opportunity for ethnicity as a new dimension of representation at that level! Better still, why not a system of proportional representation for the upper house, based on cultural, linguistic, social, and regional appurtenance rather than inherited or ascribed privilege and wealth? If parents giving evidence to the Scarman Inquiry could censure the curriculum of the school for insufficiently recognising the value of the distinctive traditions of the various ethnic minorities, could they not equally appraise the 'Lords'?[5] In the Scarman Report, the need is emphasised for 'recognition of and action to meet the special problems and needs of the ethnic minorities, based on an acceptance of them as full and equal members of a culturally diverse society'.[6] Can they be full and equal, yet excluded?

Affirmative action is already practised against regional and socioeconomic criteria. The poor, the unemployed, those in 'distant' regions, where their sight does not offend the privileged and those at the centre of power in society; the one-parent families, the sick, the infirm, the mentally handicapped and many others are all, quite properly and justly, recipients of affirmative action in a humane and compassionate society. Scarman had no doubt that the racial disadvantage and consequent inequality in British society was of such proportions that only a direct co-ordinated attack, involving positive discrimination for a time for ethnic minorities could deal with it adequately,[7] and educational policy is at the very heart of the necessary measures. How to implement that positive discrimination for a time, for how long and in which areas, towards which groups, is a question for which the use of Section 11 of the 1966 Local Government Act is no longer an adequate response, if it ever was.

The issues surrounding language seem to me to be much less intractable than those concerning affirmative action. There is no reason of equality or justice why people should not be encouraged to retain or develop their linguistic gifts, provided that they are competent in the national language and therefore not disadvantaged. It is surely no great burden, where there are concentrations of one linguistic group in a community or catchment area to offer them an opportunity to spend time on their home language or mother tongue. It might even be possible – as was previously the case with Latin – once again to offer an opportunity for the learning of a non-home language or non-mother tongue within the school curriculum, provided that that does not dominate or skew the curriculum for others. Such issues are susceptible to pragmatic solution at local level provided that there is a sensible and sensitive, agreed national policy. But, of course, there is no such national policy which could reflect the fact that the political realities of Europe and the world have changed since before the First World War, let alone the linguistic composition of the United Kingdom. Unless alienation is to heighten, such a national policy on languages, reflecting today's reality, and commanding the widest measure of national consensus possible, is urgently needed. There are high prizes of a cultural and economic kind available to us as a consequence of such a commonsense, widely legitimated policy, which afford each the human right to be and remain bilingual.

Educational development

In preceding chapters I have frequently repeated the need for multicultural education to be seen as a holistic process affecting all persons, institutions and systems. I have drawn attention to the fact that any feasible policy and practice in multicultural education has to address not only the structures and relationships inherent within institutions and systems, not only the curricula and materials which are the stock-in-trade of education's function, not only the assessment, examinations and methods of control and governance, but also the underlying and often subliminal values and assumptions which give those other matters their form and purpose. From that point of view, it is essential that policies to correct for current ethnocentrism in educational provision, and drawing on the broader societal context already outlined above, should recognise the interdependent complexity and ever-changing prismatic quality of cultural and social phenomena in democratic pluralism.

If intercultural competence is to be developed as a major dimension of multicultural education and, indeed, it is indispensable, then not only common learning structures and contents are necessary, but common learning situations in which children of different ethnic, racial, credal, regional and social backgrounds may strive together towards the ideals inherent within a new covenant for education, based on the charter of rights and freedoms advocated above. This inevitably means that some in schools and the broader system will have to cede some of their current educational privileges in the interests of achieving a more harmonious society for their children's sake, so that those children may develop the competence to make their dilemmas and conflicts creative and fruitful, rather than sterile and disruptive. In other cases, it will involve schools ceding some of their former autonomy and reflecting more critically on what they are doing about major issues such as racism in British society. A report on Catholic schools dating from 1984, for instance, stated frankly and openly:

> . . . many schools did not see dealing with racism as part of their task . . . We found no evidence of attempts to explain or deal with the structural or institutional aspects of racism in British society . . . The fact that, of the fifty schools visited, only six had a black governor . . . is an obvious matter of concern in this respect.[8]

It will be apparent that dealing with issues of racism and other forms of prejudice is a task for all schools that wish to pursue an education appropriate to a multicultural society, even if they themselves are monocredal, 'monocultural', monosocial or 'monoethnic'. Conversely, those seeking to implement multicultural education will need to seek constructive, conceptual and political coalitions more rigorously than hitherto, rather than pursue a politically and culturally more isolationist approach which focusses exclusively on one aspect of multicultural education.

Whilst teachers have, by-and-large, shown themselves remarkably resilient in the post-war period in responding to the educational demands evoked by newly perceived cultural pluralism, it is futile to expect that they can continue to care for the implementation of multicultural education, when prestigious groups, eminent individuals and major sectors in society are not only *not* committed to it, but are often actively antagonistic to it.[9] Social and moral responsibility demands that this deplorable situation should change as quickly as possible and one way to achieve this is to set down basic criteria, including multicultural ones, which would be used in inspecting and certificating all schools, both public and private. In other words, no school, whose curriculum was not attentive and responsible to multicultural principles, can be approved and permitted to continue educating children to live and work in a multicultural society, if in its very ethos, its content, practices and procedures, it is not fully committed to the fundamental principles and ethics inherent within that society. To permit otherwise would be illogical, for it would mean that certain groups of children were being specifically educated to undermine the basic tenets of a multicultural society.

Moreover, and if democracy is not to founder, there is a need for the attitudes, skills and insights associated with social action for justice to be seen as being at the very heart of the educational process. A pluralist democracy demands, as a basic competence in its education system, the ability successfully to advocate and achieve the eradication of discrimination and the inception of peaceful progress. This ability is as fundamental a basic as the three 'R's.

Then, too, as I have advocated in the section of this chapter on civil rights, a democratic pluralist society has to gather its children to its education system rather than alienate them from it: regardless of their mother-tongue. In other words, the multitude of mother-tongues which our society is now privileged to embrace must find legitimate expression in the education system, but differentially according to demand in different regions, areas and schools. Several countries have already taken account of what this means in law and in practice: the United States, Canada, Sweden. But most 'older' Western societies still cling to a concept of languages forged on the anvil of nineteenth-century power politics rather than tempered for the realities of a multilingual society. The link with human rights is self-evident. Freedom to legitimate cultural diversity cannot be liberty in practice, if the aim of the state's education system is to exclude legitimate linguistic diversity and therefore eventually eradicate it. Linguistic diversity in society has as its logic linguistic diversity in school. As the Secretary of State for Wales wrote in 1980: 'while there are people who want to speak it, Governments will respond with the means of supporting it and giving it strength'.[10]

He was speaking of Welsh, of course, and accepting the need for additional finance (affirmative action) to support – not impose – bilingualism. Equity in democracy would seem to demand such support where it is requested and educationally and financially practicable. That is not the situation at the moment, and although it would be easier under a flexible and coherent national policy for bilingualism, local authorities have the ability and autonomy, if they have the will, to commence on their own.

In the section of this chapter on human rights, I have tried to draw a balance of some of the arguments for and against positive discrimination. Here I want to refer briefly to the teacher's role in such a policy.

It is the task of all teachers to try to offer equality of educational opportunity to all the children who are in their care. It is often a difficult balancing act, but it is no part of a teacher's professional task to discriminate for or against an individual member of any cultural or social group. This does not, of course, exclude additional help, where it is needed, for that has always been part of a conscientious teacher's job. Basically, however, it is professional commonsense for the teacher that all children must be enabled to unfold intellectually and physically to their maximum, in spite of community and family backgrounds, values and traditions which may vie against this goal.

Personal and professional growth

Returning now briefly to the subject of the theme of Chapter 8, I should like to reiterate the heavy burden that the implementation of the new covenant, which is multicultural education, places on the shoulders of teachers. In the field of staff development, initiatives can be taken which can begin to heal and bridge those fissures which have been opened up in British society by religious and social class apartheid and, in some cases, privilege. Teachers from all sectors, and indeed all in education, should be involved in joint, continual and long-term staff development to enable them to acquire the values and competences which will be essential if they are to be expected to implement multicultural education.

A major dimension of multicultural education is the process of teachers evaluating their own practice and *interlearning* with other teachers and with their pupils, as well as with the broader community, in a process of mutual acculturation which is essential if cultures and societies are not to ossify and stagnate. Massive and immediate resources are needed if this important social objective is to be achieved, for, without it, pursuit of multicultural education will founder. The pressing need, therefore, is for the explicit recognition, at national, regional, institutional and personal levels, of staff development for multicultural education as a major, indeed if a harmonious society is to be guaranteed, *the* major priority for allocation of resources and commitment to in-service education.

No agenda for change in a democratic, culturally pluralist society is ever complete. Drawing on the rest of this book, this chapter has sought to identify some of the most pressing issues and dilemmas which will need to be placed on the agenda for negotiation, action and change, if the complex and interrelated nexus of policies inherent in multicultural education is to be removed from the arena of strident rhetoric and useless confrontation and eased from theory into the workshop of professional practice. It has been the theme of this book that multicultural education is both indispensable and, given the will to continue to support a pluralist democracy and educational system, practicable. Its aim is to improve the human condition and liberate the human spirit, to free mankind from culturally impoverished bondage.

Notes

1 Cultural pluralism and the educational response

1 A very helpful compilation of details concerning minorities across the globe is G. Ashworth (ed.), *World Minorities*, Sunbury, Middlesex, Quartermaine House Ltd, vol.I, 1977; vol.II, 1978; vol.III, 1980.
2 K. Watson, 'Educational Policies in Multicultural Societies', *Comparative Education*, vol.18, 1981; pp.17–31.
3 B. Bullivant, *The Pluralist Dilemma in Education*, Sydney, George Allen & Unwin, 1981.
4 S. Castles with J. Booth and T. Wallace, *Here for Good: Western Europe's New Ethnic Minorities*, London, Pluto Press, 1984, pp.85–6.
5 L. Wirth, 'The Problem of Minority Groups', in R. Linton (ed.), *The Science of Man in the World Crisis*, New York, Columbia University Press, 1945.
6 M. Gordon, *Assimilation in American Life*, New York, Oxford University Press, 1964.
7 M. Gordon, 'Towards a Theory of Ethnic Group Relations', in W. Glaser and D. Moynihan (eds), *Ethnicity: Theory and Experience*, Cambridge, Harvard University Press, 1975.
8 B.M. Bullivant, *Pluralism: Cultural Maintenance and Education*, Clevedon, Avon, Multilingual Matters Ltd, 1984.
9 J. Lynch, 'Interculturalism and Multiculturalism: Educational Responses to Cultural Pluralism in Western Europe', in J.A. Banks and J. Lynch (eds), *Multicultural Education in Western Societies*, Eastbourne, Holt Saunders, 1986.
10 I have discussed the three ideologies in a book which considers in greater detail educational policy options for responding to cultural pluralism in Western democracies. See Banks and Lynch (eds), *op.cit.*
11 The concept of cultural and social reproduction utilised in this book is taken from P. Bourdieu and J.C. Passeron, *La Reproduction: Elements pour Une Théorie du Système d'Enseignement*, Paris, Editions de Minuit, 1970. See also a classic study of social reproduction processes,

P. Willis, *Learning to Labour: How Working Class Kids get Working Class Jobs*, London, Saxon House, 1977.

12 See the report of the Commission on Migrants' Languages and Culture in School and Adult Education in Sweden, *Different Origins – Partnership in Sweden, Education for Linguistic and Cultural Diversity*, Stockholm, Utbildningsdepartment, 1984 (SOU 1983:57).

13 I have used a similar typology in one of my previous publications. See J. Lynch, *Education for Community*, London, Macmillan, 1979, p.56.

14 W. Stephan, 'Education in Multicultural Societies: Towards a Framework for Comparative Analysis', paper presented at the 11th Conference of the Comparative Education Society of Europe in Wurzburg, July 1983.

15 My debt to the writings of Habermas will be apparent throughout this book. The immediate reference is to J. Habermas, *Legitimation Crisis*, Boston, Beacon Press, 1973.

16 J.R. Mallea, 'Cultural Diversity and Canadian Education', in J.R. Mallea and J.C. Young, *Cultural Diversity and Canadian Education*, Ottawa, Carleton University Press, 1984, p.13, drawing on the work of R.A. Schermerhorn, *Comparative Ethnic Relations: A Framework for Theory and Research*, New York, Random House, 1970.

17 J.A. Banks, *Multiethnic Education: Theory and Practice*, Boston, Allyn & Bacon, 1981.

18 Schermerhorn, *op.cit.*

19 R.K. Merton, 'Discrimination and the American Creed', in R.K. Merton, *Sociological Ambivalence and Other Essays*, New York, The Free Press, 1976.

20 S. Hall, 'Teaching Race', *Multicultural Education*, vol.9, 1980.

21 Although it is not made explicit in the Report, I am assuming that this is also the meaning to be attributed to the title of the Swann Report. See Committee for Inquiry into the Education of Children from Ethnic Minority Groups, *Education for All* (The Swann Report), London, HMSO, 1985 (Cmnd. 9453).

22 This 'stirring beyond democratization' and its implications for education are adumbrated in greater detail in the final chapter of J. Lynch and H.D. Plunkett, *Teacher Education and Cultural Change*, London, Allen & Unwin, 1973.

2 Approaches to multicultural education: international perspectives

1 For details, see United Nations, *Human Rights: A Compilation of International Instruments*, New York, United Nations, 1978 and United Nations, *Human Rights: International Instruments, Signatures, Ratifications, Accessions etc.* (1 September 1983), New York, United Nations, 1983.

2 'Universal Declaration of Human Rights', Article 2, in United Nations, *op.cit.* (1978) p.1.

3 *Ibid.*, pp.111–12.

4 *Ibid.*, pp.23–4.

5 Unesco, General Conference, *Declaration on Race and Racial Pre-*

judice, Paris, Unesco, 1978. (Adopted 27 November by the General Conference.)

6 J.A. Banks, 'Race, Ethnicity and Schooling in the United States: Past Present and Future', in J.A. Banks and J. Lynch (eds), *Multicultural Education in Western Societies*, Eastbourne, Holt Rinehart, 1986.

7 J.A. Banks, *Multiethnic Education: Theory and Practice*, Boston, Allyn & Bacon, 1981.

8 J.A. Banks, 'Multiethnic Education: Development, Paradigms and Goals', in J.A. Banks and J. Lynch, *op.cit.*

9 D.M.Gollnick and P.C. Chinn, *Mulitcultural Education in a Pluralist Society*, St Louis, Wesley, 1983.

10 G. Gay, 'Multiethnic Education: Historical Developments and Future Prospects', *Phi Delta Kappan*, vol.64, 1983, pp.560–3.

11 G.C. Baker, *Planning and Organising for Multicultural Instruction*, Reading, Mass., Addison-Wesley Publishing Company, 1983.

12 C.A. Grant, 'The Teacher and Multicultural Education', in M.J. Gold *et al.*, *In Praise of Diversity: A Resource Book for Multicultural Education*, Washington, DC, Teacher Corps, Association of Teacher Educators, 1977.

13 C.A. Grant and S.L. Melnick, 'Developing and Implementing Multicultural In-Service Teacher Education', paper presented at the National Council of States on In-Service Education, New Orleans, 17–19 November 1976.

14 For an overview of the development of Glazer's thinking across two crucial decades, see N. Glazer, *Ethnic Dilemmas 1964–1982*, Cambridge, Mass., Harvard University Press, 1983.

15 S. Bowles and H. Gintis, *Schooling in Capitalist America*, New York, Basic Books, 1976.

16 C. Jencks *et al.*, *Inequality: A Reassessment of the Effect of Family and Schooling in America*, New York, Basic Books, 1972.

17 P.A. Katz (ed.), *Towards the Elimination of Racism*, New York, Pergamon, 1976, gives a very useful overview and analysis of the field.

18 See, for example, M. Ramirez and A. Casteñada, *Cultural Democracy: Bicognitive Development and Education*, New York, Academic Press, 1974; P. Gurin *et al.*, 'Internal External Control in the Maturational Dynamics of Negro Youth', in *Journal of Social Issues*, vol.XXV, no.3, 1969, pp.29–53; and J.A. Vasquez, 'Bilingual Education's Needed Third Dimension', *Educational Leadership*, vol.37, no.2, 1979, pp.166–8.

19 For instance, C.E. Cortes, 'The Role of Media in Multicultural Education', in D.M. Gollnick *et al.*, *Multiculturalism in Contemporary Education*, Indiana, Indiana University School of Education, 1980, pp.38–49.

20 Details taken from Ontario Human Rights Commission, *Annual Report 1983–1984*, Toronto, Ontario, 1984, p.9. See also D. Ray and V. D'Oyley (eds), *Human Rights in Canadian Education*, Dubuque, Iowa, Kendall Hunt Publishing Company, 1983.

21 Details taken from Minister of State for Multiculturalism, *Multiculturalism and the Government of Canada*, Ottawa, Minister of Supply and Services, 1984.

22 Canada, House of Commons, Special Committee on Participation of Visible Minorities in Canadian Society, *Equality Now!* (First Report), Hull, Quebec, Canadian Government Publishing Centre, March 1984.

23 D.M. Collenette, 'Statement on Equality Now', Ottawa, Multiculturalism Canada, April 1984.

24 Government of Canada, 'Response to *"Equality Now"* ', Ottawa, Minister of Supply and Services, 1984.

25 See Government of Canada, *The Canadian Constitution, 1982*, Ottawa, Publications Canada, 1982 and two helpful, explanatory documents: Canadian Unity Information Office, *The Charter of Rights and Freedoms: A Guide for Canadians*, Ottawa, Publications Centre, 1984, and the Public Legal Education Society, *The Canadian Charter of Rights and Freedoms: A Guide for Students*, Vancouver, BC, The People's Law School Society, 1984.

26 Multiculturalism Canada, *National Strategy on Race Relations*, Ottawa, Minister of State, March 1984.

27 See, for example, North York Board of Education, *Race and Ethnic Relations Policy and Procedures*, North York, Ontario, Board of Education, 1982 and City of North York, Committee on Community, Race and Ethnic Relations, *Handling of Racial/Ethnic Incidents in Educational Institutions*, North York, Ontario, 1984.

28 For example, British Columbia Teachers' Federation, *Policies and Procedures for Race Relations* (adopted on 23 June 1984 by the Executive Committee), Vancouver, BC, 1984.

29 Ontario Human Rights Commission, *Annual Report 1983/4*, Toronto, Ontario, Office of the Commission, June 1984. See also Commission des droits de la personne du Québec, *Charte des Droits et Libertés de La Personne*, Quebec, 1982.

30 See, for example, J. Cummins, *Bilingualism and Special Education: Issues in Assessment and Pedagogy*, Clevedon, Avon, Multilingual Matters Ltd, 1984.

31 M. Laferrière, 'Racism in Education: Old and New', in D. Ray and D. D'Oyley, *op.cit.*, pp.153–75.

32 See the contributions to the 'brainstorming' symposia, subvented by the Multiculturalism Directorate in Ottawa, J.R. Mallea and J.C. Young (eds), *Cultural Diversity and Canadian Education*, Ottawa, Carleton University Press, 1984, and R.J. Samuda, J.W. Berry and M. Laferrière, *Multiculturalism in Canada*, Toronto, Allyn & Bacon, 1984.

33 D. Wood, *Multicultural Canada*, Toronto, Ontario, Ontario Institute for Studies in Education, 1978.

34 K. Moodley, 'Canadian Multicultural Education: Promises and Practice', in J.A. Banks and J. Lynch (eds), *op.cit.*

35 See, for example, K. Moodley, 'Canadian Multiculturalism as Ideology', *Ethnic and Racial Studies*, vol.6, no.3, 1983, pp.320–31.

36 For details of this early period up to 1980, see J. Lynch, 'Community Relations and Multicultural Education in Australia', in T. Corner (ed.), *Education in Multicultural Societies*, London, Croom Helm, 1984, pp.137–55.

37 The Australian Ethnic Affairs Council, *Australia as a Multicultural Society*, Canberra, Australian Government Publishing Service, 1977.

38 Review Group on Post Arrival Programmes and Services to Migrants, *Migrant Services and Programmes*, Canberra, Australian Government Publishing Service, 1978.

39 Commonwealth Education Portfolio, *Discussion Paper on Education in a Multicultural Australia*, Canberra, 1979.

40 Australian Ethnic Affairs Council, *Australia as a Multicultural Society*, Canberra, Australian Government Publishing Service, 1977.

41 Council of the Australian Institute of Multicultural Affairs, *Looking Forward*, Melbourne, AIMA, 1984.

42 See, for example, A.J. Grassby, *The Tyranny of Prejudice*, Melbourne, AE Press, 1984.

43 Australian Council on Population and Ethnic Affairs, *Multiculturalism for All Australians: Our Developing Nationhood*, Canberra, Australian Government Publishing Service, 1982; and Department of Immigration and Ethnic Affairs, *National Consultations on Multiculturalism and Citizenship Report*, Canberra, Australian Government Publishing Service, 1982.

44 B.M. Bullivant, *Race, Ethnicity and Curriculum*, Melbourne, The Macmillan Company of Australia, 1981, and *Pluralism, Cultural Maintenance and Evolution*, Clevedon, Avon, Multilingual Matters Ltd, 1984.

45 See, in particular, J. Smolicz, *Culture and Education in a Plural Society*, Canberra, Curriculum Development Centre, 1979.

46 B.M. Bullivant, 'Multicultural Education in Australia: An Unresolved Debate', in J.A. Banks and J. Lynch (eds), *op.cit.*

47 An overview recapitulation of developments and an attempt to set them in an ideological, conceptual framework may be found in J. Lynch, 'Multicultural Education in Western Europe: Practices and Promises', in J.A. Banks and J. Lynch (eds), *op.cit.*

48 See L. Porcher, *L'Education des Enfants des Travailleurs Migrant en Europe: L'Interculturalisme et la Formation des Enseignants*, Strasbourg, Conseil de la Co-operation Culturelle, 1979 (also available in English, 1981, see below).

49 The United Kingdom, for example, was providing the required mother-tongue instruction for less than 2.2 per cent of eligible children. See Commission of the European Communities, 'Report from the Commission to the Council on the Implementation of Directive 77/486/EEC on the Education of the Children of Migrant Workers', Brussels, EEC, 1984.

50 J.S. Gundara, C. Jones and K. Kimberley, 'The Marginalisation and Pauperisation of the Second Generation of Migrants in France, the Federal Republic of West Germany and Great Britain, Relating to the Education of the Children of Migrants', Brussels, Commission of the European Communities, 1982 (Research Contract No. 82002).

51 See The Council of Europe, *The European Convention on Human Rights*, Strasbourg, 1978.

52 Council of Europe, *Human Rights Education in Schools: Concepts, Attitudes and Skills*, Strasbourg, 1984.

53 See, for example, L. Porcher, *L'Enseignment aux Enfants Migrants*, Paris, Didier, 1984 and his earlier work for the Council of Europe such as *The Education of Children of Migrant Workers in Europe: Inter-*

culturalism and Teacher Training, Strasbourg, Council of Europe, 1981.

54 See, for example, M. Mauviel, 'Les français et la diversité culturelle', *Education Permanent*, vol.75, 1984, pp.67–82.

55 See U. Boos-Nünning *et al.*, *Aufnahmeunterricht, Muttersprachlicher Unterricht, Interkultureller Unterricht*, Munich, R. Oldenbourg Verlag, 1983.

56 Swedish Commission on Migrants' Languages in School and Adult Education, *Different Origins: Partnership in Sweden: Education for Linguistic and Cultural Diversity*, Stockholm, Utbildningsdepartamentet, 1983.

57 A brief pamphlet published by the Council of Europe describes the workings of the Convention, the Commission and the Court. See Council of Europe, *The Protection of Human Rights in Europe*, Strasbourg, 1983. (To date seven protocols have been added to the original text.)

58 M.A. Gibson, 'Approaches to Multicultural Education in the United States: Some Concepts and Assumptions', *Anthropology and Education Quarterly*, vol.7, no.4, 1976, pp.7–18.

59 J. Williams, 'Perspectives on the Multicultural Curriculum', *The Social Science Teacher*, vol.8, no.4, 1979, pp.126–33.

60 J. Lynch, 'Multicultural Teacher Education in Australia: The State of the Art' (an unpublished report submitted to the Australian Education Research and Development Committee), Canberra, ERDC, 1980, cyclo, p.120.

61 J. Lynch, 'Multicultural Education in Western Europe: Practices and Promises', in J.A. Banks and J. Lynch (eds), *op.cit.*

62 J. Nixon, *A Teacher's Guide to Multicultural Education*, Oxford, Basil Blackwell, 1985, pp.38ff.

63 G. Gay, 'Changing Conceptions of Multicultural Education', *Education Perspectives*, vol.16, no.4, 1977, pp.4–9.

64 W. Stephan, 'Education in Multicultural Societies: Towards a Framework for Comparative Analysis', paper presented at the 11th Conference of the Comparative Education Society in Europe, Wurzburgh, July 1983. Reproduced in W. Mitter and J. Swift (eds), *Bildung und Erziehung* (Beiheft 2/11), Cologne, Böhlau Verlag, 1985.

65 K. Watson, 'Educational Policies in Multicultural Societies', *Comparative Education*, vol.15, no.1, 1979, pp.17–31.

66 J.A. Banks, 'Multicultural Education: Development, Paradigms and Goals', in J.A. Banks and J. Lynch (eds), *op.cit.*

67 See T.S. Kuhn, *The Structure of Scientific Revolutions*, Chicago, University of Chicago Press, 1970.

68 A useful listing of sources for teachers in this international and human rights context-setting can be found in Department of Education and Science *International Understanding* (A Handbook for Schools and Colleges), London, DES, 1979.

69 An initial essay on this topic is J. Lynch, 'Curriculum and Assessment', in M. Craft (ed.), *Education and Cultural Pluralism*, London, The Falmer Press, 1984, pp.44–56. See also Chapter 9 of this book.

3 The development of multicultural education in the United Kingdom

1 Several schemes were considered for reducing Black immigration and excluding Blacks from the civil service as is indicated by secret Cabinet papers from 1954, released at the beginning of 1985. See Press reports, 'Moves to stem black immigration', *The Guardian*, no.2, January 1985, p.2, and 'Churchill sought ways of keeping blacks out of civil service', *The Times*, no. 2, January 1985, p.4.
2 R.A. Schermerhorn, *Comparative Ethnic Relations: A Framework for Theory and Research*, New York, Random House, 1970.
3 R. Jeffcoate, *Ethnic Minorities and Education*, London, Harper & Row, 1984.
4 D. Kirp, *Doing Good by Doing Little: Race and Schooling in Britain*, Berkeley, University of California Press, 1979.
5 Details of legislation have been based on A. Lester and G. Bindman, *Race and Law*, Harmondsworth, Penguin, 1972; The Runnymede Trust and The Radical Statistics Group, *Britain's Black Population*, London, Heinemann, 1980 and appropriate CRC and CRE publications.
6 Ministry of Education, *English for Immigrants*, London, HMSO, 1963.
7 Home Office, *Second Report of the Commonwealth Immigrants Advisory Council*, London, HMSO, 1964.
8 Department of Education and Science, *Circular 7/65: The Education of Immigrants*, London, DES, 1965.
9 Department of Education and Science, *Circular 10/65: The Organisation of Secondary Education*, London, DES, 1965.
10 Department of Education and Science, *Circular 7/65, op.cit.*
11 Schools Council, *English for the Children of Immigrants* (Working Paper 13), London, HMSO, 1967.
12 Schools Council, *Teaching English to West Indian Children* (Working Paper 29), London, Evans, 1970.
13 Central Advisory Council for Education (England), *Children and Their Primary Schools* (The Plowden Report), London, HMSO, 1967.
14 Department of Education and Science, *Education Survey 13: The Education of Immigrants*, London, HMSO, 1971; Department of Education and Science, *Evaluation Survey 14: The Continuing Needs of Immigrants*, London, HMSO, 1972.
15 United Kingdom Parliament, Select Committee on Race Relations and Immigration (Session 1972–3: Education), *Report*, vol.I, Evidence and Appendices, vols II and III, London, HMSO, 1973.
16 Schools Council, *Multiracial Education: Need and Innovation* (Working Paper 50), London, Schools Council, 1973.
17 D. Lawton and B. Dufour, *The New Social Studies*, London, Heinemann, 1973.
18 L. Stenhouse, *An Introduction to Curriculum Research and Development*, London, Heinemann, 1975, pp.127–30.
19 L. Stenhouse *et al.*, *Teaching About Race Relations: Problems and Effects*, London, Routledge & Kegan Paul, 1982.
20 Community Relations Council/National Association of Teachers in Further and Higher Education, *Teacher Education for a Multicultural Society*, London, CRC, 1974.

21 Department of Education and Science, *A Language for Life* (The Bullock Report), London, HMSO, 1975.
22 Council of the European Communities, *Council Directive of 25 July 1977 on the Education of the Children of Migrant Workers*, Brussels, EEC, 1977.
23 Department of Education and Science, *Directive of the Council of the European Community on the Education of the Children of Migrant Workers*, Circular no.5/81, London, DES, 1981.
24 Commission of the European Communities, *Report from the Commission to the Council*, Brussels, EEC, 1984.
25 Department of Education and Science, *West Indian Children in our Schools* (Rampton Report), London, HMSO, 1981.
26 Department of Education and Science, 'Report by HM Inspectors on Aspects of Organisation and Curriculum in Seven Multiethnic Comprehensive Schools', London, DES, n.d., mimeo.
27 Department of Education and Science, *A Framework for the School Curriculum*, London, DES, 1980.
28 Department of Education and Science, *The School Curriculum*, London, HMSO, 1980.
29 Department of Education and Science, 'The Education of Children from Ethnic Minority Groups: Consultative Document', London, DES, 1981, mimeo.
30 S.J. Eggleston, O.K. Dunn and A. Purewal, *In-Service Teacher Education in a Multiracial Society*, Keele, University of Keele, 1981.
31 R. Giles and D. Cherrington, 'Multicultural Teacher Education in the United Kingdom: A Survey of Courses and other Provisions in British Institutions of Higher Education', London, CRE, 1981.
32 See J. Lynch, 'An Initial Typology of Staff Development Needs for Multicultural Teacher Education', in G.K. Verma and S. Modgil, *Multicultural Education: The Interminable Debate*, Lewes, Sussex, Falmer Press, 1985.
33 M. Craft (ed.), *Teaching in a Multicultural Society: The Task for Teacher Education*, Lewes, Sussex, Falmer Press, 1981.
34 G. Driver, *Beyond Underachievement: Case studies of English, West Indian and Asian School-leavers at Sixteen Plus*, London, Commission for Racial Equality, 1980; G. Driver and R. Ballard, 'Comparing Performance in Multiracial Schools', *New Community*, vol.11, no.2, 1979.
35 NATFHE, *Further and Teacher Education in a Multicultural Society*, London, National Association of Teachers in Further and Higher Education, 1979; NATFHE, *Evidence to the Committee of Inquiry into the Education of Children from Minority Groups*, London, National Association of Teachers in Further and Higher Education, 1980; National Union of Teachers, *Race, Education Intelligence*, London, NUT, 1978; National Union of Teachers, *In Black and White: Guidelines for Teachers on Racial Stereotyping in Textbooks and Learning Materials*, London, NUT, 1979.
36 Employment Gazette, 'Unemployment and Ethnic Origins', *Employment Gazette*, London, HMSO, June 1984.
37 M. Craft (ed.), *Education and Cultural Pluralism*, Lewes, Sussex, Falmer Press, 1984.

38 Home Office, *The Brixton Disorders* (The Scarman Report), London, HMSO, 1981.
39 Schools Council, *Multicultural Education*, London, Schools Council, 1982.
40 C. Mullard, L. Bonnick and B. King, *Racial Policy and Practice in Education*, London, Department of Sociology of Education, University of London Institute of Education, 1983, giving the results of a survey conducted in 1982.
41 J. Lynch, *The Multicultural Curriculum*, London, Batsford, 1983.
42 M. Craft, 'Press Release: Teacher Education in a Multicultural Society', University of Nottingham, 1983. (The six institutions initially involved were Brighton Polytechnic, Liverpool University, London University, Manchester Polytechnic, Nottingham University and Sunderland Polytechnic.)
43 Craft, *op.cit.*, 1981.
44 M. Craft and M. Atkins, *Training of Teachers of Ethnic Minority Community Languages*, Nottingham, The University, 1983.
45 M. Craft, 'Education for Diversity', in Craft (ed.), *op.cit.*, pp.5–25.
46 A. Craft and G. Bardell, *Curriculum Opportunities in a Multicultural Society*, London, Harper & Row, 1984.
47 J.A. Banks, 'Multicultural Education and its Critics', *The New Era*, vol.65, no.3, 1984, pp.58–65.
48 See University of London Institute of Education, 'Racist Society: Geography Curriculum', Conference Papers, 29 March 1983, mimeo.
49 Brent, London Borough of Brent Education Committee, *Education for a Multicultural Democracy*, London, Brent (2 vols.), and Berkshire LEA, *Education for Equality*, Advisory Committee on Multicultural Education, 1982.
50 Inner London Education Authority, *Anti-Racist School Policies*, London, ILEA, 1982.
51 R. Jeffcoate, *Ethnic Minorities and Education*, London, Harper & Row, 1984.
52 Council for National Academic Awards, Committee for Education, Multicultural Working Group, 'Multicultural Education: Discussion Paper', London, CNAA, 1984.
53 National Association for Multiracial Education, 'Statement on Teacher Education', London, NAME, 1984.
54 Department of Education and Science, *Race Relations in Schools*, London, DES, 1984.
55 See the papers presented to the 1984 NAME Conference, C. Mullard, 'Anti-racist Education: A Theoretical Basis' and 'Why Anti-Racist Education', April 1984.
56 Department of Education and Science, *The Organisation and Content of the 5–16 Curriculum*, London, DES, 1984.
57 See E. Cashmore and C. Bagley, 'Colour Blind', *The Times Educational Supplement*, 28 December 1984, p.13.
58 See P. Higginbotham, 'A Place for Old School Ties', *The Times Higher Education Supplement*, 21 December 1984.
59 See, for example, 'Moves to Stem Black Immigration', *The Guardian*, 2 January 1985, p.2 and 'Churchill Sought Ways of Keeping Blacks out of

Civil Service', *The Times*, 2 January 1985, p.4.
60 Committee of Inquiry into the Education of Children from Ethnic Minority Groups, *Education for All* (The Swann Report), London, HMSO, 1985 (Cmnd. 9453).
61 See, for example, N. O'Neil, *Racism and the Working Class*, London, Shakti Publications, 1982 and, more recently, R. Cochrane and M. Billing, 'I am not National Front Myself, But . . .', *New Society*, 17 May 1984. Readers should also refer to D. Milner, *Children and Race: Ten Years On*, London, Ward Lock Educational, 1983.
62 An earlier version of this chapter was given in Toronto at the November 1984 Conference of the Canadian Council for Multicultural Education.

4 National and local authority responses: policies and assumptions

1 Secretary of State for Education and Science and Secretary of State for Wales, *Education in Schools: A Consultative Document*, London, HMSO, 1977.
2 *Ibid.*, pp.6–7.
3 Department of Education and Science and Welsh Office, *A Framework for the School Curriculum*, London, DES, 1980, p.3.
4 *Ibid.*
5 Department of Education and Science and the Welsh Office, *The School Curriculum*, London, HMSO, 1981, paras 11 and 21, pp.3 and 6, and *The Curriculum from 5–16*, London, HMSO, 1985, p. 3.
6 *Ibid.*, p.10, para. 36.
7 Her Majesty's Inspectorate, *A View of the Curriculum*, London, HMSO, 1980, p.5 *et passim*.
8 Department of Education and Science, *Local Authority Arrangements for the School Curriculum*, London, HMSO, 1979.
9 *Ibid.*, p.35.
10 House of Commons, Home Affairs Committee, *Fifth Report: Racial Disadvantage*, London, HMSO, 1981, p.LXVI.
11 Maryland State Department of Education, *New Perspectives in Intercultural Education*, Baltimore, Maryland, State Department of Education, 1975, p.15.
12 *Ibid.*, pp.15–16.
13 A. Little and R. Willey, *Multiethnic Education: The Way Forward*, London, Schools Council, 1981.
14 See, for example, the views of one commentator, M. Stone, *The Education of the Black Child in Britain: The Myth of Multiracial Education*, London, Fontana, 1981.
15 A. Little and R. Willey, *Studies in the Multiethnic Curriculum*, London, Schools Council, 1983.
16 J. Lynch and C. Biott, 'Towards a Curriculum for a Multicultural Society: Interim Evaluation Report', Sunderland, Faculty of Education, November 1982, p.7, cyclo.
17 See the assertion by one of the authors of the Schools Council Report, R. Willey, *Race, Equality and Schools*, London, Methuen, 1984.
18 Birley High School, 'Multicultural Education in the 1980s: The Report

of a Working Party of Teachers at Birley High School', Manchester, City of Manchester Education Committee, 1980.

19 Department of Education and Science and Welsh Office, *Directive of the Council of European Community on the Education of Children of Migrant Workers* (Circular 5/81), London, DES, 1981.

20 Department of Education and Science, *The School Curriculum* (Circular 6/81), London, DES, 1981.

21 Home Office, *The Brixton Disorders* (The Scarman Report), London, HMSO, 1981 (Cmnd. 8427).

22 C. Mullard, L. Bonnick and B. King, *Racial Policy and Practice in Education: A Letter Survey*, London, University of London Institute of Education, 1983, pp.13 and 23.

23 C. Mullard, L. Bonnick and B. King, *Local Education Authority Policy Documents: A Descriptive Analysis of Contents*, London, University of London Institute of Education, 1983; *Process, Problem and Prognosis: A Survey of Local Education Authorities' Multicultural Education Policies and Practices* (Part One: The Multicultural Process; Part Three: The Prognosis), London, University of London Institute of Education, 1984.

24 Committee of Inquiry into the Education of Children from Ethnic Minority Groups, *Report: Education for All* (The Swann Report), London, HMSO, 1985, p.221 (Cmnd. 9453).

25 Department of Education and Science, Committee of Inquiry into the Education of Children from Ethnic Minority Groups, *Report: West Indian Children in Our Schools*, London, HMSO, 1981 (Cmnd. 8273) and The Swann Report, *op.cit.*

26 *Ibid.*, p.78.

27 Department of Education and Science, 'The Education of Children from Ethnic Minority Groups: Consultative Document', London, DES, October 1981.

28 Department of Education and Science, *Primary Education in England* (A Survey by HM Inspectors of Schools), London, HMSO, 1978, p.113.

29 Department of Education and Science, *Aspects of Secondary Education in England* (A Survey by HM Inspectors of Schools), London, HMSO, 1979, p.80.

30 *Ibid.*, p.261.

31 Department of Education and Science, *Education 5–9: An Illustrative Survey of 80 First Schools in England*, London, HMSO, 1982, pp.27 and p.28.

32 *Ibid.*, p.59.

33 Department of Education and Science, *9–13 Middle Schools* (An Illustrative Survey), London, HMSO, 1983, p.124.

34 Department of Education and Science, *The Organisation and Content of the 5–16 Curriculum*, London, DES, 1984, p.5.

35 Department of Education and Science, *Report by HM Inspectors on Aspects of Organisation and Curriculum in Seven Multiethnic Comprehensive Schools*, London, DES, 1979, p.17.

36 *Ibid.*, p.18, para. 7.3.

37 *Ibid.*, p.18, para. 7.4.

38 Scottish Education Department, *The Education of Ethnic Minorities in Strathclyde Region* (A Report by HM Inspectors of Schools), Edinburgh, SED, 1983, p.18 *et passim*.

39 'Tiptoe Round the Minefield', *Times Educational Supplement*, 11 May 1984.

40 Department of Education and Science, *Race Relations in Schools, A Summary of Discussions at Meetings in Five Local Education Authorities*, London, DES, n.d., 1984, p.7.

41 C. Brown, *Black and White Britain: The Third PSI Survey*, London, Heinemann, 1984.

42 'Unemployment and Ethnic Origin', *Employment Gazette*, June 1984.

43 See the Press Reports on the Cabinet Papers from 1954, 'Churchill sought Ways of Keeping Blacks out of Civil Service', *The Times*, 2 January 1985, p.4 and 'Moves to Stem Black Immigration', *The Guardian*, 2 January 1985, p.2.

44 J. Whyte, *Beyond the Wendy House: Sex-Role Stereotyping in Primary Schools*, London, Schools Council, 1983, and A. Kelly, J. Whyte and B. Smail, *Girls into Science and Technology: Final Report*, Manchester, University of Manchester, 1984.

45 Universities Central Council on Admissions, *Statistical Supplement to the Twenty-First Report 1982/3*, Cheltenham, UCCA, 1984.

46 Department of Education and Science, *Report by HM Inspectors on Sir John Cass's Foundation and Red Coat Church of England Secondary School, City of London and Tower Hamlets*, London, DES, 1984.

47 Department of Education and Science, *Report by HM Inspectors on Muslim Girls High School, Dewsbury, West Yorkshire*, London, DES, 1984.

48 Department of Education and Science, *Education Observed*, London, DES, 1984, p.3.

49 Department of Education and Science, *Education Observed 2*, London, DES, 1984, p.3.

50 Survey conducted by the author by visiting the LEAs and requesting their multicultural and/or anti-racist policy statements.

51 Inner London Education Authority, *Education in a Multiethnic Society: An Aide-Memoire for the Inspectorate*, London, ILEA, 1981.

52 City of Bradford Metropolitan Council, Local Administrative Memorandum 2/82: 'Education for a Multicultural Society: Provision for Pupils of Ethnic Minority Communities', Bradford, November 1982.

53 City of Bradford Metropolitan Council, Directorate of Educational Services, 'Local Administrative Memorandum 6/83: Racialist Behaviour in Schools', Bradford, November 1983.

54 *Ibid.*, pp.3–4.

55 City of Birmingham District Council, Education Sub-Committee, 'Report of the Chief Education Officer: Education for a Multicultural Society Report on the Response from Schools', Birmingham, Education Department, 14 February 1984, p.1.

56 *Ibid.*, pp.2–3.

57 London Borough of Brent, Education Committee, *Education for a Multicultural Democracy: Book One*, London, 1983, p.7.

58 R. Jeffcoate, *Ethnic Minorities and Education*, London, Harper & Row, 1984, pp.150–51.
59 Royal County of Berkshire, Department of Education, 'Education for Racial Equality: Policy Paper 1; General Policy: Policy Paper II: Implications, Policy Paper 3: Support', Reading, 1983.
60 Inner London Education Authority, *Race, Sex and Class* (Volumes 1–6), London, ILEA, 1983–5.
61 *Ibid.*, Vol.III, p.5.
62 D. Dorn, 'LEA Policies on Multiracial Education', *Multiethnic Education Review*, vol.2, no.2, 1983, pp.3–5.
63 Borough of Sunderland, Education Department, 'A Policy for Multicultural Education in Sunderland', Sunderland, August 1983; Borough Council of South Tyneside, Education Committee, 'Multicultural Education: A General Statement of Policy', South Shields, July 1983.
64 Department of Education and Science, *The School Curriculum* (Circular 8/83), London, DES, December 1983.
65 See, for example, City of Newcastle-upon-Tyne, *Curriculum Policy Statement* (Draft for Consultation), Newcastle-upon-Tyne, n.d., 1984, p.7, and London Borough of Merton, Education Department, *The School Curriculum: A Policy Statement*, London, February 1984, p.9, and *Working Paper on the Curriculum and Organisation in Schools*, London, April 1984, pp.15–16.
66 See City of Birmingham District Council, Education (Schools and Special Education) Sub-Committee, 'Report of the Chief Education Officer: Education for a Multicultural Society: Report on the Response from Schools', Birmingham, 14 February 1984, and London Borough of Hillingdon, 'Education for a Multi-Cultural Society: A Statement of Policy', Uxbridge, Middlesex, The Education Department, 1984.
67 See City of Newcastle-upon-Tyne, *The Council and Racial Equality*, November 1984.
68 Several Scottish Authorities were co-operating with the Consultative Committee on the Curriculum IMEP Project (International and Multicultural Education Project), based at Jordanhill College of Education, which adopted a conceptual framework which linked environmental and development education, peace education and international and multicultural education. See J. Dunlop, *IMEP Working Papers 1–3*, Glasgow, Jordanhill College of Education, 1982–5.

5 Curriculum planning, implementation and evaluation

1 See, for example, E.M. Brittan, 'Multiracial Education 2', *Education Research*, vol.18, no.2, 1976, pp.96–107.
2 All London Teachers Against Racism and Facism (ALTARF), *Teaching and Racism* (an ALTARF Discussion Document, 4/c), London, ALTARF, 1978.
3 *Ibid.*, p.20.
4 Quoted in National Union of Teachers, *All Our Children*, London, NUT, January 1978.
5 *Ibid.*, p.2.

6 H.E.R. Townsend and E.M. Brittan, *Multiracial Education: Need and Innovation*, London, Evans/Methuen Educational, 1973.

7 *Ibid.*, p.84.

8 National Union of Teachers, *Race, Intelligence, Education*, London, NUT, 1978.

9 National Union of Teachers, *In Black and White*, London, NUT, 1979.

10 National Union of Teachers, *Education for a Multiracial Society*, London, NUT, 1982, p.2.

11 Assistant Masters and Mistresses Association, *Education for a Multicultural Society*, London, AMMA, 1981.

12 Assistant Masters and Mistresses Association, *Our Multicultural Society: The Educational Response*, London AMMA, 1982. See also the report of an AMMA conference, *Positive and Negative Discrimination in Multicultural Britain*, London, AMMA, 1983.

13 Birley High School, *Multicultural Education in the 1980s*, Manchester, City of Manchester Education Committee, 1980.

14 See C. Duncan, 'Portrait of a Multicultural School: Some Implications for Practice', in T. Corner (ed.), *Race and the Curriculum*, Glasgow, University of Glasgow Department of Education, 1985, pp. 6–14.

15 City of Bradford Metropolitan Council Directorate of Educational Services, 'Local Administrative Memorandum 6/83: Racialist Behaviour in Schools', Bradford, City of Bradford Metropolitan Council, November 1983.

16 Wyke Manor School, Bradford, 'Statement and Guidelines', 1984.

17 J. Shallice, 'Formulating an Anti-Racist Policy at the Skinners Company's School', in The English Centre, *The English Curriculum: Race*, London, ILEA English Centre, n.d. (1982?).

18 *Ibid.*, p.93.

19 North Westminster Community School, 'Towards a Multicultural Philosophy', in *ibid.*, p.94.

20 *Ibid.*, pp.94–6.

21 'Quinton Kynaston Policy on Racist Behaviour', quoted in London University Institute of Education, *Racist Society: Geography Curriculum* (Papers for a Conference on 29 March 1983), London, 1983.

22 R. Jeffcoate, 'A Multicultural Curriculum Beyond the Orthodoxy', *Trends in Education*, vol.4, 1979, pp.8–12, and *Positive Image*, London, Chameleon Books, 1979, pp.32–3.

23 R. Jeffcoate, 'Curriculum Planning in Multiracial Education', *Educational Research*, vol.18, no.3, 1976, pp.192–200.

24 For the amended version, see L. Cohen and L. Manion, *Multicultural Classrooms*, London, Croom Helm, 1983, p.189.

25 *Ibid.*

26 J. Lynch, *The Multicultural Curriculum*, London, Batsford, 1983.

27 *Ibid.*, p.59.

28 P. Walkling, 'The Idea of a Multicultural Curriculum', *Journal of Philosophy of Education*, vol.14, no.1, 1980, pp.87–95.

29 J.A. Banks, *Multiethnic Education: Theory and Practice*, Boston, Allyn & Bacon, 1981, pp.257–79. See also the adaption in Cohen and Manion, *op.cit.*, pp.191–5.

30 M. Saunders, *Multicultural Teaching*, London, McGraw-Hill, 1982,

p.11, slightly amended.
31 *Ibid.*, p.19.
32 L. Stenhouse *et al.*, *Teaching About Race Relations: Problems and Effects*, London, Routledge & Kegan Paul, 1982, pp.273–7, slightly adapted and abridged.
33 J. Nixon, *A Teacher's Guide to Multicultural Education*, Oxford, Basil Blackwell, 1985, pp.75–80.
34 D. Hicks, 'Two sides of the Same Coin: An Exploration of Links between Multicultural Education and Development Education', *New Approaches to Multiracial Education*, vol.7, no.2, 1979, pp.1–5.
35 Nixon, *op.cit.*, pp.91–3.
36 D. Ruddell, 'Racism Awareness: An Approach for Schools', *Multiracial Education*, vol.11, no.1, 1982, pp.3–9.
37 J. Twitching and C. Demuth, *Multicultural Education*, London, British Broadcasting Association, 1981, pp.161–74.
38 J.H. Katz, *White Awareness: Handbook for Anti-Racist Training*, Oklahoma, University of Oklahoma Press, 1978.
39 J. Lynch, 1983, *op.cit.*
40 For example, the Universal Declaration of Human Rights of the United Nations, 1948; The European Convention on Human Rights, 1950; The International Covenant on Civil and Political Rights, 1966; and the International Convention on the Elimination of all forms of Racial Discrimination, 1966; ratified, subject to minor reservations, by the United Kingdom on 7 March 1969 (see Cmnd. 4108, August 1969). See Chapter 2 of this book.
41 For example, the 1976 Race Relations Act.
42 Reproduced in R.K. Merton, 'Discrimination and the American Creed', in R.K. Merton, *Sociological Ambivalence and other Essays*, New York, The Free Press, 1976, pp.189–216.
43 S. Hall, 'Teaching Race', *Multicultural Education*, vol.9, 1980, and 'The Whites of their Eyes: Racist Ideologies in the Media', in G. Bridges and R. Brunt (eds), *Silver Linings*, London, Lawrence & Wishart, 1981.
44 A.K. Spears, 'Institutionalized Racism and the Education of Blacks', *Anthropology and Education Quarterly*, vol.9, no.2, 1978.
45 A.M. Rose, 'The Causes of Prejudice', in M.L. Barron (ed.), *American Minorities*, New York, Alfred A. Knopf, 1962.
46 G.E. Simpson and J.M. Yinger, *Racial and Cultural Minorities*, New York, Harper & Row, 1965.
47 Contained as separate chapters in P.A. Katz (ed.), *Towards the Elimination of Racism*, New York, Pergamon, 1976, pp.157–308.
48 J.A. Banks, 'Reducing Prejudice in Students: Theory, Research and Strategies', A paper presented at the Kamloops Spring Institute for Teacher Education, Faculty of Education, Simon Fraser University, Burnaby, British Columbia, 3 February 1982.
49 J.A. Banks, *Multiethnic Education: Theory and Practice*, Boston, Allyn & Bacon, 1981.
50 United States Commission on Human Rights, *Affirmative Action in the 1980s: Dismantling the Process of Discrimination*, Washington, D.C., Clearing House Publications (65), 1981.
51 Gains achieved by deliberate teaching about race are non-persistent in

the long run without reinforcement. See L. Stenhouse, G. Verma and R. Wild (eds), *Teaching about Race Relations: Problems and Effects*, *op.cit.*, especially Chapter XXII, 'A Researcher's Speculations', by Stenhouse.

52   T. Ardono *et al.*, *The Authoritarian Personality*, New York, Harper, 1950.

53   B. Bettleheim and M. Janowitz, *Dynamics of Prejudice*, New York, Harper, 1950.

54   G. Myrdal, *An American Dilemma: The Negro Problem and Modern Democracy*, New York, Harper, 1944.

55   A. Dorn and B. Troyna, 'Multicultural Education and the Politics of Decision Making', *Oxford Review of Education*, vol.8, 1982, pp.175–85.

56   R.L. Garcia, *Teaching in a Pluralist Society*, New York, Harper & Row, 1982, particularly pp.81–90.

57   Stenhouse *et al.*, *op.cit.*, 1982.

58   F.J. Sciara and D. Cunningham, 'Racial Prejudice in Young Children: A Case for Multicultural Education', 1982, Conference paper for the Annual Conference of the Indiana Association for the Education of Young Children, 1982.

59   J. Nixon, 'Teaching about Race Relations', *Secondary School Theatre Journal*, vol.19, no.3, pp.16–18.

60   R. Jeffcoate, *Positive Image: Towards a Multiracial Curriculum*, London, Chameleon, 1979.

61   M.A. Ijaz and I.H. Ijaz, 'A Cultural Program for Changing Racial Attitudes', *History and Social Science Teacher*, vol.17, no.1, 1981, pp.17–20.

62   L.H. Dunbar, 'The Utilization of Values Clarification in Multicultural Education as a Strategy to Reduce Prejudicial Attitudes of Eighth Grade Students', Northern Arizona University doctoral thesis, 1980.

63   T.H. Chapman, 'Simulation Game Effects on Attitudes Regarding Racism and Sexism', Maryland University, Cultural Study Centre, *Research Report*, vol.8, no.74, 1974.

64   An interesting example of a human relations approach and its effects on in-service teachers in G. Blackburn, 'An Examination of the Effects of Human Relations Training on the Attitudes of Certified In-Service Teachers in Minnesota', University of Washington, Seattle, Ph.D. thesis, 1980.

65   C. Adelman *et al.*, *A Fair Hearing for All: Relationships Between Teaching and Racial Equality*, Early Reading, Bulmershe College of Higher Education, 1984, Bulmershe Research Publication No.2.

66   The only project in the United Kingdom which has so far attempted to link these areas is the IMEP Project. Banks, in his concept of the ethno-national model of courses and programmes as the goal of curriculum reform, links multiethnic education and global education. See J.A. Banks, *Multiethnic Education: Theory and Practice*, Boston, Allyn & Bacon, 1981.

67   P.S. Kowalczewski, 'Race and Education: Racism, Diversity and Inequality, Implications for Multicultural Education', *Oxford Review of Education*, vol.8, no.2, 1982, pp.145–61.

68 J. Lynch and C. Biott, 'Towards a Curriculum for a Multicultural Society: Evaluation of a DES Regional Course', Sunderland, November 1982.
69 Stenhouse *et al.*, *op.cit.*, 1982.
70 Lynch, *op.cit.*
71 J.A. Banks, *Teaching Strategies for Ethnic Studies*, Boston, Allyn & Bacon, 1984.
72 C. Biott, J. Lynch and W. Robertson, 'Supporting Teachers' Own Progress Towards Multicultural Education', *Multicultural Teaching*, vol.11, no.2, 1984, pp.39–41.
73 G. Gay, 'Developmental Prerequisites for Multicultural Education in the Social Studies', in L.W. Rosenwig (ed.) *Developmental Perspectives in the Social Studies*, Washington D.C., National Council for the Social Studies (Bulletin 66), 1982, pp.67–81. See also G.S. Pate, 'Research on Prejudice Reduction: Findings and Implications', mimeo, 1974.
74 Some parts of this last section derive from a previous article. See J. Lynch, 'Human Rights, Racism and the Multicultural Curriculum', *Educational Review*, Summer 1985.
75 The matrix, developed for the International and Multicultural Project (IMEP) of the Scottish Consultative Committee on the Curriculum, based at Jordanhill College in Glasgow, is the most advanced organiser of such coalitions across the five domains of multicultural education, peace education, development education, human rights and environmental education. See Consultative Committee on the Curriculum, International and Multicultural Education Programme, *Working Papers 1–3*, Glasgow, Jordanhill College of Education, 1982–5, and *Report on the IMEP Conference, 15–16 May, 1984*, Glasgow, Jordanhill College of Education, 1985.
76 See, for example, Vancouver School Board, *Guidelines for the Implementations of the VSB Race Relations Policy*, British Columbia, 1984.

6 School, parents and the community

1 D.W. Ryan and T.B. Greenfield, *The Class Size Problem*, Toronto, Ministry of Education, Ontario, 1975.
2 M. Rutter *et al.*, *Fifteen Thousand Hours: Secondary Schools and their Effects on Children*, London, Open Books, 1979.
3 B.S. Bloom *et al.*, 'The State of Research on Selected Alterable Variables in Education', Chicago, Department of Education, University of Chicago, 1980.
4 H.J. Walberg, 'Improving the Productivity of America's Schools', *Educational Leadership*, vol.41, no.8, 1984, pp.19–27.
5 R.S. Bloom, 'The Search for Methods of Group Instruction as Effective as One-to-One Tutoring', *Educational Leadership*, vol.4, no.8, 1984, pp.4–17.
6 An interesting summary of such factors for a developing country is J.N. Johnstone, 'Out of School Factors and Educational Achievement in Indonesia', *Comparative Education Review*, vol.27, no.2, 1983, pp.278–95.

7 Cultural Advisory Council for Education, *Early Leaving*, London, HMSO, 1954.
8 Central Advisory Council for Education (England), *Half Our Future* (The Newsom Report), London, HMSO, 1963, especially pp.70–1.
9 Schools Council, *Young School Leavers* (Enquiry 1), London, HMSO, 1968, p.242.
10 Central Advisory Council for Education (England), *Children and their Primary Schools* (The Plowden Report), London, HMSO, 1967.
11 J. Lynch and J. Pimlott, *Parents and Teachers*, London, Macmillan Education, 1976.
12 Department of Education and Science, Committee of Inquiry, *A Language for Life* (The Bullock Report), London, HMSO, 1975, paras 5.37–5.40 and 20.16.
13 Department of Education and Science and Welsh Office, *A New Partnership for Our Schools* (The Taylor Report), London, HMSO, 1977.
14 See, for example, G. Driver, 'Cultural Competence, Social Power and School Achievement', *New Community*, Spring/Summer 1977, and M. Hammersley, 'The Mobilization of Pupil Attention', in M. Hammersley and P. Woods (eds), *The Process of Schooling*, London, Routledge & Kegan Paul, 1976.
15 Department of Education and Science and Welsh Office, *Local Authority Arrangements for the School Curriculum* (Report on the Circular 14/77 Review), London, HMSO, 1979.
16 *Ibid.*, p.155.
17 *Ibid.*, pp.64–6.
18 Department of Education and Science, *Report by H.M. Inspectors on Aspects of Organisation and Curriculum in Seven Multiethnic Comprehensive Schools*, London, DES, 1979, p.9.
19 Department of Education and Science, *Race Relations in Schools: A Summary of Discussion in Five Local Education Authorities*, London, DES, 1983, pp.5–7.
20 Department of Education and Science, *West Indian Children in Our Schools* (The Rampton Report), London, HMSO, 1981.
21 House of Commons, Home Affairs Committee, *Fifth Report (Racial Disadvantage)*, London, HMSO, 1981, vol.1, p.LXIII.
22 *Ibid.*, p.xli.
23 D.P. Weikart and L.J. Schweinhart, *Changed Lives: The Effects of the Perry Pre-School Program on Youths Through Age 19*, Ypsilanti, Michigan, High/Scope Press, 1984, and Press Release by the Foundation summarising the results and dated 14 September 1984.
24 Home Office, *The Brixton Disorders, 10–12 April, 1981* (The Scarman Report), London, HMSO, 1981, p.106.
25 Home Office, *The Brixton Disorders, op.cit.*, p.106 *et passim* (Cmnd. 8427).
26 Secretary of State for Education and Science and Secretary of State for Wales, *Parental Influence at School* (A New Framework for School Government in England and Wales), London, HMSO, 1984.
27 See S. Tomlinson, *Home and School in Multicultural Britain*, London, Batsford, 1984, pp.120–3.
28 A. MacBeth, *The Child Between*, Glasgow, University of Glasgow,

Department of Education, 1983, quoted in Tomlinson, *op.cit.*

29 European Economic Community, 'Public Statement by Representatives of 40 Parent Organisations', Luxembourg, EEC, 1983, quoted in Tomlinson, *op.cit.*

30 J. Lynch, *The Multicultural Curriculum*, London, Batsford, 1983, p.97.

31 F. Morrell, 'Policy for Schools in Inner London', in G. Grace (ed.), *Education and the City* (Theory, History and Contemporary Practice), London, Routledge & Kegan Paul, 1984, pp.195–209.

32 Congress of the United States, *Education for All Handicapped Children Act of 1975* (Public Law 94–142, 94th Congress, 3–6, 29 November 1975).

33 London Borough of Brent, Teachers Association, *Multicultural Education in Brent Schools*, London, Brent Education Committee in conjunction with the Brent Teachers Assocation (NUT), June 1980.

34 Adapted from London Borough of Brent Education Committee, *Education for a Multicultural Democracy: Book 2*. London, Borough of Brent, 1983, pp.23–4.

35 This checklist is based on a number of policy statements and, in particular, City of Bradford Metropolitan Council, Directorate of Education, *Local Administrative Memoranda 2/82* and *6/83*, Bradford, LEA, 1982/3.

36 D. Joly, *The Opinions of Mirpuri Parents in Saltley, Birmingham about their Children's Schooling*, Birmingham, The Centre for the Study of Islam and Christian-Muslim Relations, 1984, p.23.

37 *Ibid.*, p.24.

38 M. Stone, *The Education of the Black Child in Britain: The Myth of Multiracial Education*, London, Fontana, 1981.

39 M. Chevannes, 'Supplementary Education: The Black Arrow Night School Project', *The Social Science Teacher*, vol.8, no.4, 1979, pp.136–7.

40 *Ibid.*, p.137.

41 J.S. Nagra, 'Asians Supplementary Schools: A Case Study of Coventry', *New Community*, vol.9, no.3, 1981, pp.431–6.

42 J. Nixon, *op.cit.*, p.130.

43 M. Tsow, *Mother Tongue Maintenance*, London, Commission for Racial Equality, 1984, pp.52–4.

44 *Ibid.*, p.56.

45 House of Commons, Home Affairs Committee, *The Chinese Community in Britain*, London, HMSO, 1985.

46 Joly, *op.cit.*, p.17.

47 V. Edwards, 'Language Issues in Schools' in M. Craft (ed.), *Education and Cultural Pluralism*, London, Falmer Press, 1984, pp.79–91.

48 National Association for Multiracial Education, 'Policy Statement: Mother-Tongue and Minority, Community Languages in Education', Mickleover, Derby, n.d. (1981?).

49 Commission of the European Communities, 'Report from the Commission to the Council', Brussels, EEC, 10 February 1984.

50 H. Hester, 'Language in the Multicultural Primary Classroom: Broadsheets', London, Schools Council/University of London Institute of Education, 1983 and J. Bleach, 'Language for Learning Project: News-

letters', London, Schools Council/University of London Institute of Education, 1983.

51 H. Rosen and T. Burgess, *Language and Dialects of London School-children*, London, Ward Lock Educational, 1980.

52 O. Rees and F. Fitzpatrick, 'Report on the Mother-Tongue and English Teaching Project (MOTET): Summary', Bradford University of Bradford/Bradford College, 1981.

53 Linguistic Minorities Project, *Linguistic Minorities in England*, London, University of London Institute of Education, 1983, p.43. For a brief résumé, see The Linguistic Minorities Project, 'Bilingualism and Mother-Tongue Teaching in England' in M. Craft (ed.), *Education and Cultural Pluralism*, *op.cit.*, pp.95–116.

54 *Ibid.*, p.100.

55 J. Wilding, *Ethnic Minority Languages in the Classroom?* (A Survey of Asian Parents in Leicester), Leicester, Leicester City Council, 1981.

56 Joly, *op.cit.*, p.15.

57 Commission for Racial Equality, *Ethnic Minority Community Languages*, London, CRE, July 1982.

58 Council of the European Communities, 'Council Directive of 25 July, 1977 on the Education of the Children of Migrant Workers', *Official Journal of the European Communities*, no.2, 199/32, 6 August 1977. This Directive was incorporated into Department of Education and Science, *Circular 5/81*, London, DES, 31 July 1981.

59 M. Craft and M. Atkins, *Training Teachers of Ethnic Minority Community Languages*, Nottingham, University School of Education, 1983.

60 Skolorverstyrelsen, National Swedish Board of Education, *The Curriculum for the Compulsory School 1980*, Stockholm, Information Section, 1980.

61 K.A. Baker and A.A. de Kanter, *Effectiveness of Bilingual Education: A Review of the Literature*, Rosslyn, Virginia, National Clearing-house for Bilingual Education, 1981.

7 Children and learning

1 M. Rutter *et al.*, *Fifteen Thousand Hours: Secondary Schools and their Effects on Children*, London, Open Books, 1979.

2 W.A. Goodenough, 'Multiculturalism as the Normal Human Experience', *Anthropology and Education Quarterly*, vol.7, 1976, pp.4–7.

3 A very useful overview of the history and research on the relationship between culture and cognition is M. Cole and S. Scribner, *Culture and Thought: A Psychological Introduction*, New York, John Wiley, 1974.

4 M. Donaldson, *Children's Minds*, London, Fontana, 1978.

5 M. Cole *et al.*, *The Cultural Context of Learning and Thinking*, New York, Basic Books, 1971.

6 W. Doyle, 'Classroom Tasks and Student Abilities', in P.L. Peterson and H.J. Walberg (eds), *Research on Teaching: Concepts, Findings and Implications*, Berkeley, Calif, McCutchan, 1979.

7 N. Bennett, *The Quality of Pupil Learning Experiences*, London, Lawrence Erlbaum Associates, 1984, p.214.

8 Home Office, *The Brixton Disorders (6–12 April 1981)* (The Scarman Report), London, HMSO, 1981, p.106.

9 S.S. Stodolsky and G. Lesser, 'Learning Patterns in the Disadvantaged', *Harvard Educational Review*, vol.37, no.4, 1967, pp.22–69.

10 H. Gardner, *Frames of Mind* (The Theory of Multiple Intelligence), London, Heinemann, 1984.

11 N. Kogan, *Cognitive Styles in Infancy and Early Childhood*, New York, Erlbaum, 1977.

12 C. Bagley, 'Cultural Diversity, Migration and Cognitive Styles: A Study of British, Japanese, Jamaican and Indian Children', in G.K. Verma and C. Bagley, *Race Relations and Cultural Differences*, London, Croom Helm, 1984, pp.217–46. Also to be found in J.R. Samuda *et al.* (eds), *Multiculturalism in Canada*, Toronto, Allyn & Bacon, 1984, pp.368–81.

13 L. Laosa, 'Multicultural Education: How Psychology can Contribute', *Journal of Teacher Education*, vol.28, 1977, pp.26–30.

14 Bagley, *op.cit.*, p.218.

15 P. Ghuman, 'An Exploratory Study of Witkin's Dimension in Relation to Social Class, Personality Factors and Piagetian Tests', *Social Behaviour and Personality*, vol.5, 1977, pp.87–91.

16 P. Ghuman, 'A Comparative Study of Cognitive Styles in Three Ethnic Groups', paper given at the Annual Conference of the British Psychological Society, September 1981, quoted in Bagley, *op.cit.*

17 H. Machtiger, 'An Exploration of the Relationship of Cognitive Styles to Learning Disabilities in Primary School Children', Ph.D. thesis, London, University of London, 1974, quoted in Bagley, *op.cit.*

18 M. Ramirez and A. Casteñada, *Cultural Democracy, Bicognitive Development and Education*, New York, Academic Press, 1974.

19 J.A. Vasquez, 'Bilingual Education's Needed Third Dimension', *Educational Leadership*, vol.37, no.2, 1979, pp.166–8.

20 *Ibid.*, p.167.

21 K. Thomas, 'Intercultural Relations in the Classroom', in M. Craft (ed.), *Education and Cultural Pluralism*, London, Falmer Press, 1984, pp.57–77.

22 S.R. Cahir, 'Cognitive Styles and the Bilingual Educator', W.E. Lambert *et al.* (eds), *Faces and Facets of Bilingualism*, Washington, D.C., National Clearinghouse for Bilingual Education, Center for Applied Linguistics, 1981, pp.24ff.

23 *Ibid.*, p.27.

24 C.J. Nine-Curt, *Teacher Training Packs for a Course on Cultural Awareness*, Falls River, Mass, National Assessment and Dissemination Center for Bilingual Education, 1976.

25 R.D. Russell, 'Black Perceptions of Guidance', *The Personnel and Guidance Journal*, vol.48, 1970, pp.721–9.

26 J.B. Rotter, 'Generalised Expectancies for Internal Versus External Control of Reinforcement', *Psychological Monographs*, vol.8, no.1, 1966.

27 G.W. Mayeske, 'Educational Achievement among Mexican Americans: A Special Report from the Educational Opportunities Survey', *Integrated Education*, vol.6, 1968, pp.32–6.

28 J.A. Vasquez, *Locus of Control, Social Class and Learning*, Los Angeles, California. National Dissemination and Assessment Center, California State University, 1978.

29 *Ibid.*, p.14.

30 R.L. Birdwhistell, *Kinesics and Context*, New York, Ballantine Books, 1970.

31 E.T. Hall, *The Hidden Dimension*, Garden City, Anchor Press, 1966.

32 M.R. Key, *Paralanguage and Kinesics*, Metuchen, Scarecrow Press, 1975.

33 D. Barnes, *Practical Curriculum Study*, London, Routledge & Kegan Paul, 1982, p.79.

34 *Ibid.*, p.80.

35 F. Musgrave, 'Education and Culture Concept', in F.A.J. Ianni and E. Storry (eds), *Cultural Relevance and Educational Issues*, Boston, Little Brown & Company, 1873, pp.12–28.

36 The work of the Johnson brothers in the United States and of Biott in the United Kingdom is important in this respect. See C. Biott, *Getting On Without The Teacher*, Sunderland, Sunderland Polytechnic Centre for Educational Research and Development, 1984.

37 M.J. Taylor, *Caught Between* (A review of research into the Education of Pupils of West Indian Origin), Windsor, Berks, NFER-Nelson, 1981, p.206.

38 *Ibid.*, p.209.

39 Quoted in C. Harrington, *Bilingual Education, Social Stratification and Cultural Pluralism*, New York, ERIC Clearinghouse on Urban Education, 1978.

40 I have taken the concept of conscientisation – identification with the social and cultural circumstances of the learner – from the work of the Brazilian adult educator, Paulo Freire. See, for example, P. Freire, *Pedagogy of the Oppressed*, Harmondsworth, Penguin, 1972.

41 H.C. Triandis, 'Culture Training, Cognitive Complexity and Interpersonal Attitudes', in R.W. Brislin *et al.* (eds), *Cross-Cultural Perspectives on Learning*, New York, Halsted Press, 1975, pp.39–77.

42 G. Gay, 'On Behalf of Children: A Curriculum Design for Multicultural Education in the Elementary School', *The Journal of Negro Education*, vol.8, no.3, pp.324–40.

43 See P.J. Bohannan, 'Field Anthropologists and Classroom Teachers', in F.A.J. Ianni and E. Storry (eds), *Cultural Relevance and Educational Issues*, *op.cit.*, pp.179–89.

8 Professional growth and development

1 S.J. Eggleston, D.K. Dunn and A. Purewal, *In-Service Teacher Education in a Multiracial Society*, Keele, Staffs., The University of Keele, 1981.

2 Council for National Academic Awards, Committee for Education, Working Group on Multicultural Education, 'Notes on Multicultural Education and the Professional Preparation and In-Service Development of Teachers', London, CNAA, October 1984.

3 National Association for Multiracial Education, 'Statement on Teacher Education', Birmingham, July 1984.
4 C. Biott, J. Lynch and W. Robertson, 'Supporting Teachers' Own Progress Towards Multicultural Education', *Multicultural Education*, vol.II, no.2, 1984, pp.39–41.
5 E. Lee, 'Racism Awareness Seminar Series', City of North York, Ontario, Board of Education, 1984, cyclo (slightly amended).
6 *Ibid.*, pp.2–3.
7 G. Gay, 'Why Multicultural Education in Teacher Preparation Programmes', *Contemporary Education*, vol.LIV, Winter 1983, pp.79–85.
8 G. Gay, 'Interfacing CBTE and Multicultural Education in Social Studies Teacher Preparation', in D. Felder (ed.), *Competency Based Teacher Education: Professionalizing Social Studies Teaching*, Washington, DC, National Council for the Social Studies, 1978, chapter six, pp.85–101. (Slightly amended and amplified.)
9 J. Lynch, 'An Initial Typology of Perspectives on Staff Development for Multicultural Teacher Education', in G.K. Verma *et al.*, *Multicultural Education: The Interminable Debate*, Lewes, Sussex, Falmer Press, 1985.
10 J.A. Banks, 'Multicultural Education: Development Paradigms and Goals', in J.A. Banks and J. Lynch (eds), *Multicultural Education in Western Societies*, Eastbourne, Holt Saunders, 1985.
11 J.A. Banks, *Multiethnic Education: Theory and Practice*, Boston, Allyn & Bacon, 1981.
12 C.A. Grant and S.L. Mellnick, 'Developing and Implementing Multicultural In-Service Teacher Education', paper presented at the National Council of States on In-Service Education, New Orleans, 17–19 November 1976.
13 J. Lynch, in G.K. Verma *et al.* (eds), 1985, *op.cit.*
14 G.C. Baker, *Planning and Organizing for Multicultural Instruction*, Reading, Mass., Addison Wesley Publishing Company, 1983, pp.51–60.
15 See J.A. Banks, *Multiethnic Education: Theory and Practice*, Boston, Allyn & Bacon, 1981, diagram p.31 *et passim*.
16 C. Duncan, 'Portrait of a Multicultural School: Some Implications for Practice', in T. Corner (ed.), *Race and the Curriculum*, Glasgow, University Department of Education, 1985, pp.6–14.
17 I have based this brief description on internal papers and documents made available to me by Carlton Duncan, to whom I am most grateful. The description is my own and Mr Duncan bears no responsibility for it.
18 R. Willey, *Race, Equality and Schools*, London, Methuen, 1984, pp.73–4.
19 J. Nixon, *A Teacher's Guide to Multicultural Education*, Oxford, Basil Blackwell, 1985, pp.133ff.
20 This section of the paper draws on Schools Council, *An Introduction to Evaluation*, London, Schools Council, 1979.
21 Adapted from C. Adelman and R. Alexander, *The Self Evaluating Institutions*, London, Methuen, 1982, pp.23–4.
22 J. Elliott, *Action-Research: A Framework for Self Evaluation in Schools*, Cambridge, Cambridge Institute of Education, 1981 (Schools

Council Programme 2: Working Paper 1 of the Teacher-Pupil Interaction and the Quality of Learning Project), pp.i-ii.

23 See W.I. Stenning and R. Stenning, 'The Assessment of Teachers' Performance: Some Practical Considerations', *Schools Organisations and Management Abstracts*, vol.3, no.2, 1984, pp.77–90.

24 B. Thomas and C. Novogrodsky, *Combating Racism in the Workplace: A Course for Workers*, Toronto, Ontario, Cross Cultural Communication Centre, 1983.

25 For example, Council on Interracial Books for Children, *Unlearning Asian American Stereotypes*, New York, CBIC Resource Centre, 1982, which includes a sound cassette, a filmstrip, teachers' guide and children's book.

26 University of Nottingham, School of Education, 'Lifestyles', Nottingham, 1984.

27 Notwithstanding similar attempts in Great Britain, the pack developed by the City of North York in Ontario is of particular interest. See City of North York, *Handling of Racial Ethnic Incidents in Educational Institutions*, North York, 1984, based on *Race and Ethnic Relations Policy and Procedures*, North York, 1984.

9 Assessment and the multicultural school: practice and promise

1 An early version of this chapter was given as a talk at the International Centre for Intercultural Studies of the University of Bradford in Autumn 1983.

2 The information in this paragraph is drawn from J.R. Mercer, 'Testing and Assessment Practices in Multicultural Education', in J.A. Banks, *Education in the 80's: Multiethnic Education*, Washington, National Education Association, 1981, pp.93–104.

3 The term 'societal curriculum' is taken from C.E. Cortes, 'The Societal Curriculum: Implications for Multiethnic Education', in Banks, *op.cit.*, pp.24–32.

4 G.K. Verma, 'The Democratization of Test Construction: A response to the Problems of Measurement in a Multi-ethnic Society', University of Bradford, International Centre for Intercultural Studies, 1983, mimeo.

5 J. Kagan, 'The IQ Puzzle: What are we Measuring?', *Inequality in Education*, July 1973, pp.5–13. (Published by the Centre for Law and Education, Harvard University.)

6 The term 'physics envy' is taken from S.J. Gould, *The Mismeasure of Man*, New York, Norton, 1981. I am grateful to Professor Harvey Goldstein of the University of London Institute of Education for drawing my attention to this devastating indictment of tests and testing.

7 A.R. Jensen, 'How much can we boost I.Q. and scholastic achievement?', *Harvard Educational Review*, vol.39, 1969, pp.1–123.

8 H.J. Eysenck, *Race, Intelligence and Education*, London, Temple Smith, 1971.

9 As Milner points out, approximately one-half of the alleged 'black deficit' can be eradicated when a black tester administers a test for black

children. See D. Milner, *Children and Race: Ten Years on*, London, Ward Lock, 1983, p.173. The research which he cited on this issue is H.G. Canady, 'The Effect of Rapport on the I.Q.: A New Approach to the Problem of Social Psychology', *Journal of Negro Education*, vol.5, 1936, pp.209–19.

10 See, for example, J.R. Flynn, *Race, I.Q. and Jensen*, London, Routledge & Kegan Paul, 1980, and, in a briefer form, National Union of Teachers, *Race, Education, Intelligence*, NUT, 1978. The two sides of the British debate are summarised in parallel by their protagonists, H.J. Eysenck and S. Rose, 'Race, Intelligence and Education', *New Scientist*, 15 March 1979, pp.849–52.

11 A good overview of examinations is provided in Schools Council, *Exams Brief: A School Examinations Guide for Employers*, Schools Council n.d.

12 For an account of the early historical development, see J. Roach, *Public Examinations in England 1850–1900*, Cambridge, Cambridge University Press, 1971.

13 Department of Education and Science, *Statistical Bulletin 1/83*, DES, January 1983, Table 2.

14 Schools Council, *Comparability in GCE: A Review of the Boards of Studies 1964–1977*, May 1978, p.14, Tables V and VII.

15 A.S. Wilmott and C.G. Hall, *'O' Level Examined: The Effect of Question Choice*, Schools Council, 1976, p.157.

16 Assessment of Performance Unit, *Exposure and Performance: An Investigation of Test Validity within the Context of the APU Monitoring Programme*, London, APU, Department of Education and Science, 1983.

17 Social class is a more powerful factor than either unemployment or ethnicity in staying on at school and examination results achieved. Department of Education and Science, *Statistical Bulletin, 12/83*, September 1983, particularly Table 4, and *Statistical Bulletin 13/84*. The sex dimension of inequality is clarified by two recent reports. See J. White, *Beyond the Wendy House: Sex Role Stereotyping in Primary Schools*, London, Schools Council, 1983, and A. Kelly, J. White and B. Smail, *Girls into Science and Technology: Final Report*, Manchester, The University Department of Sociology, 1984.

18 B. Goacher, *Selection Post-16: The role of Examination Results*, London, Methuen Educational, 1984 (Schools Council Examination Bulletin 45).

19 D.L. Nuttall, 'The Myth of Comparability', *Journal of the National Association of Inspectors and Educational Advisers*, Autumn, 1979, pp. 16–18.

20 These figures derive from D. Smith, *Racial Disadvantage in Britain*, Harmondsworth, Penguin, 1977 and are quoted in B. Carrington, 'Schooling an Under-class: The Implication of Ethnic Differences in Attainment', *Durham and Newcastle Research Review*, vol.IX, no.47, Autumn 1981, pp.293–305.

21 The term *ethclass* is taken from the work of an Australian academic. See K. Marjoribanks, *Ethnic Families and Children's Achievements*, Sydney, George Allen & Unwin, 1979.

22 B.L. Coard, *How the West Indian Child is made Educationally Sub-Normal in the British School System*, London, Beacon, 1971.

23 H.E.R. Townsend, *Immigrant Pupils in England – The LEA Response*, NFER, 1971.

24 S. Tomlinson, *Educational Subnormality: A Study of Decision-Making*, Routledge & Kegan Paul, 1981, chapter 7.

25 J.H. Taylor, *The Halfway Generation: A Study of Asian Youth in Newcastle-upon-Tyne*, NFER, 1976.

26 G. Driver and R. Ballard, 'Comparing Performance in Multiracial Schools: South Asian Pupils at 16', *New Community*, vol.VII, Summer 1979, pp.143–53.

27 D. Brooks and K. Singh, *Aspirations versus Opportunities: Asian and White School Leavers in the Midlands*, Walsall CRC and Leicester CRC in conjunction with the Commission for Racial Equality, 1978.

28 A. Little, 'The Educational Achievement of Ethnic Minority Children in London Schools', in G. Verma and C. Bagley (eds), *Race and Education Across Cultures*, Heinemann, 1975.

29 J. Essen and M. Ghodsian, 'The Children of Immigrants: School Performance', *New Community*, vol.VII, no.3, 1979, pp.442–9.

30 G. Driver, 'How West Indians do Better at School (Especially the Girls)', *New Society*, vol.51, no.902, 1980, pp.111–14, and G. Driver, *Beyond Underachievement*, Commission for Racial Equality, 1980.

31 M. Craft and A.Z. Craft, 'The Participation of Ethnic Minority Pupils in Further and Higher Education', *Educational Research*, vol.25, no.1, 1983, pp.10–19.

32 S. Scarr *et al.*, 'Developmental Status and School Achievements of Minority and Non-Minority Children from Birth to 18 Years in a British Midlands Town', *British Journal of Development Psychology*, vol.1, 1983, pp.31–48.

33 S. Tomlinson, 'The Educational Performance of Ethnic Minority Children', *New Community*, vol.VIII, 1980, pp.213–34.

34 S. Tomlinson, 'The Educational Performance of Children of Asian Origin', *New Community*, vol.X, no.3, 1983, pp.381–92.

35 *Ibid.*, p.391.

36 In the context of the complexity of the picture it may no longer be functional to speak of the educational performance of 'ethnic minority pupils' *en gros*, which in any case only serves to mask the real inequalities. From this point of view, I tend to agree with Jeffcoate that the issue is one of democratic equality, with some racial groups receiving less than their fair share due to racial discrimination and prejudice. See R. Jeffcoate, *Ethnic Minorities and Education*, London, Harper, 1984.

37 Jenkins and Troyna quote that 'black unemployed youngsters tend to be better qualified, in formal terms, than their white equivalents . . . [to be] more ambitious and more likely to engage in further education' and they conclude, 'there is no guarantee that parity in the market for educational credentials will bring equality in the job search', See R. Jenkins and B. Troyna, 'Educational Myths, Labour Market Realities', in B. Troyna and F.I. Smith, *Racism, School and the Labour Market*, Leicester, National Youth Bureau, 1983, p.11.

38 The statistical support for these assertions may be found in Runnymede

Trust, *Race and Immigration Bulletin*, no.159, September 1983, pp.6–11.

39 Commission for Racial Equality, *Young People and the Job Market: A Survey*, London, CRE, 1982.

40 M. Campbell and D. Jones, *Asian Youths in the Labour Market: Transition to Work Project*, Bradford, Bradford College, 1982, and D. Smith, *Unemployment and Racial Minorities*, 1981, p.51.

41 Department of Employment, 'Unemployment and Ethnic Origin', *Employment Gazette*, June 1984.

42 C. Brown, *Black and White Britain: The Third PSI Survey*, London, Heinemann Educational Books/Policy Studies Institute, 1984.

43 Committee of Inquiry into the Education of Children from Ethnic Minority Groups, *Interim report: West Indian Children in Our Schools*, London, HMSO, 1981.

44 Jenkins and Troyna, *op.cit.*, pp.5–16.

45 The evidence for these factors is summarised in Inner London Education Authority, *Race, Sex and Class: Achievement in Schools*, London, ILEA, 1983.

46 K. Roberts *et al.*, 'Young, Black and Out of Work' in Troyna and Smith, *op.cit.*, pp.17–28. See also findings of the Commission for Racial Equality survey in Nottingham which found that in over half the cases white applicants were selected in preference to equally well-qualified blacks. Commission for Racial Equality, *Half a Chance?: A Report on Job Discrimination against Young Blacks in Nottingham*, CRE, 1980.

47 Some teachers have, however, unilaterally broken out of the vice of standardised testing in the search for a better way of helping children. See E. Plackett, 'How I stopped testing and learnt to live without it', in Inner London Education Authority, English Centre, *The English Curriculum: Race* (Material for Discussion), London, ILEA English Centre, 1983, pp.81–3.

48 J. Mortimore and P. Mortimore, *Secondary School Examinations: The Helpful Servants, not the Dominating Master*, London, Tinga Tinga/Heinemann, 1984.

49 Schools Council, *Programmes of Work: Programme Five – Improving the Examinations System*, London, Schools Council, March, 1981.

50 See, for example, N. File, *Assessment in a Multicultural Society: History at 16*, Longmans/Schools Council, 1983 and subsequent publications in the series, see also A. Craft and G. Bardell (eds), *Curriculum Opportunities in a Multicultural Society*, London, Harper & Row, 1984, some of the chapters for which were based on the above programme of work.

51 National Foundation for Educational Research, *Educational Abilities Scales*, Windsor, Berks., NFER/Nelson, 1984. See also recent developments in multiple intelligence theory, as an alternative to single figure intelligence quotients to measure children's abilities, E. Gardner, *Frames of Mind: The Theory of Multiple Intelligences*, Heinemann, 1984.

52 HMI (Wales), *Assessment and Monitoring of Progress in Secondary Schools*, Welsh Office/HMSO, 1983, p.29. With regard to graded tests the work arising from the agreement between the ILEA and the University of London Schools Examinations Board is exemplary. See

University of London, Schools Examinations Board, 'Graded Assessments', 'Newsheets Nos 1 and 2', March and October 1984.

53 Department of Education and Science, *Press Notice 1/84* (Education Secretary Explains Bold and Ambitious Objective to Raise Standards), 6 January 1984.

54 P. Black, W. Harlen and T. Orgee, *Standards of Performance: Expectations and Reality*, London, Department of Education and Science, 1983.

55 Schools Council, *Primary Practice*, Methuen, 1983.

56 P. Levy and H. Goldstein (eds), *Tests in Education*, London, Academic Press, 1984.

57 Scottish Council for Research in Education, *Pupils in Profile*, SCRE, 1977.

58 HMI (Wales), *op.cit.*

59 J. Balogh, *Profile Reports for School Leavers*, London, Schools Council/Longman, 1982, and B. Goacher, *Recording Achievement at 16*, London, Schools Council/Longman, 1983.

60 A. Harrison, *Profile Reporting of Examination Results*, London, Schools Council, 1983 (Schools Council Examination Bulletin 43).

61 See, for example, B. Maxfield, *Computer Aided Profiling*, London, Department of Education and Science, Further Education Unit, 1983.

62 An extensive bibliography on Computer-Assisted Tailored Testing may be obtained from the ERIC Clearinghouse on Tests, Measurement and Evaluation in Princeton, USA. See also ERIC-Update, *Computerized Adaptive Testing* from the same source, for a helpful resource.

63 Department of Education and Science/Welsh Office, *Records of Achievement for School Leavers*, London, DES/WO, 1983 (Draft Policy Statement, November 1983).

64 See, for example, the decision by Leicestershire County Council to allow parents and guardians to inspect pupil records in primary and secondary schools. R. Garner, 'County Ends Secrecy over Pupils' Records', *Times Educational Supplement*, no.3486, 22 April 1983, p.1.

65 An interesting article by a headteacher on the problems associated with this practice and the 'opaque' legal situation is R. Honeyford, 'The School Attendance of British Asian Children', *Headteachers Review*, Winter, 1983, pp.16–19. See also, 'NAHT seeks way to stop term time travel among Asians', *The Times Educational Supplement*, 30 December 1983.

66 For the evidence of increased 'testing' by teachers, see C. Gipps *et al.*, *Testing Children: Standardized Testing in Local Authorities and Schools*, London, Heinemann, 1984.

67 See Inner London Education Authority, *Race, Sex and Class*, London, ILEA, 1983 (a series of five publications); City of Bradford Metropolitan Council, Directorate of Educational Services, 'Local Administrative Memorandum 2/82: Education for a Multicultural Society: Provision for Pupils of Ethnic Minority Communities', Bradford, 1982 and 'Local Administrative Memorandum 6/83: Racialist Behaviour in Schools', Bradford, 1983. Also Schools Council, *Education of*

Children from Ethnic Minority Groups (Pamphlet 19), 1983, especially pp.19–23.
68 The Report of a local Schools Council-supported group suggests a useful first list of criteria for judging pupils' contributions to co-operative, self-directed group work. See C. Biott, 'Getting on Without the Teacher', Sunderland, The Polytechnic, 1983, cyclo, pp.22–23, and C. Biott and M. Clough, 'Co-operative Group Work in Primary Classrooms', *Education 3–13*, vol.11, no.2, 1983, pp.33–36.
69 United Kingdom, Parliament, *Education Act 1980*, London, HMSO, 1980, especially section 8.
70 See E. Ogilvie, *Gifted Children in Primary Schools*, Macmillan Education, 1973, p.51, quoted in Schools Council, *Primary Practice*, Methuen Educational, 1983, p.121.
71 See Schools Council, *op.cit.*, p.134.
72 R.B. Moore, *Racism in the English Language*, New York, Council on Interracial Books for Children Inc., 1976.
73 This chapter was completed before the appearance of the Swann Report, but the attention of the reader is drawn, in particular, to Chapter Three of that Report. See 'Achievement and Underachievement', in Committee of Inquiry into the Education of Children from Ethnic Minority Groups, *Report: All Our Children* (The Swann Report), London, HMSO, 1985 (Cmnd. 9453), pp.58–190 *et passim*.

10 Diversity, equity and cohesion: agenda for action

1 W. Brandt (Chairman), *Report of the Independent Commission on International Development Issues (North-South: A Programme for Survival)*, London, Pan Books, 1980.
2 W. Brandt (Chairman), *Report of the Brandt Commission (Common Crisis: North-South: Co-operation for World Recovery)*, London, Pan, 1983.
3 N. Glazer, *Ethnic Dilemmas 1964 – 82*, Cambridge, Mass., Harvard University Press, 1983, pp.182–208.
4 B. Whitaker (ed.), *Minorities*, London, Pergamon, 1985.
5 Home Office, *The Brixton Disorders 10–12 April, 1981* (The Scarman Report), London, HMSO, 1981, p.104.
6 *Ibid.*, p.112.
7 *Ibid.*, p.135.
8 Department of Christian Doctrine and Formation of the Bishop's Conference of England and Wales, Working Party on Catholic Education in a Multiracial, Multicultural Society, *Report: Learning From Diversity* (A Challenge for Catholic Education), London, Catholic Media Office, 1984, p.47.
9 See the results of recent research conducted at Aston University in Birmingham, reported in the education press, E. Cashmore and C. Bagley, 'Colour Blind', *The Times Educational Supplement*, 28 December 1984, p.13; J. Judd, 'Public Schools are criticised for Race Views', *The Observer*, 30 December 1984, p.5; and B. Doe,

'Independents Blind to Multicultural Approach', *The Times Educational Supplement*, 21 December 1984, p.1.
10 Secretary of State for Wales, the Right Honourable Nicholas Esmonds, MP, *The Welsh Language: A Commitment and a Challenge* (The Government's Policy for the Welsh Language), Cardiff, The Welsh Office, 1980, p.iii.

Subject index

Figures in italics refer to tables

Adult Language Use Survey, 120
Advisory Centre for Education, 106
All-London Teachers Against Racism
    and Fascism (ALTARF), 80
Asians, 118, 132, 165, 167–8, 169
assessment, 141, 159; a. and
    examination guidelines, 178–9;
    Assessment of Performance Unit,
    164–5; biased against West Indians,
    166; Binet testing, 160; comparability
    and equality of examinations, 163–5,
    170–1; contextual guidelines, 176–7;
    continuous a., 172, 173–4; ethnic
    dimension of examinations, 165–8;
    formal examinations, 163; historical
    development of, 159–60; intelligence
    and race, 161–2; intelligence tests,
    161; Jensen controversy, 161–3;
    multicultural a., 174–6, 179–80; need
    for reform, 172–3; new tests, 172; new
    types of, 172–3; 'objective' tests, 160–
    1, 162; 'profiling', 172, 173; scepticism
    of psychological testing, 161; school
    achievement tests, 161; teachers and,
    179–80; use of computers in, 173;
    Wechsler Scale, 160
Assessment of Performance Unit, 164–
    5, 172
assimilation, 5, 6, 11, 42, 44
Assistant Masters and Mistresses
    Association (AMMA), 81
Association for Teaching in the Social
    Services, 48
Association of Teachers for the
    Education of Pupils Overseas
    (ATEPO), 81

Australia, 3, 5, 31–2; *Australia as a
    Multicultural Society*, 29, 30; Child
    Migrant Education Programme, 29;
    Curriculum Development Centre,
    29–30; developments in multicultural
    education, 28–31; Education
    Research and Development
    Committee, 30; Institute of
    Multicultural Affairs, 30; National
    Advisory and Co-ordinating
    Committee on Multicultural
    Education, 31; Racial Discrimination
    Act (1975), 28; racism in, 30; White
    Australian Policy, 28

Belgium, 6
bilingualism, 27–8, 29, 48, 121, 122–3,
    127, 133
Birley High School, Manchester, 62, 82
blacks, 22, 23, 25–6, 67–8, 161; *see also*
    West Indians
Bradford College, 63, 120
Bradford Metropolitan Council Local
    Education Authority, 63, 71–2, 82,
    120
Bradford, University of, 63, 120
Brandt Commission, 184
British Advisory Committee on Race
    Relations Research, 132
British Nationality Act (1948), 43
British Nationality and Status of Aliens
    Act, 43
Brixton riots, 50, 62, 109–10
Bullock Report, 48, 107

Canada, 5, 6, 31–2, 122; academics and
    multicultural education, 27–8;
    biculturalism in, 26; Bill of Rights

Subject index

National Federation for Educational
Research, 172
National Foundation for Educational
Research, 81
National Union of Teachers (NUT), 50,
80–1
Newsom Report, 106
North/South Report, 184
North Westminster Community School,
84
Nottingham, University of, 155

parents, 103, 104; blacks ps., 110; Green
Paper on parental influence, 110;
home-school partnership, 106–9, 110–
11, 112–16, 123–4, 130–1; importance
of mother-tongue to, 121;
involvement in primary schools, 107;
involvement in supplementary
schools, 117; LEAs and, 107–9;
measures for parental involvement,
114; parent-teacher associations, 113;
parents associations in the EEC, 111;
ps. from ethnic minorities, 110–12;
phases of involvement in school
system, 111–12; Public Law, 94–142;
112; survey of Mirpuri parents, 116
Plowden Report, 46, 106
pluralism, 5–6, 13
Policy Studies Institute, 67–8
pupils, 136–9; cognitive styles and, 127–
33; importance of home environment,
105; importance of parent-teacher
partnership, 106–7; leadership, 137;
peer tutoring, 137; progress in
schools, 158; variables in school
experience, 105–6

Quintin Kynaston School, London, 52,
84

race relations: in Canada, 27; in schools,
108; in United Kingdom, 45, 66; *Race
Relations in Schools*, 67; teaching
about, 92, 94
Race Relations Acts: 1965, 45; 1968,
46–7; 1976, 48–9, 75
Race Relations Board, 45, 47, 48
racial discrimination, 20
racism, 21–2, 25, 84, 187; ALTARF
document on teaching and r., 80; anti-
racist education, 143–4, 150; anti-
racist school policies, 82–4; anti-racist
training, 95; awareness of, 94;
definition of, 97; discrimination, 96,

97, 98; in Australia, 30, 31; in United
Kingdom, 43–4, 52–3, 58, 59, 68–9,
71–2, 74–5, 189; need to combat, 153–
6; NUT and, 80, 81; prejudice, 95–7;
prejudice reduction, 98–100, 104,
151; seminars on racism awareness,
146–7; stereotyping, 97; theories of
prejudice acquisition, 97–8
Rampton Report, 63, 108–9

Scarman Report, 50, 62, 109, 110, 130,
185
schools, 68–9, 77–8; anti-racist policies,
82–4; definitions of multicultural
education, 82; discourse with parents,
104; discourse with the community,
104; ethnic minorities, 107–9;
governing bodies, 110; home-school
partnership, 106–9, 110–11, 112–16,
123–4, 158; parent governors, 108–9;
phases of involvement in s. system,
111–12; policies for multicultural
schools, 79, 113–14; principles for s.
policy on multicultural education, *83,
93*; supplementary ss., 116–19, 123–4
Schools Council, 48, 51, 61, 62, 145, 152,
171, 173; 'Education for a Multiracial
Society', 47; English for Immigrant
Children, 46; mother-tongue project,
120; *Multiracial Education: Needs and
Innovation*, 47; primary report, 172–
3; Working Paper, 50, 81; *Young
School Leavers, Enquiry 1*, 106
schools: individual: Islamic Studies
School, Coventry, 118; North
Westminster Community School, 84;
Quintin Kynaston School, London,
52, 84; Wyke Manor School,
Bradford, 82, 152
schools: supplementary, 116–19, 127
Scottish Council for Research in
Education, 173
Secondary Pupils Survey, 120–1
slavery, 21–2, 25–6
socialisation, 128, 129, 131, 133, 139
societies, multicultural, 3–4, 11, 95
staff development, 158; American
proposals, 147–8; evaluation, 153–5;
experience of Wyke Manor School,
152; improving professional practice,
141, 142–3; in-service training, 155;
initial principles for, 149–50, *151*, 156,
157, 158; need for, 142–4; need for
open learning, 152; need to control
racism, 153–6; propositions about,

Name index

Name index